The Origins of
the Christian
Mystical Tradition

The Origins of the Christian Mystical Tradition

From Plato to Denys

ANDREW LOUTH

CLARENDON PRESS · OXFORD

Oxford University Press, Walton Street, Oxford OX2 6DP

London Glasgow New York Toronto
Delhi Bombay Calcutta Madras Karachi
Kuala Lumpur Singapore Hong Kong Tokyo
Nairobi Dar es Salaam Cape Town
Melbourne Wellington
and associate companies in
Beirut Berlin Ibadan Mexico City Nicosia

Oxford is a trade mark of Oxford University Press

Published in the United States
by Oxford University Press, New York

First published 1981
First published in paperback 1983

British Library Cataloguing in Publication Data
Louth, Andrew
The origins of the Christian mystical
tradition from Plato to Denys.
1. Mysticism — Early church, ca. 30–600
I. Title
248'.22'09015   BV5075   80–41057

ISBN 0-19-826668-5

Typeset in Great Britain by
King's English Typesetters Limited, Cambridge
and printed by
The Thetford Press Limited, Thetford, Norfolk

Preface

THE origin of this book was a series of lectures on 'Mystical Theology in the Fathers' given in the Faculty of Theology at the University of Oxford. Shortly afterwards Mother Jane, SLG, very kindly asked me if I would repeat the course at the Convent of the Incarnation in Oxford for the benefit of those Sisters of the Love of God who wished to hear them. A gratifyingly large number did. Since then the lectures have been revised and rewritten and later stages of the book have been given as talks at the Convent of the Incarnation, and also to the Sisters of the Precious Blood, at Burnham Abbey. I owe a very great deal to these opportunities of sharing my thoughts with them and responding to their questions and criticisms. The circle of indebtedness extends much wider, but there are various particular debts of which I am especially conscious. In the chapter on Philo, I received help and encouragement from Dr C. T. R. Hayward, now at the University of Durham, and Robin Lane Fox, now at New College; Dr O. M. T. O'Dono-van, now at Wycliffe College, Toronto, read an early version of the chapter on Augustine and made many acute and helpful observations; Sister Jocelyn Mary, SLG, gave me much help in understanding the doctrine of the Dark Night in St. John of the Cross. Naturally, none of them is responsible for the use I have made of their ideas. I was also greatly helped by being able to count on the accurate and intelligent typing of Mrs Anne Borg. But my greatest debt is to Sister Edmée, SLG, who has suffered all the stages of the fashioning of this book: I owe more than I can tell to her encouragement and criticisms, which have saved me from many asperities of style and obscurities of thought.

The final form of the book retains one particular feature of the original lectures: extensive quotation from the philosophers and Fathers discussed. This was intended to give the original hearers some sort of feel for the thought and vision of these ancient writers. I beg the reader not to skip them: they are the most important part.

Oxford,
Feast of SS Cyril and Methodius,
1980.

ANDREW LOUTH

Acknowledgements

The author and publisher gratefully acknowledge permission to reproduce the following copyright translations:

John Burnaby: Extracts from *De Trinitate*, Books VIII–X, XIV and XV from *Augustine: Later Works*, vol. VIII, The Library of Christian Classics (1955). Reprinted by permission of SCM Press Ltd., London, and The Westminster Press, U.S.A.

F. H. Colson et al: Extracts from *Philo's Works* (10 vols. 1929–62). Reprinted by permission of The Loeb Classical Library (Harvard University Press: William Heinemann).

F. M. Cornford: Extracts from *The Republic of Plato*, translated by F. M. Cornford (1941), by permission of Oxford University Press.

R. P. Lawson: Extracts from *Origen: The Song of Songs, Commentary and Homilies*, (Vol. 26, Ancient Christian Writers Series, 1957). Reprinted by permission of the Paulist Press, New York.

Stephen Mackenna: Extracts from *Plotinus: The Enneads* (1969). Reprinted by permission of Faber & Faber Ltd., and Pantheon Books, a Division of Random House, Inc.

Extracts from *From Glory to Glory* by Jean Danielou, translated by Herbert Musurillo. Copyright © 1961 by Charles Scribner's Sons. Reprinted by permission of the publisher.

F. J. Sheed: Extracts from *The Confessions of St. Augustine* (1944). Reprinted by permission of Sheed and Ward Ltd.

Contents

Introduction

THE aim of this book is to outline the development of mystical theology in the Patristic period as far as Dionysius or Denys the Areopagite in the late fifth century. This was a formative period for mystical theology, as for other areas of theology. Not that nothing happened later — a mistake less likely to be made, perhaps, in the case of mystical thought — but that in the Fathers' pioneering attempts to understand the relation of the soul to God there emerge the basic patterns of thought which later theologians will take for granted. The study of Patristic mystical theology is, then, important for any study of Christian mysticism, as well as having its own intrinsic interest.

This formative period for mystical theology was, of course, the formative period for dogmatic theology, and that the same period was determinative for both mystical and dogmatic theology is no accident since these two aspects of theology are fundamentally bound up with one another. The basic doctrines of the Trinity and Incarnation, worked out in these centuries, are mystical doctrines formulated dogmatically. That is to say, mystical theology provides the context for direct apprehensions of the God who has revealed himself in Christ and dwells within us through the Holy Spirit; while dogmatic theology attempts to incarnate those apprehensions in objectively precise terms which then, in their turn, inspire a mystical understanding of the God who has thus revealed himself which is specifically Christian.

Put like that it is difficult to see how dogmatic and mystical theology could ever have become separated; and yet there is little doubt that, in the West at least, they have so become and that 'dogmatic and mystical theology, or theology and "spirituality" [have] been set apart in mutually exclusive categories, as if mysticism were for saintly women and theological study were for practical but, alas, unsaintly men.'[1] That this divorce need not be permanent can be seen from the achievement of such modern theologians as Karl Barth and Hans Urs von Balthasar; that there was no such divorce with the Fathers is widely recognized: 'the work of the Fathers embodies to a peculiar degree an integration of devotion and reason'[2], though this remark assumes that Patristic theology integrates things properly distinct and so unconsciously takes their separation for granted.

One of the results of this Western divorce between theology and spirituality is that it tends to be transferred to the study of the Fathers, so that the student of Patristics knows the Origen of the *De Principiis* and *Contra Celsum*, or the Gregory of Nyssa of the *Contra Eunomium* and his other polemical writings, but not the Origen of the homilies and commentaries (which form the bulk of his work), nor the Gregory of the *Life of Moses* or the *Homilies on the Song of Songs*. Even Augustine's *De Trinitate* is approached as an exercise in speculative theology[3] rather than as an attempt to give an account of the ascent of the soul to God, the God whom it knows from Scripture to be God the Holy Trinity. But, in the Fathers, there is no divorce between dogmatic and mystical theology; and part of the aim of this book is to redress the balance by discussing their mysticism which is at the heart of their theology, the issues raised in their dogmatic theology being profoundly affected by and, indeed, resolved at the level of their mystical theology.

One general and fundamental problem of Patristic theology is its relationship to contemporary Hellenistic culture, dominated as it was by ways of thinking which had their roots in Plato; and it was in terms of such methods of thought that Christian theology found its first intellectual expression. To

---

[1] Thomas Merton, *Seeds of Contemplation* (new edition, Anthony Clarke, 1972),197; quoted also in my *Theology and Spirituality* (SLG Press, revised edition, 1978), a paper in which the relation of these two is more fully discussed.

[2] M. F. Wiles, *Working Papers in Doctrine* (SCM Press, 1976, 100.

[3] Unfortunately the most accessible version of selections from *De Trinitate*, in the Library of Christian Classics, vol. VIII (1955), edited by John Burnaby, very much encourages this impression — something Jaroslav Pelikan complained about in his *Development of Christian Doctrine* (Yale UP, 1969), 124.

quote Endre von Ivánka: 'The phenomenon which characterizes the whole of the first millennium of Christian theological thought . . . is the use of Platonism as the form for [its] philosophical expression and the framework of the world-picture in terms of which the proclamation of revealed truths was made — in other words, Christian Platonism.'[4] 'Christian Platonism' has meant many things, but in our period Christianity and Platonism met primarily on the level of mysticism, for, by the second century, Platonism 'was characterized by its predominantly religious and theocentric world view . . . This age was attracted not so much by Plato the ethical teacher or political reformer, as by Plato the hierophant who (according to an old legend) had been conceived of Apollo and born of the virgin Perictione . . . Second-century Platonism is theological and otherworldly.'[5]

This kind of Platonism, known to us as 'Middle Platonism',[6] was 'mystical'; it was concerned with the soul's search for immediacy with God, a concern which was intensified with Plotinus and neo-Platonism. Christian mystical theology found here very amenable material, so much so that one of the great living authorities on Hellenistic religion, Père A.-J. Festugière, can say: 'When the Fathers "think" their mysticism they platonize. There is nothing original in the edifice.'[7] Such is the importance of Platonism for an understanding of Christian mystical theology that the first three chapters of this book are concerned with the Platonist tradition: with Plato, with Philo (who can be regarded as a representative of Middle Platonism and whose writings were influential among the Fathers), and with Plotinus. Only then will we look at the development of mystical theology in the Fathers and see the extent to which Platonism determines their thought, but also the extent to which this Platonic influence is resisted and rejected. And we will see that this resistance and rejection

---

[4] *Plato Christianus* (Einsiedeln, 1964), 19. For a survey of recent research on this problem see E. J. Meijering, *God Being History* (Amsterdam, 1975), 'Zehn Jahre Forschung zum Thema Platonismus and Kirchenväter' 1–18.

[5] R. E. Witt, *Albinus and the History of Middle Platonism* (reprint, Amsterdam, 1971), 123.

[6] The most recent discussion of Middle Platonism is by J. Dillon, *The Middle Platonists* (Duckworth, London, 1977).

[7] *Contemplation et vie contemplative selon Platon* (Paris, 3rd edn., 1967), 5.

becomes sharper, and ultimately final, with the full emergence of the fundamental Christian doctrine of *creatio ex nihilo* — creation out of nothing.

Central to Platonism is its conviction of man's essentially spiritual nature: it is in virtue of his having a soul that man can participate in the realm of eternal truth, the realm of the divine. The mystical strand in Platonism (which is proper and fundamental to it) develops from this notion of man's essentially spiritual nature, from the belief of his kinship with the divine. But, for Christianity, man is a creature; he is not ultimately God's kin, but created out of nothing by God and only sustained in being by dependence on His will. There is an ontological gulf between God and his creation, a real difference of being. Only in Christ, in whom divine and human natures are united, do we find One who is of one substance with the Father. At this point Christianity and Platonism are irreconcilable, and the conflict between them came to a head in the Arian controversy — a crucial moment in the development of the Church's dogmatic theology, and equally, as we shall see in chapter five, in the development of the Christian mystical tradition.

Intimately linked with this is the bearing of the doctrine of the Incarnation on mystical theology. Within the Platonic framework, the soul's search for God is naturally conceived of as a return, an *ascent* to God; for the soul properly belongs with God, and in its ascent it is but realizing its own true nature. Christianity, on the other hand, speaks of the Incarnation of God, of his *descent* into the world that he might give to man the possibility of a communion with God that is not open to him by nature. And yet man *is* made in the image of God, and so these movements of ascent and descent cross one another and remain — as a fact of experience — in unresolved tension. The way in which mystical theology grapples with this apparently quite contrary emphasis within the Christian tradition will concern us in most chapters.

But what, we might ask, is mysticism and mystical theology? Can there, indeed, be such a thing as Christian mystical theology? There are many — particularly Protestants — who say not; yet the phenomenon seems persistent, however impossible. The stimulus of a book called *The Protestant Mystics* was the categorical assertion — by a Protestant — that 'there are *no* Protestant mystics'.[8] We shall see that this tension between the mystical and the anti-mystical is not absent from the Fathers. Like monasticism, mysticism is not a religious phenomenon peculiar to Christianity, and it is disputed whether it is essential to Christianity at all. But it can be characterized as a search for and experience of immediacy with God. The mystic is not content to know *about* God, he longs for union with God. 'Union with God' can mean different things, from literal identity, where the mystic loses all sense of himself and is absorbed into God, to the union that is experienced as the consummation of love, in which the lover and the beloved remain intensely aware both of themselves and of the other. How the mystics interpret the way and the goal of their quest depends on what they think about God, and that itself is influenced by what they experience: it is a mistake to try to make out that all mysticism is the same.[9] Yet the search for God, or the ultimate, for His own sake, and an unwillingness to be satisfied with anything less than Him; the search for immediacy with this object of the soul's longing: this would seem to be the heart of mysticism.

Here we come to a particular point which we shall meet in the ensuing pages, the Greek word *nous* and its derivatives. *Nous* is usually translated as 'mind' or 'intellect'. Part of the problem is that neither of these words is as rich in derived forms as the Greek *nous* (they have, most significantly, no verb). But beyond that, the words 'mind' and 'intellect' and their derivatives (intellection, intellectual, etc.) have quite different overtones from the Greek *nous*. The most fundamental reason for this is a cultural one: the Greeks were pre-Cartesian, we are all post-Cartesian. We say, 'I think, therefore I am', that is, thinking is an *activity* I engage in and there must therefore be an 'I' to engage in it; the Greeks would say, 'I think, therefore there is that which I think — *to noeta*'. What I think is something going on in my head; what the Greek thinks, *to noeta*, are the objects of thought that (for example, for

[8] Anne Fremantle and W. H. Auden, *The Protestant Mystics* (London, 1964), vii, quoting W. T. Stace.
[9] The literature on this subject is vast, but see in particular R. H. Zaehner, *Mysticism — Sacred and Profane* (London, 1957).

Plato) exist in a higher, more real world.[10] This means that
nous and its derivatives have a quite different *feel* from our
words, mind, mental, intellect, intellection, etc. Our words
suggest our reasoning, our thinking; *nous, noesis*, etc. suggest an
almost intuitive grasp of reality. To quote Festugière:

> It is one thing to approach truths by reason, it is quite another to
> attain to them by that intuitive faculty called *nous* by the ancients,
> the 'fine point of the soul' by St Francis de Sales, and the 'heart' by
> Pascal.[11]

By means of *nous*, Festugière goes on to say, the soul

> aspires to a knowledge that is a direct contact, a 'feeling' (*sentiment*),
> a touching, something seen. It aspires to a union where there is total
> fusion, the interpenetration of two living things.[12]

Nous, then, is more like an organ of mystical union than
anything suggested by our words 'mind' or 'intellect'. And yet
nous does mean mind; *noesis* is a deeper, simpler, more
contemplative form of thought, not something quite other
than thinking. It is essential, therefore, to give what we might
call a mystical connotation to words which normally we
understand in a limited sense. Stephen MacKenna puts the
problem vividly in the preface to his translation of Plotinus'*Enneads*:

> A serious misapprehension may be caused, to take one instance
> among several, by incautiously reading into terms used by Plotinus
> meanings or suggestions commonly conveyed by those words in the
> language of modern philosophy or religion; on the other hand, there
> is in places almost a certainty of missing these same religious or
> philosophical implications or connotations where to the initiate the
> phrase of Plotinus conveys them intensely.
>
> Thus it is not easy, without knowledge and the training of habit,
> to quiver with any very real rapture over the notion of becoming
> 'wholly identified with the Intellectual-Principle'.[13] When it is
> understood and at each moment deeply realized that 'The Intellec-
> tual-Principle' is the highest accessible 'Person' of the Godhead, is
> very God, is the Supreme Wisdom immanent within the human soul

---

[10] See Festugière's discussion of this, *Contemplation* 220 ff, 247–9.
[11] *La Révélation d'Hermès Trismégiste* (Paris, 1944), I 63.
[12] Ibid. 65.   [13] MacKenna's term for *nous*.

and yet ineffably superior to all the Universe besides, then perhaps
we may feel the great call to the devotion that has such a reward.[14]

MacKenna's solution is consistently to use 'intellect' and its
derivatives for *nous* and its derivatives, and the cumulative
effect of such strangeness is to rouse in the reader a sense of
the special meaning this group of words has for Plotinus. Such
a solution is not really possible in our case as we are dealing
with several writers who, while they do make use of this word,
use others too, and have no completely consistent vocabulary
among themselves. But by mentioning the problem here I
hope the reader will be able to bear in mind the very different
connotation the word *nous* has in Greek from any equivalents
we may use. As we can see, it is a word that is at the very heart
of the vocabulary of any Greek mystical theology.

Our introduction has raised a number of general issues. In
the following chapters we shall be concerned primarily with
elucidating the meaning of the various philosophers, theologians, and men of prayer we are studying. Awareness of these
issues will inform our approach but will not always be at the
forefront of our minds. In the last chapters, however, we shall
return to these general issues and try to discuss them in the
light of what we have learned in the course of our study.

[14] *Plotinus: The Enneads*, tr. S. MacKenna, revised by B. S. Page (4th edn.,
London, 1969), xxv.

I. PLATO

IT could be argued that mystical theology, or perhaps better, a doctrine of contemplation, is not simply an element in Plato's philosophy, but something that penetrates and informs his whole understanding of the world. We find it first in his understanding of Socrates' discussions with his friends about the various moral virtues in the early dialogues. The Socratic way was not to teach, but to elicit from his friends an understanding of virtue that, he said, they already had — confusedly, it is true, but none the less genuinely. Their understanding only needed to be *awakened*. Plato enshrines this principle in the myth that originally men's souls contemplated the eternal truths or realities — the Forms or Ideas — but that birth and being joined to a body is a painful process which causes the soul to forget. It forgets the perfect vision of Truth and Beauty it once had and moves in a dazed way in a world of change and illusion. Knowledge — true knowledge — is remembering what the soul once knew. Plato sees the world in which we live — a world of change and conjecture and opinion — as a world in which knowledge is impossible. For knowledge must be certain, and the object of knowledge must therefore, he says, be immutable, eternal. And nothing in this world satisfies those requirements. The recovery of true knowledge of Truth and Beauty, of what alone is Real, is the object of philosophy. Such knowledge in its perfection is impossible in this life, so philosophy is a preparation for dying and being dead (*Phaedo*,64A).[1]

This quest is for several objects: for Being, in the *Phaedo*; for

---

[1] References to Plato are to the OCT edition. Various translations have been used: those from which quotations have been taken have been indicated.

the Good, in the *Republic;* for Beauty, in the *Symposium* and the *Phaedrus;* for the One, or the Limit, in the *Philebus*. But, in all of them, the quest takes the form of searching for that which transcends the changing and shifting nature of this world — both the mutability of the world we perceive through the senses and the varying and uncertain opinions held by men of the world. It is a search for knowledge — not mere conjecture or opinion — and a knowledge characterized by more than certainty or infallibility. It involves the discovery of what is truly real, eternal, and immutable. Knowledge (*episteme, noesis*) is for Plato more than knowledge *about*: it implies identity with, participation in, that which is known.[2] We find an example of this in the characteristic claim and insistence of Socrates that *virtue* is knowledge. Obviously in one sense it is not. I can perfectly well know what courage is without being courageous. But is that really to know, Socrates wondered? For Plato real knowledge is more than intellectual awareness — it implies the orientation of the whole person so that one participates in the realm of Ideas or Forms.

Now, all this implies several things about the relationship between the soul and the realm of Forms; and the way in which the interrelationship is developed can only be understood if we realize the religious dimension of Plato's thought. Plato is not just taking up the search of the Presocratics for the true understanding of the nature of things: he is also taking up (as indeed some of the Presocratics did) the religious strivings of man.[3] The realm of the Forms is the divine world. The Forms have, more truly than any of the gods of mythology had, the characteristics of the divine: eternity and immortality. Plato refers to the realm of the Forms in the *Phaedrus* (247C) as *topos hyperouranios*, a place above the heavens — clearly the dwelling-place of the gods. In virtue of its capacity to know the Forms the soul is a denizen of this realm, it belongs to that place above the heavens, it is divine. It is the 'same necessity' (*Phaedo* 76E6) which underlies both the existence of the Ideas and the pre-existence (and, with that, the immortality) of the soul; because of the *syngeneia* (kinship)

---

[2] Cf. W. Jaeger, *Paideia* II 65 ff.; A.-J. Festugière, *Contemplation*, 5.
[3] W. Jaeger, *Theology of the Early Greek Philosophers* (1947), *passim*.

between the souls and Ideas, which is to say, that they are of the same kind, the same nature. So the search of the soul for knowledge of the Forms is, in a sense, its homecoming. The soul is naturally divine and seeks to return to the divine realm. And it does this in the act of contemplation — *theoria* — of Being, Truth, Beauty, Goodness. This act of *theoria* is not simply consideration or understanding; it is union with, participation in, the true objects of true knowledge. It bespeaks, as Festugière says again and again, 'un sentiment de présence' — a feeling of presence, of immediacy.[4] Now what this *theoria* is may become clearer as we proceed.

How does the soul return to this *theoria* of the Forms that it once had in its pre-mundane existence? What sort of return is it anyway? Perhaps we can begin to understand this most easily by recounting Plato's long allegory of the Cave from the seventh book of the *Republic*:

Here is a parable to illustrate the degrees in which our nature may be enlightened or unenlightened. Imagine the condition of men living in a sort of cavernous chamber underground, with an entrance open to the light and a long passage all down the cave. Here they have been from childhood, chained by the leg and also by the neck, so that they cannot move and can only see what is in front of them, because the chains will not let them turn their heads. At some distance higher up is the light of a fire burning behind them; and between the prisoners and the fire is a track with a parapet built along it, like the screen at a puppet-show, which hides the performers while they show their puppets over the top.

Now, behind this parapet imagine persons carrying along various artificial objects, including figures of men and animals in wood or stone or other materials, which project above the parapet. Naturally, some of these persons will be talking, others silent. ... A strange picture, and a strange sort of prisoners — like ourselves. For in the first place prisoners so confined would have seen nothing of themselves or of one another, except the shadows thrown by the fire-light on the wall of the Cave facing them, and they would have seen as little of the objects carried past. Now, if they could talk to one another, would they not suppose that their words referred only to those passing shadows which they saw? And suppose their prison had an echo from the wall facing them? When one of the people crossing behind them spoke, they could only suppose that the sound

---

[4] See, for example, *Contemplation*, 5, 343.

came from the shadow passing before their eyes. In every way, then, such prisoners would recognize as reality nothing but the shadows of those artificial objects.

Now consider what would happen if their release from the chains and the healing of their unwisdom should come about in this way. Suppose one of them was set free and forced suddenly to stand up, turn his head, and walk with eyes lifted to the light; all these movements would be painful, and he would be too dazed to make out the objects whose shadows he had been used to see. What do you think he would say, if someone told him that what he had formerly seen was meaningless illusion, but now, being somewhat nearer to reality and turned towards more real objects, he was getting a truer view? Suppose further that he were shown the various objects being carried by and were made to say, in reply to questions, what each of them was. Would he not be perplexed and believe the objects now shown him to be not so real as what he formerly saw? And if he were forced to look at the fire-light itself, would not his eyes ache, so that he would try to escape and turn back to the things which he could see distinctly, convinced that they really were clearer than these other objects now being shown to him? And suppose someone were to drag him away forcibly up the steep and rugged ascent and not let him go until he had hauled him out into the sunlight, would he not suffer pain and vexation at such treatment, and, when he had come out into the light, find his eyes so full of its radiance that he could not see a single one of the things that he was now told were real?

He would need, then, to grow accustomed before he could see things in that upper world. At first it would be easiest to make out shadows, and then the images of men and things reflected in water, and later on the things themselves. After that, it would be easier to watch the heavenly bodies and the sky itself by night, looking at the light of the moon and stars rather than the Sun and the Sun's light in the day-time.

Last of all, he would be able to look at the Sun and contemplate its nature, not as it appears when reflected in water or any alien medium, but as it is in itself in its own domain. And now he would begin to draw the conclusion that it is the Sun that produces the seasons and the courses of the year and controls everything in the visible world, and moreover, is in a way the cause of all that he and his companions used to see. (514A–516C)[5]

Plato himself provides his own commentary on this allegory:

[5] The translation in this and other passages from the *Republic* is by F. M. Cornford (Oxford, 1941).

Every feature in this parable is meant to fit our earlier analysis. The prison dwelling corresponds to the region revealed to us through the sense of sight, and the fire-light within it to the power of the Sun. The ascent to see the things in the upper world you may take as standing for the upward journey of the soul into the region of the intelligible; then you will be in possession of what I surmise, since that is what you wish to be told. Heaven knows whether it is true; but this, at any rate, is how it appears to me. In the world of knowledge the last thing to be perceived and only with great difficulty is the essential Form of Goodness. Once it is perceived, the conclusion must follow that, for all things, this is the cause of whatever is right and good; in the visible world it gives birth to light and to the lord of light, while it is itself sovereign in the intelligible world and the parent of intelligence and truth. Without having had a vision of this Form no-one can act with wisdom, either in his own life or in matters of state. (517A–C)

The Cave is the world revealed to us by our senses. It is a world characterized by unreality. And yet, it is the world we are used to — it is what we think of as 'reality'. The soul, which really belongs to the divine realm of the Forms or Ideas, has made itself at home in this world of unreality revealed to us through the senses. Plato's concern, then, is with the soul's search for true reality. The allegory of the Cave shows us some of the problems that this search involves; and the first of these is to see that there is a problem at all — to see that we need to search for reality, and are not in touch with it already. The first stage is an awakening — an awakening to the fact that we are far from home, far from the soul's true abode, the realm of the Forms. Having been awakened, the soul must then unlearn its apprehensions of false reality and begin to accustom itself to true reality. Plato sees this as a gradual process: in terms of the allegory, the prisoners move from seeing shadows and hearing echoes to seeing the artificial objects which produced those shadows and echoes — a move from unconscious deception to seeing what it is that deceives us. Then, if the prisoner will go further in the pursuit of reality, it will be as if he were dragged forcibly up a steep and rugged ascent, a painful process, leading to his coming into the daylight — a daylight that dazzles his weakened eyes and blinds him. Once out of the cave, he will only be able to grasp the reality now within his reach by a gradual process of becoming accustomed to it. First he looks at shadows — shadows of real things this time — and reflections. Then at the night sky, and at the world by the light of the stars and the moon. Finally he will be able to see things as revealed by the Sun itself, and actually contemplate the Sun and its nature, and see that it is from the Sun that the seasons and the course of the year and everything in the visible world proceed.

A long and gradual process of detachment from false reality and attachment to, and growing familiarity with, true reality: that is what Plato sees as the soul's ascent.

The first step, then, is an awakening: a realization that we are immersed in what only appears to be reality, that our knowledge is mere opinion (*doxa*). What was most striking about the historical Socrates was the way he brought men to a state of acknowledged ignorance and perplexity (*aporia*). It is this that we find in the early 'Socratic' dialogues, and in what Xenophon tells us about Socrates.

There then follows a process of detachment from false reality and attachment to true reality, a process of *paideia*, of education, or correction. This is the concern of the rest of the *Republic*, and also of several other dialogues — and Plato discusses it from several points of view. In the *Republic* (as also in the *Laws*) he is concerned with a specific programme of *paideia*. Elsewhere he is concerned with specific aspects of this training of the soul, but nowhere does he forget that what we are concerned with is an awakening and re-orientation of the soul: an awakening of the soul to its true life, and a re-orientation of the soul towards that life. So he says:

We must conclude that education is not what it is said to be by some, who profess to put knowledge into a soul which does not possess it, as if they could put sight into blind eyes. On the contrary, our own account signifies that the soul of every man does possess the power of learning the truth and the organ to see it with; and that, just as one might have to turn the whole body round in order that the eye should see light instead of darkness, so the entire soul must be turned away from this changing world, until its eye can bear to contemplate reality and that supreme splendour which we have called the Good. Hence there may well be an art whose aim would be to effect this very thing, the conversion of the soul, in the readiest way; not to put the power of sight into the soul's eye which already has it, but to ensure that, instead of looking in the wrong direction, it is turned the way it ought to be.   (518B–D)

The soul looks 'in the wrong direction' because it is bound to the world that is revealed to it by the senses. To be detached from this world will mean for it to be detached from the senses and the body. So, an important element in the soul's ascent is detachment from the body and the realization of itself as a spiritual being. This is put very sharply in the *Phaedo*: the man who really wishes to attain to knowledge of reality must seek to purify himself — to purify himself from the body and become pure in himself. Such a person will be one who:

approaches each thing, so far as is possible, with the reason alone, not introducing sight into his reasoning nor dragging in any of the other senses along with his thinking, but who employs pure, absolute reason in his attempt to hunt down the pure, absolute essence of things, and who removes himself, so far as is possible, from eyes and ears, and, in a word, from his whole body, because he feels that its companionship disturbs the soul and hinders it from attaining truth and wisdom.   (65E–66A)

Philosophy is thus an attempt to live now a life we can only really live beyond death; it is a preparation for death.

For, if pure knowledge is impossible while the body is with us, one of two things must follow, either it cannot be acquired at all, or only when we are dead: for then the soul will be by itself apart from the body, but not before. And while we live, we shall, I think, be nearest to knowledge when we avoid, as far as possible, intercourse and communion with the body, except what is absolutely necessary, and are not filled with its nature, but keep ourselves pure from it until God himself sets us free. And in this way, freeing ourselves from the foolishness of the body and being pure, we shall, I think, be with the pure and shall know of ourselves all that is pure — and that is, perhaps, the truth. For it cannot be that the impure attain the pure.   (66 E–67 A)[6]

This process of purification has two dimensions: moral and intellectual. Moral purification is the practice of the moral

---

[6] In all passages from the *Phaedo* I have used the translation by H. N. Fowler, in the Loeb Classical Library (1914).

virtues: justice, prudence, temperance, and courage. This is
seen as a way of purifying the soul from the effect of union
with the body. Failure to achieve any of the virtues means that
the soul is unduly influenced by the body. In particular
temperance and courage are seen as the virtues by which the
soul, or rather the rational part of the soul, the mind or *nous*,
controls the desiring part of the soul (the source of all desires,
to epithymetikon) and the passionate part of the soul (the source
of impulses or passions — particularly anger — *to thymikon*).
Lack of these virtues means lack of control, and that means
that the soul is at the mercy of the irrational parts of the
human make-up. The aim of acquiring these virtues is not the
possession of these virtues themselves, but the consequence
they secure — tranquillity, and lack of distraction for the soul.

Moral purification, understood in this way, is clearly part of
philosophy as *melete thanatou*, practice of dying; it is one way in
which the soul seeks to be released and separated from the
body (which is how Plato defines death — *Phaedo* 67 D). In the
Phaedo such purification is presented thus harshly. Elsewhere
in Plato — especially in the *Republic* and the *Laws* — it is
clearly seen that such purification is something that requires
positive attention to and training of the body: the body, and
the whole way of life of the philospher, is taken up into the life
of contemplation. Plato speaks of *mousike paideia*, education
through music, which, while including more than we mean by
music, also involves sensitivity to rhythm and form. So he
speaks of the 'decisive importance of education in poetry and
music: rhythm and harmony sink deep into the recesses of the
soul and take the strongest hold there, bringing that grace of
body and mind which is only to be found in one brought up in
the right way' (*Republic* 401 D). Such *mousike paideia* means
that the soul is deeply sensitive to *beauty*; and it is beauty that
characterizes the form of true reality.[7] Understood like this,
moral purification might be regarded as attuning the body to
the true end of the soul, which is contemplation of true reality.

But there is another, and more important, dimension to the
purification the soul must undergo on its ascent to the real,
and that is intellectual purification. This intellectual purifica-

---

[7] See Jaeger, *Paideia* III. 228 ff.

tion Plato subsumes under the name of dialectic, and the
purpose of dialectic is to accustom the soul to contemplation,
noesis. In the *Republic* Plato discusses what sorts of study will
best serve dialectic, and he singles out two: mathematics, the
science of number and measure; and dialectic proper, the
search for the essence of things, an attempt to find the
principles of things and the highest principle of all, the Idea of
the Good on which all other Ideas depend. These two
intellectual exercises he calls *egertika tes noeseos*, for they
awaken and exercise the understanding (*nous*). And they do
this because both mathematics and dialectic abstract from
what the senses present to us; they accustom the mind to deal
with objects apart from the senses, pure reality (*ousia*).

That sounds very abstract — and indeed it is — but Plato
infuses it with passion. He speaks of the 'pursuit of being'
(*Phaedo* 66 C) using the imagery of the hunt; of the soul
'approaching and mingling with the truly real and begetting
understanding and truth' (*Rep.* 490B). There is, too, the
passionate description of the soul's recognition of true beauty
in the form of the beloved in the *Phaedrus*: 'when one who is
fresh from the mystery, and saw much of the vision, beholds a
godlike face or bodily form that truly expresses beauty, first
there comes upon him a shuddering and a measure of that awe
which the vision inspired, and then reverence as at the sight of
a god . . .' (251 A).[8]

These two strands — the austerely abstract and the passionate — are fused in the account of the pursuit of beauty
found in Diotima's speech in the *Symposium*:

He who aspires to love rightly, ought from his earliest youth to make
a single form the object of his love, and therein to generate
intellectual excellences. He ought, then, to consider that beauty in
whatever form it resides is the brother of that beauty which subsists
in another form; and if he ought to pursue that which is beautiful in
form it would be absurd to imagine that beauty is not one and the
same thing in all forms and would therefore remit much of his ardent
preference towards one, through his perception of the multitude of
claims upon his love. In addition, he would consider the beauty
which is in souls more excellent than that which is in form. So that

[8] Translated by R. Hackforth (1952). I have followed this translation throughout.

one endowed with an admirable soul, even though the flower of his form were withered, would suffice him as the object of his love and care, and the companion with whom he might seek and produce such conclusions as tend to the improvement of youth; so that it might be led to observe the beauty and the conformity which there is in the observation of its duties and the laws, and to esteem little the mere beauty of the outward form. The lover would then conduct his pupil to science, so that he might look upon the loveliness of wisdom; and that contemplating thus the universal beauty, no longer like some servant in love with his fellow would he unworthily and meanly enslave himself to the attractions of one form, nor one subject of discipline or science, but would turn towards the wide ocean of intellectual beauty, and from the sight of the lovely and majestic forms which it contains, would abundantly bring forth his conceptions in philosophy; until, strengthened and confirmed, he should at length steadily contemplate one science, which is the science of this universal beauty.   (*Symp.* 210 A–D)[9]

Here Plato describes how love is subjected to the process of intellectual purification. It is a process of abstraction and simplification — abstraction both qualitative and quantitative. Thus, the soul is led from that which is perceived by the senses to that which is independent of the senses and perceived by the mind alone — a movement from the material to the spiritual. It is led, too, from concern for the many and various to what is single and unique. And yet it is still love. It is not love drained by abstraction and become indifferent, but a love intensified and deepened as the soul plunges into 'the wide ocean of intellectual beauty'.

When the soul has thus been led through this process of moral and intellectual purification, when it has been dragged up 'the steep and rugged ascent', what does it find? It is this that Diotima describes in the continuation of the speech from the *Symposium* already quoted.

He who has been disciplined to this point in Love, by contemplating beautiful objects gradually, and in their order, now arriving at the end of all that concerns Love, on a sudden beholds a beauty wonderful in its nature. This is it, O Socrates, for the sake of which all the former labours were endured. It is eternal, unproduced, indestructible, neither subject to increase nor decay: not, like other

---

[9] Translated by Shelley, in *The Nonesuch Shelley*, 865 ff.

things, partly beautiful and partly deformed; not at one time beautiful and at another time not; not beautiful in relation to one thing and deformed in relation to another; not here beautiful and there deformed; not beautiful in the estimation of one person and deformed in that of another; nor can this supreme beauty be figured to the imagination like a beautiful face, or beautiful hands, or any portion of the body, nor like any discourse, nor any science. Nor does. it subsist in any other that lives or is, either in earth, or in heaven, or in any other place; but it is eternally uniform and consistent, and mono-eidic with itself. All other things are beautiful through a participation of it, with this condition, that although they are subject to production and decay, it never becomes more or less, or endures any change. When any one, ascending from a correct system of Love, begins to contemplate this supreme beauty, he already touches the consummation of his labour.

(*Symp.* 210 D–211 B)[10]

'A beauty wonderful in its nature': this is the goal of the soul's ascent, the rapturous vision of Beauty in itself, the Form of Beauty. But, we should note that it is not simply the highest Form that is discerned, rather the summit of the soul's contemplation is something that transcends what it has known before. What is revealed is eternal: it neither is born nor dies; it does not increase or diminish; it is free of all relativity, as to nature, or duration, as to any of its aspects, or as to place; it can be represented neither by image (*phantasia*) nor by definition (*logos*), it does not manifest itself in another, but is unique in itself. What is revealed is ineffable. As Festugière notes,[11] it is not so much the highest Form, rather it transcends the realm of the Forms: this is quite clear from the fact that it does not admit of definition, *logos*.

This understanding of the Form of the Beautiful as transcending the realm of the Forms is very like what we find in the *Republic* concerning the Form of the Good. Plato compares the Idea of the Good in the realm of the Ideas to the sun in the realm of sensible reality, and extends this analogy to a comparison between *noesis*, understanding, perception in the intelligible realm, and sight, perception in the sensible realm:

---

[10] Ibid. 866 ff.
[11] *Contemplation*, 229 ff. Cf. also 343 ff.

You know what happens when the colours of things are no longer irradiated by the daylight but only by the fainter luminaries of the night; when you look at them, the eyes are dim and seem almost blind, as if there were no unclouded vision in them. But when you look at things on which the Sun is shining, the same eyes see distinctly and it becomes evident that they do contain the power of vision . . . Apply this comparison, then, to the soul. When its gaze is fixed upon an object irradiated by truth and reality, the soul gains understanding and knowledge and is manifestly in possession of intelligence. But when it looks towards that twilight world of things that come into existence and pass away, its sight is dim and it has only opinions and beliefs which shift to and fro, and now it seems like a thing that has no intelligence . . .

This, then, which gives to the objects of knowledge their truth and to him who knows them his power of knowing, is the Form or essential nature of Goodness. It is the cause of knowledge and truth; and so, while you may think of it as an object of knowledge, you will do well to regard it as something beyond truth and knowledge and, precious as these both are, of still higher worth. And, just as in our analogy, light and vision were to be thought of as like the Sun, but not identical with it, so here both knowledge and truth are to be regarded as like the Good, but to identify either with the Good is wrong. The Good must hold a yet higher place of honour . . .

But I want to follow up our analogy still further. You will agree that the Sun not only makes the things we see visible, but also brings them into existence and gives them growth and nourishment; yet he is not the same thing as existence. And so with the objects of knowledge: these derive from the Good not only their power of being known, but their very being and reality; and Goodness is not the same thing as being, but even beyond being, surpassing it in dignity and power.   (508 C–509 B)

This explains why it is that the soul's understanding is enfeebled if it tries to understand things that do not belong to the realm of the Forms — it is as if it tried to observe this world at night. The Form of the Good is the Sun of the intelligible realm; and this means that it is the source of all perception in that realm — that is, of understanding. It is the 'cause of knowledge and truth'. And, so Plato argues, it is, in a sense, *beyond* knowledge and truth. It is in the light of the Idea of the Good that we have true knowledge. And he goes on to say that the Good is even 'beyond being, surpassing it in dignity and power'. The Idea of the Good is not simply the most truly real, but the source itself of all true reality. It is beyond knowledge, and so contemplation of the Good — like contemplation of the Beautiful in the *Symposium* — cannot be simply called knowledge (*episteme*), as can contemplation of the other Forms. The Good is unknowable, and the soul can only touch it, or be united with it.[12]

Contemplation of the Form of the Good or the Beautiful is, then, something that transcends the more usual contemplation of the other Forms (though that is rare enough). This is brought out in another way in the passage from the *Symposium* we have just quoted, when Diotima, as reported by Socrates, says that 'he who has been disciplined to this point in Love ... now arriving at the end of all that concerns Love, *on a sudden* beholds a beauty wonderful in its nature.' 'On a sudden' — *exaiphnes*. The final vision of the Beautiful is not attained, or discovered: it *comes upon* the soul, it is revealed to the soul. It is outside the soul's capacity; it is something given and received. One might speak here of rapture or ecstasy: particularly as such language brings out another idea contained in the world *exaiphnes*, that the final vision is not just *suddenly* present, but suddenly *immediate* to the soul.[13]

The unknowability of the ultimately Real, the source of all reality, and the state of ecstasy that comes upon the soul as it comes into the presence of the ultimately Real clearly go together. The Form of the Good is unknowable, and so, if the soul is to know it, it must in that act of knowing break through the normal limits of knowledge: it is in ecstasy that one knows the Unknowable. Such a connection is not merely implicit. Plato himself makes it in his Seventh Letter, when speaking of the ultimate knowledge, which is the goal of the philosophic quest: 'for it does not admit at all of verbal expression like other studies, but, as a result of continued application to the subject itself and communion therewith, it is brought to birth in the soul on a sudden (*exaiphnes*), as light that is kindled by a leaping spark, and thereafter it nourishes itself' (*Ep.* VII, 341 CD).

This ultimate contemplation — *theoria* — of the Good or the

---

[12] Cf. *Rep.* 490 B (quoted above) and *Symp.* 212 A, both of which use the metaphor of touching.   [13] See Festugière, *Contemplation*, 343, n. 1.

Beautiful is the end of dialectic, but it is not something we can produce or practise — as we can practise dialectic. This ultimate *theoria* comes: we can be ready for it, we can prepare for it, we cannot, however, elicit it, for it is *theoria* of that which is beyond knowledge, beyond the reach of the powers of our understanding.

The Highest Being, the One or the Good, is in truth ineffable. One touches it, one is united with it by *theoria*, but one cannot define it. Circumscribed, it would be no more than an essence. But it transcends all essences, being the principle that determines them as essence, and holds them all in being. The whole task of the master must be reduced to a sort of leading by the hand. He guides the disciple, he prepares him, in his manners and in his spirit, for the contemplative act, but he can neither produce this act nor communicate the result of it. Contemplation is a life lived by a person.[14]

We noted at the beginning of this chapter that there is a religious dimension to Plato's doctrine of contemplation; that for him the realm of the Forms is the divine realm, eternal, immortal, situated beyond the heavens; that the soul belongs to this realm and that in contemplation it realizes its kinship with the Forms, the divine inhabitants of the realm beyond the heavens. In contemplation, then, we might say, the soul realizes its kinship with the divine; that in its flight from this world it becomes *divine*. Plato does indeed say that: 'flight hence is assimilation to God so far as that is possible' (*Theaetetus* 176 B).

Here is an important strand in Plato's understanding of the soul's ascent, but his thought is very rich and contains many possibilities. Plato's ideal is always to pass beyond this world, but this is not necessarily expressed so sharply as in the *Theaetetus'* image of flight. In the *Timaeus* there is a much more positive view of the cosmos: it is called a 'visible god', and the soul's ascent begins by its being attuned to the cosmos, in particular to the movement of the heavenly bodies.

We are creatures not of earth but of heaven, where the soul was first born, and our divine part attaches us by the head to heaven, like a plant by its roots, and keeps our body upright . . . A man who has given his heart to learning and true wisdom and exercised that part

---

[14] Ibid. 191.

of himself is surely bound, if he attains to truth, to have immortal and divine thoughts, and cannot fail to achieve immortality as fully as is permitted to human nature; and because he has always looked after the divine element in himself and kept his guardian spirit in good order he must be happy above all men. There is of course only one way to look after anything and that is to give it its proper food and motions. And the motions in us that are akin to the divine are the thoughts and revolutions of the universe. We should each therefore attend to those motions and by learning about the harmonious circuits of the universe repair the damage done at birth to the circuits in our head, and so restore understanding and what is understood to their original likeness to each other.

(90 A–D)[15]

This is, in some respects, in marked contrast to what we find elsewhere in Plato — in particular, to his rejection of astronomy in the *Republic* (528 E–530 C). But, it is important, as it shows how Plato could understand the soul's assimilation to God not simply as rejection of the world, but as transcending the cosmos by means of the cosmos itself. It is also important as an early witness to the idea that God is perceptible through the cosmos and that contemplation of the cosmos (and especially of the heavens) could lead the soul to God. This tradition, further developed in the *Epinomis* (whether Plato's or not), and the early Aristotle's *De Philosophia*, and found in Cicero, Philo, and the treatise ascribed to Aristotle, *De Mundo*, had great influence between the time of Plato and the beginning of the Christian era.[16]

None the less, whether Plato envisages a stage of attunement to, or harmony with, the cosmos or not, his ultimate aim is the vision of the Forms and, beyond and above them, of the Supreme Form of the Good or the Beautiful. Having attained this stage — something only finally possible beyond death — the soul rejoins the company of the gods. 'The society of the gods none shall join who has not sought wisdom and departed wholly pure: only the lover of knowledge may go thither'

---

[15] Translation by H. D. P. Lee (1965).

[16] On this see A.-J. Festugière, *La Révélation d'Hermès Trismégiste*, II: *Le Dieu cosmique* (Paris, 1949), *passim*, and, in more general terms, his *Personal Religion among the Greeks* (Berkeley, 1954), Chapters 7 and 8.

(*Phaedo* 82 B–C). There, in the 'place beyond the heavens', the soul achieves its homecoming:

> Of that place beyond the heavens none of our earthly poets has yet sung, and none shall sing worthily. But this is the manner of it . . . It is there that true Being dwells, without colour or shape, that cannot be touched; reason alone, the soul's pilot, can behold it, and all true knowledge is knowledge thereof. Now even as the mind of a god is nourished by reason and knowledge, so also is it with every soul that has a care to receive her proper food; wherefore when at last she has beheld Being she is well content, and contemplating truth she is nourished and prospers . . . Such is the life of the gods.
>
> (*Phaedrus* 247 C–248 A)

'Such a life as this', says Diotima to Socrates, 'spent in the contemplation of the beautiful, is the life for man to live' (*Symp.* 211D). This contemplation of true beauty is *bios biotos*, the life worth living. But we would misunderstand Plato if we left it there. The vision of the Good and the Beautiful, of the source of true reality, enables one to understand how all true reality fits together. The realm of the Forms becomes something one can understand as a whole, not as a collection of disorganized *aperçus*. A man who has seen the truth like that is the man who can help his fellow men, help them to order their lives. For Plato this is expressed in his conviction that in the true form of the city-state the rulers would be men who had attained contemplation and were thus able to discern the principles governing human life. Plato recognizes that one who has enjoyed this supreme vision will be reluctant to leave contemplation of it; he recognizes too that one who sees clearly will not necessarily (or even probably) be credited with possession of true wisdom by others; yet he seeks in his writings, in various ways, to show how the contemplation of the Good is something to be used for the benefit of others.

How this is to be is less clear. Plato thought in terms of a city-state; but the city-state was about to pass into history. There is, moreover, a strand in Plato that can see no hope for the city-state. But the undertow of his thought is deeper than mere historical contingency, for he is concerned with true wisdom, not with mere appearance, with the fundamental orientation of man's soul, rather than with his behaviour. But however deeply he interiorized the notion of virtue, he could not relinquish a concern for the society in which men lived, as his unfinished *Laws* bears witness. This tension between the contemplative and the statesman was bequeathed by Plato to later ages.

II. PHILO

WITH Philo we move from the world of classical Greece, a world of city-states, to the period of the Roman Empire. Philo was born towards the end of the first century BC and died in the middle of the first century AD. He was thus a contemporary of Christ, though there is no reason to suppose he had heard of him, and an elder contemporary of most of the writers of the New Testament, some of whom he may have influenced. A Jew of one of the wealthiest families in Alexandria, he was very much at home in the Hellenistic world. His education was Greek and it is unlikely that he knew much Hebrew; but he was a devout Jew, none the less, and defended the traditional customs of his faith. The bulk of his writings consists of commentaries on parts of the Pentateuch in the Septuagint version.

He is important for our purposes for two reasons. First, as a representative of Middle Platonism, the Stoicized form Platonism had taken from the beginning of the first century BC, which provides the intellectual background of many of the Fathers, and is the form in which the idea of the soul's ascent to God is understood. Secondly, Philo is important in himself, for there is no doubt that his writings had a very considerable influence on the Alexandrian tradition in Greek patristic theology. In fact, were it not for his influence on Christians, we should probably know little, if anything, about him, for his works have been preserved for us by Christians, not by Jews. We know of no Jew who mentions him by name until the fifteenth century.

One of the contrasts between Middle Platonism and Plato himself is that there is in Middle Platonism a much clearer conception of a transcendent God. With Plato there is not so

much an idea of God, as an idea of the divine, and it is the
world of the Forms that is the realm of the divine. So, with
Plato, we found it more appropriate to approach his mystical
theology by considering his doctrine of contemplation. With
most Middle Platonism, despite the clearer notion of God, this
would probably still be the most obvious approach, but with
Philo the doctrine of God is central. Though in many ways his
understanding of God is similar to contemporary notions of
God as the One, the Ultimate, it breathes a different spirit:
God is for him not only a philosophical principle, he is the
God of Abraham, Isaac, and Jacob, a God who reveals
Himself, a God about whom Philo thinks and ponders because
He is important to him in Himself. Philo was first and
foremost a Jew. So in consideration of Philo's mystical
theology, it is more suitable to consider first his doctrine of
God. For it is God who is the object of Philo's quest, and it is
His nature that will determine the nature of this quest.

For Philo[1] God is unknowable in Himself and is only made
known in His works. Negative theology must be something of
an ill-begotten child, for the claims made to paternity are so
diverse; but Philo certainly has some claim to be called the
Father of negative theology. God is unknowable in Himself:
His essence cannot be encompassed by human conceptions.
God can only be known as He relates Himself to us. Philo here
utilizes a distinction — not original to him — which was to
have a great career: the distinction between God's essence and
His activities or energies. God is unknown in Himself, but
known in His activities. The distinction is often expressed in
the form of the distinction between He who is, as God
declared Himself to be in the book of Exodus, and His powers
(*dynameis*).

The doctrine of God's unknowability is frequently iterated
throughout the writings of Philo and the theme is often
introduced by the famous sentence from Plato's *Timaeus*: 'To
discover the maker and father of this universe is indeed a hard

[1] The edition of Philo's works used is that of F. H. Colson and G. H. Whitaker
(Loeb Classical Library), which largely follows Cohn and Wendland (Berlin,
1896–1915), and the Loeb translation has been used, with occasional modifications.
References to individual treatises by section with the Loeb abbreviations of the titles
(which are given in vol. x, p. xxxv f.)

task' (28 C). Not that it is difficult to be convinced of the bare existence of God; Philo is far from scepticism. God's existence can easily be apprehended, and to prove it Philo usually falls back on an argument from the order and beauty of the cosmos. Or perhaps not so much an argument as *contemplation* of the order and beauty of the cosmos — especially of the heavens — leading to a sense of awe and wonder at the splendour of God's work, and a *conviction* of his existence (see, e.g., *Leg. All.* iii. 97–9). But what the Deity is in essence is not only difficult but, he says, perhaps impossible to solve. Why? Philo's most frequent contention is that knowledge of God is beyond human capacity, because man's creaturely state prevents such knowledge. It is not — and here we have a characteristically Platonist strain — because God out of envy denies man knowledge of Himself. So God addresses Moses thus:

I freely bestow what is in accordance with the recipient; for not all that I can give with ease is within man's power to take, and therefore to him that is worthy of my grace I extend all the boons which he is capable of receiving. But the apprehension of Me is something more than human nature, yea, even the whole heaven and universe, will be able to contain. Know thyself, then, and do not be led away by impulses and desires beyond thy capacity, nor let yearning for the unattainable uplift and carry thee off thy feet, for of the obtainable nothing shall be denied thee. (*Spec. Leg.* i. 43 ff.)

Know thyself — that should be Moses' aim. Sometimes the difficulty, even the impossibility, of such self-knowledge, is given by Philo as a reason for God's unknowability:

Do not however suppose that the Existent which truly exists is apprehended by any man; for we have in us no organ by which we can envisage it, neither in sense, for it is imperceptible by sense, nor yet in mind . . . And why should we wonder that the Existent cannot be apprehended by men when even the mind in each of us is unknown to us? For who knows the essential nature of the soul? (*Mut.* 7, 10)

God is unknowable in Himself, and knowable only in so far as He can be related to us. This means more than Aristotle's idea that the individual is unknowable, that only universals can be known[2] — something which applies to all individuals, not just to God. What Philo means is that God cannot simply fall within the terms of a relationship: if we know Him, it is because He has established a relationship with us. So, in that sense, God is unknowable in Himself, and knowable only in so far as He relates himself to us. God's *ousia* is inaccessible to us; he relates to us through his powers or *dynameis* (or the *energeiai* of his *dynameis*): God is unknowable in his *ousia* and knowable in his *dynameis*.

These powers of God are very important for Philo and act as intermediaries between the absolute oneness and simplicity of God, He who is, and the multiplicity of the world. Several times he identifies these powers with Plato's Ideas (e.g. *Spec. Leg.* i.48). Philo never delimits the number of the powers; he says, indeed, that they are in themselves unknowable (*Spec. Leg.* i.47). Two, however, are particularly important for him, the kingly and the beneficent — or, occasionally, the kingly and the creative. They manifest God as, respectively, Him who rules, and Him who showers benefits upon man. Through His rule, and through His goodness, God makes Himself known to man and can be known by man.[3]

God, then, is unknowable in Himself because of His simplicity and man's incapacity, but He can reveal Himself according to man's capacity and does so, especially as Ruler and as the Bountiful. God is known because He makes Himself known: in a certain sense all knowledge of God is of grace. So, in *De Specialibus Legibus* (i. 49ff.), we find God's answer to Moses' request to see Him face to face concluding thus:

Do not, then, hope ever to be able to apprehend Me or any of My powers in Our essence. But I readily and with right goodwill will admit you to share of what is attainable. That means that I bid you come and contemplate the universe and its contents, a spectacle apprehended not by the eye of the body but by the unsleeping eyes of the mind. Only let there be a constant and profound longing for wisdom which fills its scholars and disciples with verities glorious in their exceeding loveliness.

[2] *Metaphysics* III. 1003 a13 ff.
[3] This idea of God manifested through His rule and bounty reflects a Hellenistic, rather than a biblical, notion of kingship.

Philo continues: 'When Moses heard this he did not cease from his desire, but kept the yearning for the invisible aflame in his heart.' That is a pattern we often find in Philo: contemplation of the cosmos, leading to knowledge of God's existence and enjoyment of His benefits, but beyond that a yearning to know the unknown God. What sort of yearning is it? And what satisfaction does Philo envisage its finding? It is this yearning to know the unknowable God that leads to the mystical dimension of Philo's thought.

In *De Abrahamo* Philo discusses the appearance to Abraham of the three angels at the oak of Mamre. *Three* men appear to Abraham, and yet Abraham addresses them as 'My Lord' (singular), and, on at least one occasion, the text introduces their words by saying, 'The Lord (singular — in the Hebrew, Yahweh) said'. Philo explains that the three men represent God and His two principal powers, the creative and the kingly, and he says:

... the central place is held by the Father of the Universe, who in the sacred scriptures is called He that is as His proper name, while on either side of Him are the senior powers, the nearest to Him, the creative and the kingly. The title of the former is God, since it made and ordered the universe; the title of the latter is Lord, since it is the fundamental right of the maker to rule and control what he has brought into being. So the central Being, with each of His powers as His squire, presents to the mind which has vision the appearance sometimes of one, sometimes of three; of one when the mind is highly purified and, passing beyond not merely the multiplicity of other numbers, but even the dyad which is next to the unit, presses on to the ideal form which is free from mixture and complexity, and being self-contained needs nothing more; of three when, as yet uninitiated into the highest mysteries, it is still a votary only of the minor rites and unable to apprehend the Existent alone by Itself and apart from all else, but only through Its actions, as either creative or ruling. This is, as they say, a 'second-best voyage'; yet all the same there is in it an element of a way of thinking such as God approves. But the former state of mind has not merely an element. It is in itself the divinely-approved way, or rather it is the truth, higher than a way of thinking, more precious than anything which is merely thought.

(*Abr.* 121-3)

There are two points to remark on. First, the use of the vocabulary of the mystery religions — initiation, greater mysteries, lesser mysteries — which we shall find elsewhere in Philo, and frequently in the Christian Fathers. Although the language goes back to the Eleusinian mysteries, it probably does not indicate any direct influence of mystery cults, for Plato had used such language of the soul's ascent to contemplation,[4] and by Philo's time it had become a literary tradition. But it does highlight the religious quality, the sense of awe and privilege in the soul's deepening quest for God. Secondly, it is knowledge of *to on*, the Existent One, by itself alone and apart from anything. else, that is the 'greater mystery' — the soul passes into the inner sanctuary of knowledge of God when it passes beyond knowing God through His activities.

Philo goes on to explain further by distinguishing three classes of men who seek God from different motives — a theme which is endlessly taken up in the Fathers. The first kind, he says, 'worship the solely Self-Existent and nothing can make them swerve from this, because they are subject to the single attraction which leads them to honour the One. Of the other two types, one is introduced and made known to the Father by the beneficial, the other by the kingly power' (*Abr.* 125). There are those who serve God through love of God alone, those who serve Him from hope of reward, and those who serve Him through fear of punishment; the motives are in a descending order of purity and praiseworthiness. Yet all are accepted by God, as Philo makes clear when he represents God as saying

My first praises will be set apart for those who honour Me for Myself alone, the second to those who honour Me for their own sakes, either hoping to win blessing or expecting to obtain remission of punishment, since, though their worship is for reward and not disinterested, yet all the same its range lies within the divine precincts and does not stray outside. But the prizes set aside for those who honour Me for Myself will be gifts of friendship; those whose motive is self-interest do not show friendship, but for that I do not count them as aliens. For I accept both him who wishes to enjoy My beneficial power and thus partake of blessings and him who propitiates the dominance and authority of the master to avoid chastisement. For I know well that they will not only not be

---

[4] e.g. *Symp.* 210 A

worsened but actually bettered through the persistence of their worship and through practising piety pure and undefiled. For, however different are the characters which produce in them the impulses to do My pleasure, no charge shall be brought against them, since they have one aim and object, to serve Me.

(*Abr.* 128–30)

Philo's compassion towards those who serve God out of fear is remarkable and humane, and in contrast not only with the Rabbis, from whom Philo probably acquired this triple distinction, but also with many of the Fathers

Although God, then, is knowable through the activity of His Powers, there is a quest of the soul for the unknowable God in Himself, beyond and apart from the powers. If we recall how earlier we saw Philo distinguishing between God in Himself and God as He relates Himself to us through the powers, we can say that the mystical quest of the soul is the result of its longing for God Himself alone, and apart from the benefits of His relationship to us — it is a quest of pure love.

How is this quest pursued? and what is the end of the quest? First, let us deal with 'how?'. A fairly common account of the way discloses three stages: conversion to pure religion, self-knowledge, and knowledge of God. For instance, in the treatise *De Migratione Abrahami*:

In this way the mind gradually changing its place will arrive at the Father of piety and holiness. Its first step is to relinquish astrology, which betrayed it into the belief that the universe is the primal God instead of being the handiwork of the primal God, and that the causes and movements of the constellations are the causes of bad and good fortune to mankind. Next it enters upon the consideration of itself, makes a study of the features of its own abode, those that concern the body and sense-perception, and speech, and comes to know, as the phrase of the poet puts it: 'All that existeth of good and of ill in the halls of thy homestead'. The third stage is when, having opened up the road that leads from self, in hope thereby to come to discern the Universal Father, so hard to trace and unriddle, it will crown maybe the accurate self-knowledge it has gained with the knowledge of God Himself. It will stay no longer in Haran, the organs of sense, but withdraw into itself. For it is impossible that the mind whose course still lies in the sensible rather than the mental should arrive at the contemplation of Him that is.   (*Mig.* 195ff.)

The first stage is conversion to pure religion. In this passage
it is expressed in terms of conversion from a belief in astrology,
from a belief, that is, that the heavens rule the affairs of men
and are, in fact, divine, to a belief in a transcendent God who
created the universe. Philo's rejection of this 'cosmic religion'
is a rejection of the dominant form of cultured piety in the
Hellenistic world.[5] What he offers men is not some experience
of oneness with the cosmos, but a communion with the
Creator God Himself. The first stage is to see that the universe
is not all there is, but something created, beyond which there
is the Creator. The second stage is by way of self-knowledge in
which the soul comes to know itself. This involves the
acquiring of moral purity, through which the soul asserts its
sovereignty over the body, and is discussed by Philo in terms
familiar from Plato. But for Philo the soul is not an essentially
divine being that belongs to the divine realm and is seeking in
contemplation to recover its pristine state. The soul is a
creature, created by God, and nothing in itself. This means
that self-knowledge is not *identified* with knowledge of God; in
self-knowledge the soul does not realize the world of the Ideas
within itself (as in Plotinus, and perhaps in Plato), rather, in
self-knowledge the soul comes to realize its own nothingness
and is thrown back on God, Him who is. This is put very
dramatically in a passage in *de Somniis*, which speaks of
Abraham:

who gained much progress and improvement towards the acquisi-
tion of the highest knowledge: for when most he knew himself, then
most did he despair of himself, in order that he might attain to an
exact knowledge of Him Who in reality is. And this is nature's law:
he who has thoroughly comprehended himself, thoroughly despairs
of himself, having as a step to this ascertained the nothingness in all
respects of created being. And the man who has despaired of himself
is beginning to know Him that is. (*Som.* i. 60)

This recognition that the soul is a creature also leads to an
emphasis on the fact that the soul's capacity to know God is
not a natural capacity, but rather something given by God:

[5] For this see F. Cumont's seminal article, 'Le Mysticisme astral dans l'antiquité',
Bulletin de l'Académie Royale de Belgique (Classe des Lettres) 5 (1909), 256–86, and A.-J.
Festugière, *La Révélation*, II: *Le Dieu cosmique* and more briefly, *Personal Religion*, chap.
VII: 'Man and the World'.

Let us not, then, the pupils of Moses, be any longer at a loss as to how man came to have a conception of the invisible God. For Moses himself learnt it by a divine communication, and has taught us how it was. He stated it thus. The Creator wrought for the body no soul capable by itself of seeing its Maker but, accounting that it would be greatly to the advantage of the thing wrought should it obtain a conception of Him who wrought it, since this is what determines happiness and blessedness, He breathed into him from above of His own Deity. The invisible Deity stamped on the invisible soul the impression of Itself, to the end that not even the terrestrial region should be without a share in the image of God.   (*Det.* 86)

The soul can conceive of God because it has received from God some participation in Himself. So Philo sees man's spiritual capacity not as something natural but as God-given; man's relationship to God is a possibility given to him by God. In his insistence on this we can sense something of a contrast between Philo and Plato. Nevertheless, what Philo says draws on Plato's idea in the *Timaeus* (41C: cf. 90 A ff.) that immortal souls are the direct creation of the demiurge, while what is mortal is made by lesser gods.

The way then is, with some modifications, the way that we have already found in Plato — a movement from the material to the spiritual, from the external to the interior, from the transient to the eternal — and the method is one of purification, both moral and intellectual. The end of the way is something outside the soul's power to attain — on the third stage the soul *hopes* for the final manifestation of God; there is no suggestion that the soul can attain this state by its own efforts. In one place, however, Philo gives an account of the soul's ascent from conversion by way of dialectic which is both profoundly Platonist, but which also suggests something quite different. It is an allegory of a passage from Leviticus (2:14), which in Philo's version runs: 'What is offered in the offering of the first-fruits is first the new, then the roasted, then the sliced, and last the ground' (*Sac.* 76). The detail is complicated, but his conclusion is: 'When then you acknowledge in a spiritual sense these four things: the "new", that is the blossom or vigour; the "roasted", that is the fire-tested and invincible reason; the "sliced", that is the division of things into their classes; the "pounded", that is the persistent practice and exercise in what the mind has grasped, you will bring an offering of the first-fruits, even the first and best offspring of the soul' (*Sac.* 87). Here we have conversion to the true religion in the first stage; in the middle two something very like Platonic dialectic, — the training of the reason and the slicing into categories; and the fourth, pounding or grinding, which Philo describes as a 'continual dwelling in and lingering over the thoughts presented to our mind'. What we have, it seems to me, is an account, veiled in allegory, of meditation, leading to a sort of contemplative mulling over. And the object of such meditation is Scripture[6] which is, for Philo, the inspired word of God; it is direct communication with God as opposed to the indirect witness of creation.

To understand this a little more we must discuss Philo's doctrine of the Word, the *Logos*. It is well known that Philo's doctrine is a development of the Stoic idea of the divine *logos* or reason that underlies and fashions all things. For Philo, with his pronounced doctrine of a transcendent God (in contrast to Stoic immanentism), the *Logos* becomes a mediator between the transcendent God and the world, and has both transcendent and immanent aspects.[7] There is however another strand in Philo's doctrine of the Word that is much less remarked on. This develops not out of the idea of the divine reason, *logos*, but from the idea of God as one who speaks — *ho legon* — an idea of God without parallel in Greek thought.[8] There is no difficulty in relating this to the idea just mentioned of the divine reason fashioning the universe, since, in the account of the creation in Genesis 1, creation is a result of God's *speaking*. It is in line with this approach that we read (*Fug.* 95) of 'the powers of Him who speaks (*tou legontos*), their leader being the creative power, in the exercise of which the Creator produced the universe by a word (by the Word?)'. Here the Word — if this is what Philo really has in mind — appears to be something distinct from the powers. Elsewhere

---

[6] The 'new, fresh, blessed thoughts from the ever ageless God' (*Sac.* 76).

[7] For this see E. Bréhier, *Les Idées philosophiques et religieuses de Philon d'Alexandrie* (Paris 1925), 83–111; J. Daniélou, *Philon d'Alexandrie* (Paris, 1958), 153–62. There is also a long discussion in H. A. Wolfson, *Philo* (Cambridge, Mass., 1947), I. 200–94, 325–59.

[8] According to J. Dillon, *The Middle Platonists* 166.

the Word is spoken of as Himself a power, albeit the highest one, the third above and between the sovereign and bountiful powers:

And in the midst between the two there is a third which unites them, Reason, for it is through reason that God is both ruler and good. Of these two powers, sovereignty and goodness, the Cherubim are symbols, as the fiery sword is the symbol of reason. For exceeding swift and of burning heat is reason and chiefly so the reason [or Word] of the Cause, for it alone preceded and outran all things, conceived before them all, manifest above them all.   (*Cher.* 28)

Why the Word appears above and between the Cherubim who represent the two senior powers can be seen from *De Fuga* where we read that the Word is:

himself the Image of God, chiefest of all beings intellectually perceived, placed nearest, with no intervening distance to the Alone truly existent One. For we read, 'I will talk with thee from above the Mercy-Seat, between the two Cherubim' (Exod. 25:21): words which show that while the Word is the charioteer of the Powers, He who talks is seated in the chariot, giving direction to the charioteer for the right wielding of the reins of the Universe.   (*Fug.* 101)

Although there seems to be some confusion as to whether the Word is the word spoken by God, or the one to whom God speaks, it seems clear enough that in the Word there is direct communication with God, as opposed to the indirect experience of Him afforded by the other powers.

The picture of the Word between the powers recalls the picture in *De Abrahamo*[9] of Him who is between the two senior powers. There we found a contrast between those who seek God for His own sake and those who seek Him for what they can obtain through the powers. There is a similar contrast here between those who seek the Word and those who seek the powers:

The man who is capable of running swiftly it bids not to stay to draw breath but pass forward to the supreme Divine Word, who is the fountain of Wisdom, in order that he may draw from the stream and,

[9] See above, 22.

released from death, gain life eternal as his prize. One less sure-footed it directs to the power to which Moses gives the name 'God', since by it the Universe was established and ordered. It urges him to flee for refuge to the creative power, knowing that to one who has grasped the fact that the whole world was brought into being a vast good accrues, even the knowledge of its Maker, which straightway wins the thing created to love Him to whom it owes its being. One who is less ready it urges to betake himself to the kingly power, for fear of the sovereign has a force of correction to admonish the subject, where a father's kindness has none such for the child . . .
(*Fug.* 97 f.)

All this seems to suggest that Philo's 'mystic way', as we have called it, where the soul seeks God for himself alone and not for the benefits it can receive through the powers, where the soul seeks God immediately and not through the media-tion of the powers, where the soul passes beyond the 'minor rites' and is admitted to the 'higher mysteries',[10] that this 'mystic way' is pursued by seeking the Word and thus a direct communion with God, in particular in meditation on the Scriptures. And this direct communing with the Word in meditation *is* to enter into the higher mysteries. The Word is the soul's food, as it seeks God in and for Himself. So Philo compares it to the manna in the wilderness:

You see of what sort the soul's food is. It is a word of God, continuous, resembling dew, embracing all the soul and leaving no portion without part in itself. But not everywhere does this word show itself, but only on the wilderness of passions and wickedness, and it is fine and delicate both to conceive and be conceived and surpassingly clear and transparent to behold, and it is as it were coriander seed. Tillers of the soil say that if you cut a coriander seed and divide it into countless pieces, each of the portions into which you cut it, if sown, grows exactly as the whole seed could have done. Such too is the word of God, able to confer benefits both as a whole and by means of every part, yes, any part you light on.
(*Leg. All.* iii. 169 f.)

This feeding on Scripture, God's communication to the soul, is very important for the understanding of Philo. It gives particularity to the importance of grace in his mystical

[10] Terms used in *Abr.*

thought. For Philo all is of grace: creation is a grace, the soul's capacity to know God is due to the grace of God.[11]. And, on the way, meditation on God's word is the soul's food. Philo's allegorical method may seem strange to us — though it is not that different from many later methods of meditating on Scripture, it simply has a different cultural context — but for him it is a real way of feeding his love for God. Philo sometimes speaks of the soul receiving from God in a way that recalls infused contemplation:

Again, shall we on whom God pours as in snow or rain-shower the fountains of His blessings from above, drink of a well and seek for the scanty springs that lie beneath the earth, when heaven rains upon us unceasingly the nourishment which is better than the nectar and ambrosia of the myths? Or shall we draw up with ropes the drink which has been stored by the devices of men and accept as our haven and refuge a task which argues our lack of true hope; we to whom the Saviour of all has opened His celestial treasure for our use and enjoyment . . .? Nay, he will not drink of a well on whom God bestows the undiluted rapture-giving draughts . . .

(*Quod Deus*, 155 ff.)

Philo here is, among other things, contrasting Scripture with pagan philosophy and pagan myths, but his language recalls St. Teresa's analogy of the Four Waters (*Life*, XI), particularly the second, third, and fourth, the fourth water being, for Teresa, infused contemplation. And, it is in terms of the fourth, the highest, that Philo describes the experience of the soul engaged on the true quest. So we must see in Philo's pondering on Scripture something that passes beyond discursive meditation to contemplation (to use the traditional terms of Western spiritual theology).

This strand in Philo's doctrine of the Word is something quite original to him. Starting from an idea of God without parallel in his philosophical milieu, Philo develops an understanding of the Word that sees meditation on Scripture, that is, God's self-disclosure, as central to the soul's search for God. This is quite new — and something that the Christian Fathers were to take up and make their own.

In Philo, then, we have a way by meditation on scripture, a

---

[11] See above, 26.

way to God as He is in Himself through attending to His self-
disclosure in His Word, and in His Word in Scripture. But
this is still only a stage: the soul that seeks God as He is in
Himself will seek to ascend beyond God's manifestation of
Himself through the Word to God in Himself:

One who has come from abroad under Wisdom's guidance arrives at
the former place, thus attaining in the divine word the sum and
consummation of service. But when he has his place in the divine
Word he does not actually reach Him who is in very essence God,
but sees Him from afar: or rather, not even from a distance is he
capable of contemplating Him; all he sees is the bare fact that God
is far away from all Creation, and that the apprehension of Him is
removed to a very great distance from all human power of thought.
                                                          (*Som.* i. 66)

But what is this apprehension of God in Himself? What is the
goal of the soul's quest? In a fairly characteristic passage,
Philo speaks of the goal of the soul's quest thus:

. . . If thou art seeking God, O mind, go out from thyself and seek
diligently; but if thou remainest amid the heavy encumbrances of
the body or the self-conceits with which the understanding is
familiar, though thou mayest have the semblance of a seeker, not
thine is the quest for the things of God. But whether thou wilt find
God when thou seekest is uncertain, for to many He has not
manifested Himself, but their zeal has been without success all
along. And yet the mere seeking by itself is sufficient to make us
partakers of good things, for it always is the case that endeavours
after noble things, even if they fail to attain their object, gladden in
their very course those who make them.   (*Leg. All.* iii. 47)

It is clear that the mind's going out of itself spoken of here has
nothing to do with ecstasy but simply means detachment from
the body and bodily concerns. There is no guarantee of
success on the quest: for God must reveal Himself, and the
soul can do nothing to elicit this disclosure — it can only
prepare. But even so, the quest by itself is sufficient satisfaction. One might say that the quest is the goal and the goal is
the quest. In any case, to be engaged on the quest for God is
what matters.

Philo has an important treatment of Moses' search for God
in *De Posteritate Caini*:

But so unceasingly does Moses himself yearn to see God and to be seen by Him that he implores Him to reveal clearly His own nature, which is so hard to divine, hoping thus to obtain at length a view free from all falsehood, and to exchange doubt and uncertainty for a most assured confidence.   (13)

Here we have what we are familiar with — the yearning to know God in and for Himself. Philo goes on: 'So see him enter into the thick darkness where God was, that is, into the innermost sanctuary — formless conceptions concerning being' (14). We note again the language of the mystery cults, the mind entering the shrine or sanctuary, the greater mysteries, knowledge of God in and for Himself. That is also made clear by Philo's words about 'formless conceptions concerning being', which I take to mean that they are beyond the realm of the forms, beyond Plato's 'place above the heavens'. It is thick darkness — for God is unknowable. Philo continues:

When therefore the God-loving soul probes the question of the essence of the Existent One, he enters on a quest of that which is beyond form and beyond sight. And out of this quest there accrues to him a vast boon, namely to apprehend that the God of real Being is apprehensible by no one, and to see precisely this, that He is incapable of being seen.   (15)

The goal of the quest, which is said to be a great boon, is to know that God cannot be known. In part this means that the quest is never-ending — the goal is always beyond because God is infinite and incomprehensible.

With the lovers of God, then, in their quest of the Existent One, even if they never find Him, we rejoice, for the quest of the Good and the Beautiful, even if the goal be missed, is sufficient of itself to give a foretaste of gladness.   (21)

The quest is a joy in itself. That we have seen before. But Philo's doubt, 'even if the goal be missed', rather than something like, 'although the goal can never be attained', makes one wonder whether there may not be some further goal to this quest. Perhaps some sort of ecstatic knowing by unknowing. But even without that possibility, Philo can be seen to have developed a mysticism of love and yearning for God in Himself, in his unknowability. God is unknowable in

Himself, but known through the activity of His powers: some souls are called on a quest to seek God in and for Himself, a quest that is unending and is itself a source of joy. That the quest is unending is occasionally related to the fact that with God alone is there stillness and quiet, change of all sorts being the permanent lot of creation.[12]

But does Philo go further? Does he speak of any kind of ecstatic union with God? We have seen that for Plato the final vision of the Idea of the Beautiful is some sort of rapture and we shall find again in Plotinus an understanding of ecstasy in which the soul is united with the One. What about Philo?

Philo does discuss ecstasy. In one place (*Quis her.* 249) he distinguishes four types of ecstasy: madness or melancholy, amazement, stillness of mind, and divine possession or frenzy. The fourth type is certainly literal ek-stasis: the mind is expelled and the divine spirit takes its place:

When the light of God shines, the human light sets; when the divine light sets, the human dawns and rises. This is what regularly befalls the fellowship of the prophets. The mind is evicted at the arrival of the divine Spirit, but when that departs the mind returns to its tenancy. Mortal and immortal may not share the same home. And therefore the setting of reason and the darkness which surrounds it produce ecstasy and inspired frenzy. (264 ff.)

That is certainly genuine ecstasy, *sortie de soi*, but it has nothing to do with mystical union: it is purely concerned with the ecstasy that produces prophecy.

The third type of ecstasy is not discussed by Philo at any length. He describes it as 'stillness of mind' and also as 'tranquillity and stillness of the mind', 'sleep of the mind'. Such terminology will later be used to describe mystic states, but Philo does not seem to have such in mind here. Parallel discussions (*Qu. Gen.* i. 24; *Leg. All.* ii. 19–37) suggest that Philo is concerned with the nature of sleep — both ordinary sleep and the metaphorical sleep to which the mind succumbs when overwhelmed by the activity of the senses — the very opposite of any mystical state.[13]

In some places, however, Philo does seem to envisage a

[12] See, e.g., *Post.* 29
[13] Cf. Bréhier, 196 ff. See also M. Harl's important introduction to her edition of *Quis Her.* (Paris, 1966. Vol. 15 of the Lyon edition of Philo).

state in which the soul passes beyond the stage of seeking. For instance, in *Leg. All* i. 84, comparing the colours of the ruby and the sapphire (which he says is green, because, doubtless, of his assimilation of the 'ruby and the sapphire' of Exod. 18:18 to the 'ruby and the green stone' of Gen. 2:12), he writes:

to him who makes the confession of praise the hue of the ruby belongs, for he is permeated by fire in giving thanks to God, and is drunk with a sober drunkenness. But to him who is still labouring the hue of the green stone is proper, for men in exercise and training are pale.

Here there seems to be a contrast between the soul that still struggles — 'in exercise and training' — and the soul that is 'drunk with sober drunkenness'. 'Sober drunkenness' suggests some sort of ecstatic state, and other language in this passage seems to suggest that Judah, of whom the ruby is a symbol, has attained a state of ecstasy. For instance,

the very word denoting confession (*exomologesis*) vividly portrays the acknowledgement that takes a man out of himself. For whenever the mind goes out from itself and offers itself up to God, as Isaac or 'laughter' does, then does it make confession of acknowledgement towards the Existent One.   (*Leg. All.* i. 82)

But, if we look closely, it is fairly clear what sort of a contrast is being made between the ruby and the sapphire, Judah and Issachar, the soul who makes confession of praise and the soul who still labours. Philo says that here there is a contrast between the *phronimos* and the *phronon*, the man who is good and the man who seeks to do good (*Leg. All.* i. 79). But this is nothing else than the Stoic contrast between the sage, the wise man, *sophos*, *spoudaios*, *phronimos*, and the one who is seeking virtue, the one who is progressing, *prokopton*. For the Stoics there was a difference of kind between these two states, and the transition from the state of *prokopton* to that of *sophos* was a sudden and total change (Plutarch uses the word *exaiphnes* in this context[14]). For the Stoics the sage was one

---

[14] See H. von Arnim, *Stoicorum Veterum Fragmenta* (reprinted Stuttgart, 1968) III. 539. In general, on the contrast between the *sophos* and the *prokopton*, see J. M. Rist, *Stoic Philosophy* (Cambridge, 1969), 90 ff.

who possessed the good, who no longer struggled to attain it but whose actions simply *were* right. Their language about the sage was pretty ecstatic,[15] but there was no suggestion that the sage *was* an ecstatic. Far from having gone out of himself, the sage had become wholly himself, at one with himself and the whole cosmos.

It is this that Philo is thinking of when he speaks of one who is drunk with sober drunkenness, not of ecstatic union with God. The type of this is Isaac, 'Laughter', the self-taught one, the one who is taught by the Word and does not need to struggle to gain knowledge. So Isaac receives an oracle the purpose of which is:

to show him that the wise man does but sojourn in this body which our senses know, as in a strange land, but dwells in and has for his fatherland the virtues known to the mind, which God speaks and which are thus identical with divine words.   (*Conf.* 81)

It seems that we are back discussing the one who longs for God in Himself and knows the 'infused contemplation' granted to the one who pursues the quest. This is the wise man, the one for whom the longing to know God has become all-devouring, the one for whom the quest is his life and that quest endless:

Therefore, my soul, if thou feelest any yearning to inherit the good things of God, leave not only thy land, that is the body, thy kinsfolk, that is the senses, thy father's house (Gen. xii. 1), that is speech, but be a fugitive from thyself also and issue forth from thyself. Like persons possessed and corybants, be filled with inspired frenzy, even as the prophets are inspired. For it is the mind which is under the divine afflatus, and no longer in its own keeping, but is stirred to its depths and maddened by heavenward yearning, drawn by the One who truly is and pulled upward thereto, with truth to lead the way and remove all obstacles before its feet, that its path may be smooth to tread — such is the mind, which has this inheritance.   (*Quis Her.* 69 ff.)

---

[15] See Arnim *SVF* IV, Index, s.v. σόφος.

III.   PLOTINUS

PLOTINUS is more than an episode in our passage from Plato to the Fathers. In him we find the supreme exponent of an abiding element in what we might call 'mystical philosophy'. He represents man's inherent desire to return to heaven at its purest and most ineffable. Compared with him the various theories of Hellenistic philosophy appear as so many hints and suggestions. As E. R. Dodds puts it, in Plotinus 'converge almost all the main currents of thought that come down from eight hundred years of Greek speculation; out of it there issues a new current destined to fertilize minds as different as those of Augustine and Boethius, Dante and Meister Eckhart, Coleridge, Bergson and T. S. Eliot.'[1]

Of Plotinus' life we know little. Porphyry, the disciple to whom Plotinus entrusted the editing of his writings, wrote a brief account of his master which would stand as sufficient tribute to the quality of Plotinus' teaching and life even were no other available. According to Porphyry, Plotinus was extremely unwilling to talk of himself, and would not celebrate his own birthday or allow an artist to take a likeness of him. Nevertheless, some facts emerge. Born c.204, he appears to have come from Alexandria, where he studied philosophy, notably under Ammonius Saccas. Drawn to Eastern thought — Persian and Indian — he joined the army under the Emperor Gordian for his campaign against Persia. After Gordian's death Plotinus fled back to the Empire and finally settled in Rome where he taught philosophy, by which time he was about forty. Porphyry tells us he was reluctant to commit the substance of his discussions to writing, but that at last he did write various treatises, fifty-four in all, which Porphyry

[1] 'Tradition and Personal Achievement in the Philosophy of Plotinus', in E. R. Dodds, *The Ancient Concept of Progress* (Oxford, 1973), 126.

edited and arranged according to themes in six groups of nine treatises — hence *Enneads*, meaning nine.[2]

We think of Plotinus and his followers as *neo*-Platonists, innovators, marking a new departure in the Platonic tradition. But this is a modern viewpoint which they would have resisted: they saw themselves simply as Platonists. 'These doctrines are no novelties, no inventions of today; they were stated, though not elaborated, long ago. Our present teaching is simply an exposition of them — we can prove the antiquity of these opinions by Plato's own testimony' (V.1.8).[3] And, indeed, Plotinus finds the whole of his philosophy in Plato: Plato is his Scripture, and he uses quotations from him to vindicate the truth and orthodoxy of his opinions. More than that, even when he does not quote Plato directly, his language is often full of Platonic echoes. This is particularly true of his understanding of the soul's ascent to the One. Nevertheless, Plotinus is deeply original. He draws together the doctrines of Plato, and the discussions they had given rise to in the intervening centuries, into a profound and suggestive system, though the term 'system' is perhaps misleading. Plotinus does have a unifying vision; everything is fitted into a whole. On the other hand, it is not true to say there are no loose ends; nor is it the case that his system has the mechanical, geometric structure of later Athenian neo-Platonism, best exemplified in Proclus' *Elements of Theology*, which, somewhat like Spinoza's *Ethics*, is a treatise fashioned after the manner of Euclid. We can approach Plotinus' philosophy or system in two ways. It can either be seen as a great hierarchical structure, a great chain of being, or it can be seen as an exercise in introspective understanding of the self. It is the latter which will interest us most, but we shall begin with the former.

Plotinus' hierarchy is expressed in terms of three principles, or *hypostases*, or gods. Beginning with the highest, these are the One or the Good; Intelligence, *nous* (impossible to translate, it is rendered somewhat awkwardly as Intellectual-Principle[4] in MacKenna's version[5]); and Soul, *psyche*. Soul is

---

[2] On all this see Porphyry's *Life of Plotinus*, in any edition of the *Enneads*.

[3] All such references are to the *Enneads*.

[4] But see my introduction, p. vi.

[5] *Plotinus: The Enneads*, translated by S. MacKenna, revised by B. S. Page, preface by E. R. Dodds, introduction by P. Henry, SJ (Faber and Faber, 1969). This is the

the level of life as we know it, the realm of sense-perception, of discursive knowledge, of planning and reasoning. Beyond this, there is the more unified realm of Intelligence, *nous*. This is Plato's realm of the Forms. Here knower and known are one, here knowledge is intuitive: it is not the result of seeking and finding, with the possibility of error, but a possession, marked by infallibility. For Plato this was ultimate reality. For Plotinus, not so; for here, among the Forms, there is still duality, there is still multiplicity; there is the duality of knower and known, even if they are united; there is multiplicity in that there are many Forms, even if they are a harmonious unity. Beyond the realm of Intelligence, for Plotinus, is the One, which is absolutely simple, beyond any duality whatsoever, and of which, therefore, nothing can be said. It is the One, because beyond duality; it is the Good, because it has no need of anything else. It is the source of all, it is beyond being. Nothing can be affirmed truly of the One: 'we must be patient with language; we are forced for reasons of exposition to apply to the Supreme terms which strictly are ruled out; everywhere we must read "so to speak"' (*hoion*: VI.8.13). 'Generative of all, the Unity is none of all; neither thing nor quality nor quantity nor intellect nor soul; not in motion, not at rest, not in place, not in time; it is the self-defined, unique in form, or better, formless . . .' (VI.9.3).

These three *hypostases*, the One, Intelligence or *nous*, and Soul, are related by processes Plotinus calls emanation and return — *proodos* and *epistrophe*. Intelligence emanates from the One, and Soul from Intelligence: out of the utterly simple there comes multiplicity, and that multiplicity is further diversified and broken up at the level of discursive under-standing. This process of emanation is a process of 'overflow-ing', the potent simplicity of the One 'overflows' into Intelli-gence, and Intelligence overflows into Soul. Emanation is met by Return. Emanation is the One's unfolding its simplicity: Return is the Good's drawing everything to itself. Everything strives for the Good, longs to return to the Good: and this is Return. The balance of Emanation and Return produces

translation used here (with occasional modifications), of which E. R. Dodds says: 'His work must in my opinion rank as one of the very few great translations produced in our time' (see p. xiii). The Greek text used is the critical edition by P. Henry and H.-R. Schwyzer (Paris and Brussels, 1951–73).

equilibrium. This is not an explanation of the *origin* of the cosmos — for Plotinus the cosmos is eternal — it is an attempt to understand how things eternally are.

Plotinus uses several analogies to illustrate his understanding of how everything emanates from the One. Sometimes he speaks of the way warmth emanates from a fire, or light from the sun. A favourite analogy is the One as the centre of a circle, containing potentially all the circles that can emanate from it. In this analogy, Intelligence is the circle with the One as its centre, and Soul such a circle revolving round the One (IV.4.16). E. R. Dodds develops this analogy thus:

For the Outgoing his favourite image is that of an expanding circle, whose radii all take their rise in the pure simplicity of an unextended and indivisible point and carry outwards towards the circumference a trace of that potent simplicity, which fades gradually as the circle expands, but is never wholly lost. We may think of the continuously expanding and continuously weakening circle of ripples that you get when you throw a stone into still water — save that here there is no stone-thrower, and no water either: reality *is the ripples* and there is nothing else.[6]

From the One emanates *Nous*; from *Nous*, Soul. Soul emanates too, and the products of its emanations are the various forms of embodied life. These cannot emanate, for they are too weak. The furthest limit of the One's emanation is matter, which is on the brink, as it were, of being and non-being.

To emanation there corresponds, as we have seen, an answering movement of return. Everything desires to return to the One, to return to the fulness of being of which it is an outflow. And the return is back through the *hypostases*: embodied soul to Soul free from body, Soul to *Nous*, *Nous* to the One. The process of return is a movement of desire, desire nourished by and expressed in contemplation. In *Ennead* III. 8 Plotinus maintains — as a sort of play, he says, but a pretty serious sort of play — 'that all things are striving after Contemplation, looking to Vision as their one end . . . and that all achieve their purpose in the measure possible to their own kind, each attaining Vision and possessing itself of the End in its own way and degree. . . .' Genuine contemplation

[6] Dodds, op. cit., 130.

achieves return, *epistrophe*, but weak contemplation leads to something produced outside itself. Action, for instance, is a form of weak contemplation. So, the visible world is the production of the weak contemplation of Nature, which is itself the offspring of World-Soul's contemplation. This example gives us a glimpse of Plotinus' deep sense of the primacy of contemplation, and also suggests that his notion of return is an extrapolation of his sense of the *soul's* desire for return to the One. And that suggestion is, I suspect, justified.

This leads us quite directly to the other way I mentioned of looking at Plotinus' philosophy, that is, as an exercise in introspective understanding of the self. What we have so far said about Plotinus' philosophy would be misleading if it suggested that this hierarchy of the One, Intelligence, and Soul was a sort of ladder, the One being at the top, distant and remote. For Plotinus, the higher is not the more remote; the higher is the more inward: one climbs up by climbing in, as it were. Augustine's *tu autem eras interior intimo meo et superior summo meo* (thou wert more inward than the most inward place of my heart and loftier than the highest), with its suggested identification of the inward and the higher, strikes an authentically Plotinian note. As the soul ascends to the One, it enters more and more deeply into itself: to find the One is to find itself. Self-knowledge and knowledge of the ultimate are bound up together, if not identified. Ascent to the One is a process of withdrawal into oneself. So Plotinus speaks thus of the soul's ascent to the One:

'Let us flee then to the beloved Fatherland': this is the soundest counsel. But what is this flight? How are we to gain the open sea? For Odysseus is surely a parable to us when he commands the flight from the sorceries of Circe or Calypso — not content to linger for all the pleasure offered to his eyes and all the delight of sense filling his days.

The Fatherland to us is There whence we have come, and There is the Father.

What then is our course, what the manner of our flight? This is not a journey for the feet; the feet bring us only from land to land; nor need you think of coach or ship to carry you away; all this order of things you must set aside and refuse to see: you must close the eyes and call instead upon another vision which is to be waked within you, a vision, the birth-right of all, which few turn to use.

And this inner vision, what is its operation?

Newly awakened it is all too feeble to bear the ultimate splendour. Therefore the Soul must be trained — to the habit of remarking, first, all noble pursuits, then the works of beauty produced not by the labour of the arts but by the virtue of men known for their goodness; lastly, you must search the souls of those that have shaped these beautiful forms.

But how are you to see into a virtuous soul and know its loveliness?

Withdraw into yourself and look. And if you do not find yourself beautiful yet, act as does the creator of a statue that is to be made beautiful: he cuts away here, he smooths there, he makes this line lighter, this other purer, until a lovely face has grown upon his work. So do you also; cut away all that is excessive, straighten all that is crooked, bring light to all that is overcast, labour to make all one glow of beauty and never cease chiselling your statue, until there shall shine out on you from it the godlike splendour of virtue, until you shall see the perfect goodness surely established in the stainless shrine.

When you know that you have become this perfect work, when you are self-gathered in the purity of your being, nothing now remaining that can shatter that inner unity, nothing from without clinging to the authentic man, when you find yourself wholly true to your essential nature, wholly that only veritable Light which is not measured by space, not narrowed to any circumscribed form nor again diffused as a thing void of term, but ever unmeasurable as something greater than all measure and more than all quantity — when you perceive that you have grown to this, you are now become very vision. Now call up all your confidence, strike forward yet a step — you need a guide no longer. Strain and see.   (I.6.8–9)

There is much that is familiar in this passage, much that reminds us of Plato: the image of flight, from the *Theaetetus*, then, more strikingly, the echoes of Diotima's speech in the *Symposium*; only here, significantly, it is not just human beauty that awakens the soul's love, but also the beauty fashioned by the arts. But, despite similarities, the feel is different. The emphasis on withdrawal into oneself is much stronger; and the vivid image of making one's soul as a sculptor does a statue is new and striking. Another point that MacKenna's translation brings out with great deftness and beauty is the sense of the reality and wonder of that Fatherland whence the soul has come and whither it seeks to return. 'There', 'whence': such words haunt Plotinus' prose.

How is the soul to return? What is the way? As the passage just quoted suggests, it will be the way of Plato, the way of purification, moral and intellectual. But, to understand Plotinus' own characteristic understanding of the soul's ascent we must see *why* it is that the soul needs to ascend.

The soul has come from the Fatherland, but, more than that, it has *forgotten* the Fatherland. As we have seen, the process of emanation is a movement from simplicity to multiplicity, from certain possession to discursive thought, seeking understanding, carrying with it the possibility of error. And for most souls this possibility has become actuality. Plotinus puts it like this:

> The evil that has overtaken them has its source in self-will, in the entry into the sphere of process, and in the primal differentiation with the desire for self-ownership. They conceived a pleasure in this freedom and largely indulged their own motion; thus they hurried down the wrong path . . . [Such souls] no longer discern either the divinity or their own nature; ignorance of their rank brings self-depreciation; they misplace their respect, honouring everything more than themselves, all their awe and admiration is for the alien, and, clinging to this, they have broken apart, as far as a soul may, and they make light of what they have deserted . . . Admiring pursuit of the external is a confession of inferiority . . .
>
> (V.1.1).

Elsewhere he speaks of the fallen souls becoming 'dwellers in the Place of Unlikeness, where, fallen from all resemblance to the Divine, we lie in gloom and mud' (I.8.13). The 'Place of Unlikeness', a phrase taken from Plato's *Statesman* (273 D), later picked up by Augustine and bequeathed to the Middle Ages as *regio dissimilitudinis*, 'land of unlikeness', is the place of the fallen soul. Unlikeness, difference, obscures the soul's simplicity and likeness to the divine. The 'way', then, will be recovery of its simplicity, of its kinship to the divine. This will involve purification, both in the sense of the restoration of its own beauty, and in the cutting off of what has sullied that purity. The soul is to seek for itself, for its true self, and in doing that it is seeking for the divine, for the soul belongs to the divine, it has kinship with the divine. It is because of this kinship that the quest is worth pursuing, and similarly because of this kinship that it will be successful (see V.1.1.).

Plotinus has several ways of putting this. The passage above suggests that the fallen soul has become self-centred, and yet centred on a self that is not purely its self (cf. IV.8.4). Instead of calm possession of what it truly is, the soul knows a feverish clutching at what it can acquire, which blurs the soul's nature and puts it out of focus. What it grasps at as the centre of its being is not the true centre at all: there is then what we might call a certain ec-centricity (out-of-centredness) in the fallen soul. And this ec-centricity engenders tension in the soul, a tension that it feels as self-consciousness. Plotinus was, perhaps, the first to see that self-consciousness, self-awareness, can be a hindrance to the soul's progress. It is sickness of which we are aware, for example, he remarks, whereas when we are in health we are normally unaware of it (V.8.11). Again, if we are conscious of the fact that we are reading, it is a sure sign that our attention is wandering. From these examples Plotinus draws the general conclusion that:

it would seem that consciousness tends to thwart the activities upon which it is exercised, and that in the degree in which these pass unnoticed they are purer and have more effect, more vitality, and that, consequently, the Proficient arrived at this state has the truer fulness of life, life not spilled out in sensation but gathered closely within itself.   (I.4.10)

Self-consciousness is evidence of duality, of unlikeness, in the soul: as the soul returns into itself, becoming more truly what it is, this self-consciousness will evaporate. This, we shall see, is most profoundly true of union with the One. On the other hand, the capacity for self-consciousness is not just evidence of lack of simplicity, for as self-awareness, it provides a means by which the soul may reach a level of interior simplicity that transcends self-consciousness.

All that has self-consciousness and self-intellection is derivative; it observes itself in order, by that activity, to become master of its Being: and if it study itself this can only mean that ignorance inheres in it and that it is of its own nature lacking and to be made perfect by Intellection.   (III.9.9)[7]

The purpose of the way is to achieve simplicity, and the means is purification. Purification, *katharsis*, is a fundamental and much developed idea in Plotinus' thought.[8] It includes, as we would expect, the pursuit of the moral virtues. Plotinus, however, is anxious to point out how the pursuit of morality can actually hinder the soul's ascent. For morality is concerned with the soul's activity in the realm of sensible reality and can thus bind the soul the more firmly to that realm (V.9.5). For Plotinus the pursuit of virtue is only right if virtue is seen as purificatory; and to that end he draws a distinction between civic virtues, which are essentially concerned with the conduct of life here on earth, and purificatory virtues, which help the soul to detach itself from the world and prepare it for contemplation (see I.2.3). The aim of moral purification is tranquillity — then 'there will be no battling in the soul' (I.2.5) — a tranquillity that will help the soul to achieve inwardness. But more important than moral purification is intellectual purification. This includes dialectic and mental training such as we would expect. But it is best characterized rather differently. In one place, speaking of the soul's ascent, Plotinus says: 'The guiding thought is this: that beauty perceived in material things is borrowed' (V.9.2). It is real enough — Plotinus has nothing but contempt for those who vilify the cosmos — but it is *borrowed*, it is lent to the material order, it does not inhere in it. And, as we read on, we find that this is generally true: the beauty we perceive is borrowed. Even when we reach the realm of Intelligence, the realm of the Idea, which is 'veritably intellectual, wise without intermission and therefore beautiful in itself', we must look beyond: 'we must look still inward beyond the Intellectual, which, from our point of approach, stands before the Supreme Beginning, in whose forecourt, as it were, it announces in its own being the entire content of the Good, that prior of all, locked in unity, of which this is the expression already touched

---

[7] See P. Hadot, *Plotin, ou la simplicité du regard* (Paris, 1963), 36 ff.; and J. Trouillard, *La Purification plotinienne* (Paris, 1955), 34 ff.

[8] J. Trouillard, op. cit., *passim*: a profound and subtle work.

by multiplicity' (ibid.). This ability to let go and pass beyond, an activity learnt by exercise at lower levels: this is the fruit of intellectual purification. Trouillard calls this *générosité intellec-tuelle*, a rarer gift than moral generosity, and he characterizes it as *disposition d'audace, de souplesse et de dépouillement noétiques.*[9] As moral generosity liberates us from the passions, so intellec-tual generosity frees us from what is partial and fragmentary, or from what is borrowed, and takes us on to the true source of all reality.

On one occasion Plotinus gives us what seems to be an exercise in intellectual dialectic which *realizes* our identity with the intellectual realm.

Let us, then, make a mental picture of our universe: each member shall remain what it is, distinctly apart; yet all is to form, as far as possible, a complete unity so that whatever comes into view, say the outer orb of the heavens, shall bring immediately with it the vision, on the one plane, of the sun and of all the stars with earth and sea and all living things as if exhibited upon a transparent globe. Bring this vision actually before your sight, so that there shall be in your mind the gleaming representation of a sphere, a picture holding all the things of the universe moving or in repose or (as in reality) some at rest, some in motion. Keep this sphere before you, and from it imagine another, a sphere stripped of magnitude and of spatial differences: cast out your inborn sense of Matter, taking care not merely to attenuate it: call on God, maker of the sphere whose image you now hold, and pray Him to enter. And may He come bringing His own Universe with all the gods that dwell in it — He who is the one God and all the gods, where each is all, blending into a unity, distinct in powers but all one god in virtue of that one divine power of many facets. (V.8.9)

Such an exercise in abstraction and concentration we can parallel elsewhere — in Clement of Alexandria, for instance, and many later mystics. As with them, so with Plotinus, we are concerned with an act of withdrawal and concentration that enables the soul to *experience* an ultimate reality that is free of all limitations. But we might notice another thing from this passage: that purification is, in a way, dependent upon the higher reality. The stripping, the negating, of this purification

[9] Op. cit., 138.

does not effect our entry into the realm of Intelligence, rather it reveals that the soul truly belongs to that realm. It is the reality of the higher, the most inward, that makes possible our entry there — and purification is the *sign* that such is taking place.[10]

Purification, then, restores the soul to itself, realizes within it the realm of the Forms, the realm of *nous*, Intelligence. In this realm, the soul passes beyond discursive knowledge to a knowing more immediate, more intuitive. Here the mind 'thinks reality' (V.5.1); there is unity between knower and known; knowledge here is a form of possession, it is certain, infallible. 'What the reasoners seek, the wise hold: wisdom, in a word, is a condition in a thing that possesses repose' (IV.4.12).

Here is contained all that is immortal: nothing here but is Divine Mind; all is God, this is the place of every soul. Here is rest unbroken . . . All its content, thus, is perfect, that itself may be perfect throughout, as holding nothing that is less than the divine, nothing that is less than intellective. Its knowing is not by search but by possession, its blessedness inherent, not acquired . . . The Intellectual-Principle is all and therefore its entire content is simultaneously present in that identity: this is pure being in eternal actuality . . .   (V.1.4)

And yet this realm is not the ultimate; here is not the end of the soul's quest. For, here, there is still duality: beyond, there is the One. Put like that, it is a rational projection; everything must stem from what is simple, and the realm of *nous*, though more unified than anything else we have known, is not pure simplicity. But, for Plotinus, this is not simply a rational postulate: the realm of *nous* points beyond itself, and where it points, we may follow. It points beyond itself: its beauty, too, though possessed and inherent, is borrowed:

Every one of those Beings exists for itself but becomes an object of desire by the colour cast upon it from The Good, source of those graces and of the love they evoke. The soul taking that outflow from the divine is stirred; seized with a Bacchic passion, goaded by these goads, it becomes Love. Before that, even Intellectual-Principle with

---

[10] See Trouillard, 54 ff.

all its loveliness did not stir the soul; for that beauty is dead until it take the light of The Good, and the soul lies supine, cold to all, unquickened even to Intellectual-Principle there before it. But when there enters into it a glow from the divine, it gathers strength, awakens, spreads true wings, and however urged by its nearer environing, speeds its buoyant way elsewhere, to something greater to its memory: so long as there exists anything loftier than the near, its very nature bears it upwards, lifted by the giver of that love. Beyond Intellectual-Principle it passes but beyond The Good it cannot, for nothing stands above That. Let it remain in Intellectual-Principle and it sees the lovely and august, but it is not there possessed of all it sought; the face it sees is beautiful no doubt but not of power to hold its gaze because lacking in the radiant grace which is the bloom upon beauty.   (VI.7.22)

The realm of Intelligence points beyond itself: and where it points the soul may follow. How? There is no more that it can do: purification has rendered it quite transparent: it is wholly diaphanous, wholly pure, it has become what it is: Intelligence ('we are each the intelligible world': III.4.3). 'Only by a leap can we reach to this One . . .' (V.5.8). But it is not a leap we make; rather we are swept off our feet, so to speak.

Knowing of The Good or contact with it is all-important: this — we read — is the grand learning, the learning, we are to understand, not of looking towards it but attaining, first, some knowledge of it. We come to this learning by analogies, by abstractions, by our understanding of its subsequents, of all that is derived from The Good, by the upward steps towards it. Purification has The Good for goal; so the virtues, all right ordering, ascent within the Intellectual, settlement therein, banqueting upon the divine — by these methods one becomes, to self and to all else, at once seen and seer; identical with Being and Intellectual-Principle and the entire living all, we no longer see the Supreme as an external; we are near now, the next is That and it is close at hand, radiant above the Intellectual.

Here, we must put aside all the learning; disciplined to this pitch, established in beauty, the quester holds all knowledge still of the ground he rests on, but, suddenly, swept beyond it all by the very crest of the wave of Intellect surging beneath, he is lifted and sees, never knowing how; the vision floods the eyes with light, but it is not a light showing some other object, the light itself is the vision. No longer is there thing seen and light to show it, no longer Intellect and object of Intellection; this is the very radiance that brought both

Intellect and Intellectual object into being for the later use and allowed them to occupy the quester's mind. With This he himself becomes identical, with that radiance whose Act is to engender Intellectual-Principle ...   (VI.7.36)

Again we note the word *exaiphnes*, suddenly. *Suddenly* the soul is swept out of itself into union. It is not something the soul can achieve, but something that comes upon it. We must be careful, however, not to suppose that the One in any active way draws the soul up to itself in ecstasy. Plotinus takes it for granted that the One has no knowledge or awareness of anything below itself (VI.7.37.1 ff.) and denies that the One is even aware of itself in any way that we can recognize: 'nothing found elsewhere can be found There; even Being cannot be There. Nor therefore has it intellection ...' (VI.7.41).[11] What Plotinus is insisting upon is that for the soul there is, in union with the One, ecstasy, genuine ecstasy, in the sense of going out of oneself, *sortie de soi*. Strictly speaking, in this ascent, the soul does not become *nous*, nor does *nous* become the One: it passes *out of itself* into the other.[12] Such experiences of ecstasy or rapture Plotinus himself knew, as on one occasion he remarks:

Many times it has happened: lifted out of the body into myself; becoming external to all other things and self-encentred; beholding a marvellous beauty; then, more than ever, assured of community with the loftiest order; enacting the noblest life, acquiring identity with the divine; stationing within It by having attained that activity, poised above whatsoever within the Intellectual is less than the Supreme: yet, there comes the moment of descent from intellection to reasoning ...   (IV.8.1)

A passing moment of rapture. Porphyry, in his *Life*, tells us that four times was Plotinus caught up to the One during the time he knew him, and once he himself knew this state. He gives the impression that it is a rare and fleeting phenomenon. So it presumably is, as an *experience*, but we may wonder whether this is an adequate way of understanding it. As we have seen, self-consciousness is evidence of duality in the soul;

[11] See J. M. Rist, *Plotinus: the Road to Reality* (Cambridge, 1967), chap. 4: 'The One's Knowledge', 38–52.
[12] See R. Arnou, *Le Désir de Dieu dans la philosophie de Plotin* (Rome, 1967²), 220.

we should not expect to find it in the soul that is one with the One. Nor do we: Plotinus himself counters the objections of those who cannot accept the idea that in union with the One we pass beyond self-consciousness.

> Still, we will be told, one cannot be in beauty and yet fail to see it. The very contrary: to see the divine as something external is to be outside of it; to become it is to be most truly in beauty: since sight deals with the external, there can be no vision unless in the sense of identification with the object . . . This is why in that other sphere, where we are deepest in the knowledge by intellection, we are aware of none . . . (V.8.11)

And since we pass beyond self-consciousness, we cannot say that when the *experience* has passed the state of union with the divine has vanished. It would indeed seem from various passages in Plotinus that we should rather speak of a *state* of union with the One.[13] So, for instance, he speaks of the soul as holding the centre of its being to the One, which is its centre:

> In our present state — part of our being weighed down by the body, as one might have the feet under water with all the rest untouched — we bear ourselves aloft by that intact part and, in that, hold through our own centre to the centre of all the centres, just as the centres of the great circles of a sphere coincide with that of the sphere to which all belong. Thus we are secure.
>
> If these circles were material and not spiritual, the link with the centres would be local; they would lie round it where it lay at some distant point: since the souls are of the Intellectual, and the Supreme still loftier, we understand that contact is otherwise procured, that is by those powers which connect Intellectual agent with Intellectual object; indeed soul is closer to the Supreme than Intellect to its object — such is its similarity, identity, and the sure link of kindred. Material mass cannot blend into other material mass: unbodied beings are not under this bodily limitation; their separation is solely that of otherness, of differentiation; in the absence of otherness, each, in ceasing to be distinguished from the others, is immediately present to them.
>
> Thus the Supreme as containing no otherness is ever present with us . . . (VI.9.8)

Ecstasy is what happens when the soul is overwhelmed by the reality of its union with the One. As an experience it is

---

[13] See Trouillard, 98 ff.

ineffable, for since the One is beyond knowing, any contact with the One is beyond telling. As Plotinus himself puts it: 'the main source of the difficulty is that awareness of this Principle comes neither by knowing nor by the Intellection that discovers the Intellectual beings, but by a presence overpassing all knowledge' (VI.9.4). *Parousia* — presence — that is one way Plotinus will speak of awareness of the One in union; another is touching, *synaphe*. But no words are satisfactory: Plotinus is very clear on the pain of incomprehension and consequent terror the soul feels as it reaches out into this unknown:

> The soul or mind reaching towards the formless finds itself incompetent to grasp where nothing bounds it, or to take impression where the impinging reality is diffuse; in sheer dread of holding to nothingness it slips away. The state is painful; often it seeks relief by retreating from all this vagueness to the region of sense, there to rest as on solid ground, just as the sight distressed by the minute rests with pleasure on the bold . . . Soul must see in its own way; this is by coalescence, unification; but in seeking thus to know the Unity it is prevented by that very unification from recognising that it has found; it cannot distinguish itself from the object of this intuition. Nonetheless, this is our one resource if our philosophy is to give us knowledge of the One . . .   (VI.9.3.)

This is the real homecoming, the soul has arrived at last at the Fatherland. And yet the soul has become so strange to itself that what should be natural to the soul is strange and awesome. The strangeness is such that it is filled with terror and desperation and longs to return to that land of Unlikeness where, in its confused way, it feels 'at home'. Yet, as the soul in ecstasy passes out of itself, it finds its true self. It finds itself at one with the heart of all reality.

> The man formed by this mingling with the Supreme must — if he only remember — carry its image impressed upon him: he is become the Unity, nothing within him or without inducing any diversity; no movement now, no passion, no outlooking desire, once this ascent is achieved; reasoning is in abeyance and all Intellection and even, to dare the word, the very self: caught away, filled with God, he has in perfect stillness attained isolation; all the being calmed, he turns neither to this side nor to that, not even inwards to himself; utterly resting he has become very rest. He belongs no longer to the order of the beautiful; he has overpassed even the choir of the virtues; he is

like one who, having penetrated the inner sanctuary, leaves the temple images behind him — though these become once more first objects of regard when he leaves the holies; for There his converse was not with image, not with trace, but with the very Truth in the view of which all the rest is but of secondary concern.

There, indeed, it was scarcely vision, unless of a mode unknown; it was a going forth from the self, a simplifying, a renunciation, a reach towards contact and at the same time a repose, a meditation towards adjustment. This is the only seeing of what lies within the holies: to look otherwise is to fail ...

It is not in the soul's nature to touch utter nothingness; the lowest descent is into evil and, so far, into non-being: but to utter nothing, never. When the soul begins again to mount, it comes not to something alien but to its very self; thus detached, it is in nothing but itself; self-gathered it is no longer in the order of being; it is in the Supreme.

There is thus a converse in virtue of which the essential man outgrows Being, becomes identical with the Transcendent of Being. The self thus lifted, we are in the likeness of the Supreme: if from that heightened self we pass still higher — image to archetype — we have won the Term of all our journeying. Fallen back again, we waken the virtue within until we know ourselves all order once more; once more we are lightened of the burden and move by virtue towards Intellectual-Principle and through the Wisdom in That to the Supreme.

This is the life of gods and of the godlike and blessed among men, liberation from the alien that besets us here, a life taking no pleasure in the things of earth, a flight of the alone to the Alone.

(VI.9.11)

'The flight of the alone to the Alone': the very familiarity of that phrase is a measure of the influence of Plotinus. It also enshrines the essence of the mystical quest as he sees it: a solitary way that leads to the One, sovereign in solitary transcendence. The One has no concern for the soul that seeks him; nor has the soul more than a passing concern for others engaged on the same quest: it has no companions. Solitariness, isolation; the implications of this undermine any possibility of a doctrine of grace — the One is unaware of those who seek it, and so cannot turn towards them — or any positive understanding of the co-inherence of man with man. These limitations, as we shall now begin to see, disclose a radical opposition between the Platonic vision and Christian mystical theology.

IV. ORIGEN

WITH Origen we begin to discuss specifically *Christian* mystical theology. So far we have discussed the Platonic background to such theology, and in doing that we may seem to have prejudged the issue as to whether Christian mystical theology has, in fact, a Platonic background at all. However, the idea that Christian mystical theology is nothing but Platonism is a charge often made, and we shall not advance our understanding of this problem by ignoring it. Even without discussing the Fathers, we have seen that this 'Platonic background' is complicated. It is not pure Plato. What we have found in Philo and Plotinus has other philosophical debts than those to Plato. Middle Platonism, of which Philo, as we have seen, can be regarded as an example, and neo-Platonism are indebted to Aristotle and the Stoics for some of their emphases. But it is not by chance that they are called 'Platonist': Plato is their acknowledged master.

The influence of *Middle* Platonism on the Fathers is perhaps more considerable than might at first sight appear likely. Plato and Plotinus are essentially interesting for their own sakes: both were great philosophers. Philo was not, nor were the rest of the so-called Middle Platonists. Rather we find with them a kind of 'accepted wisdom', a way of looking at things which was customary in the early Patristic period and, just for that reason, was influential in the Fathers. How this influence operated, we shall see in what follows.

But even before we come to the Fathers, we have seen something more than the wisdom of pagan philosophy: with Philo we find the influence of the God of the Old Testament, of a God who created man and cares for him and chose Israel to be His people and revealed Himself in His dealings with them. Philo's concern is to show that pagan philosophy could discover nothing not already, for the Jew, a matter of revelation — and the revelation of *God*, moreover, not simply of the divine. This strand assumes even greater importance in the Christian Fathers. Whatever the influence of Platonism, they were concerned with God and not with the divine. Philo's idea of a God who speaks, who declares Himself, is given a sharper edge and more immediacy when, with the Fathers, he becomes the God who speaks and declares Himself in the life, death, and resurrection of Jesus of Nazareth. To know God is to accept that revelation, to participate in God's self-communication thus made known. So for most of the Fathers (with only rare exceptions) the 'mystical life' is the ultimate flowering of the life of baptism, the life we receive when we share in Christ's death and risen life by being baptized in water and the Holy Spirit.

When we begin to examine Origen's understanding of the soul's ascent to God this is the first point to emerge: the ascent begins, or is made possible, by what God has done for us in Christ and made effective in us by baptism. The mystical life is the working-out, the realizing, of Christ's union with the soul effected in baptism, and is a communion, a dialogue between Christ and the soul. Though this is often expressed in language drawn from Plato, when such language is used (as it is in Origen), what these Platonic-sounding concepts mean is very different from what Plato or Plotinus intended. Origen is talking about the life of the baptized Christian within the Church; Plato and Plotinus about the search for ultimate truth by an intellectual élite, either in the company of other like-minded souls, or as 'the alone to the Alone'.

Origen was deeply indebted to Platonism. As we shall see, his theology is permeated through and through by Platonic ways of thought. But his attitude to philosophy is not at all simple.[1] He studied under the philosopher, Ammonius Saccas, who was also Plotinus' master, but he studied *as a Christian*. He was not a convert from philosophy like Justin Martyr or Clement of Alexandria, and he had none of their

---

[1] See the sharply contrasting accounts in H. Koch, *Pronoia and Paideusis: Studien über Origenes und sein Verhältnis zum Platonismus* (Berlin and Leipzig, 1932) and H. Crouzel, *Origène et la philosophie* (Paris, 1962).

welcoming attitude towards philosophy which, for him, was
simply a useful study for the Christian theologian as a training
in dialectic, and something he justifies by the example of the
Israelites' 'spoiling of the Egyptians' at the Exodus.[2] According to a pupil of Origen, Gregory Thaumaturgus, this was
Origen's great gift; his capacity to press wisdom into the
service of the one Lord wherever it might be found:

This greatest gift has our friend accepted from God, this goodly
portion from heaven, to be the interpreter of God's words to men, to
understand the things of God as God's utterances, and to set them
forth to men as men hear. Therefore there was nothing unutterable
to us, for there was nothing inaccessible. We were privileged to learn
every word, Barbarian or Hellenic, mystic or published, divine or
human, traversing them all with the fullest freedom, and exploring
them, bearing off from all and enjoying the riches of the soul . . . In a
word, this was indeed our Paradise, imitating that great Paradise of
God, wherein we needed not to till the earth below, not to minister
to the body and grow gross, but only to increase the acquisitions of
our souls, like some fair plants engrafting themselves, or rather
engrafted in us by the Cause of all.[3].

But Origen's real concern was with the interpretation of
Scripture. This was the repository of all wisdom and all truth
and, as we shall see, the interpretation of Scripture lies at the
very heart of his mystical theology. It was certainly the heart
of his life's work: most of his writings consist of exposition of
Scripture.

It was, then, as an interpreter of the Bible that Origen
exercised his greatest influence on later theologians; here was
a wealth of reflection on Scripture that could not be ignored
and, as the ground of his mystical theology, was to be deeply
pervasive in its influence. For him the Song of Songs was *the*
book on the summit of the mystical life, the union of the soul
with God. This judgement Origen bequeathed to later theology, along with many of the themes he draws out in his
interpretation of the Song, in particular, the idea of the three
stages of the mystical life — the three ways later called

---

[2] See Origen's letter to Gregory Thaumaturgus (*PG* XI. 88–92) and his *Homilies on
Joshua*. (*GCS*, VII. 286–463).
[3] *Address on Origen*, XV (*PG* X. 1096 AB). Metcalfe's trans. (London, 1920), 82 f.

purificatory, illuminative, and unitive — and the notion of the
soul's spiritual senses.

Let us begin by looking at his use of the Song of Songs.
Origen's *Commentary* and *Homilies* on the Song[4] are not the
earliest examples of the genre; there is a commentary, extant
only in translation, by Hippolytus, and there is no doubt that
Origen made use of this earlier work. However, in Hippolytus'
commentary we find an ecclesiological interpretation dominant; that is, the relationship between the Bridegroom and the
Bride is interpreted as referring to the relationship between
Christ and the Church. The background to that is probably
rabbinic interpretation, which saw the Song as expressing the
relationship between God and Israel. The interpretation in
terms of Christ and the individual soul occurs only occasionally in Hippolytus. With Origen the relationship of the soul to
Christ (not that this is isolated from the theme of the
relationship of the Church to Christ) becomes more prominent: there is a mystical, as well as an ecclesiological interpretation.

How does Origen justify this use of the Song of Songs? In
the Old Testament, there are, he says at the beginning of
the first *Homily* on the Song, seven songs, and the Song of
Songs is the seventh and the most sublime. Before we can sing
this song we must have progressed through the singing of the
other six. Origen speaks of the progression through the six
songs to the Song of Songs itself thus:

You must come out of Egypt and, when the land of Egypt lies behind
you, you must cross the Red Sea if you are to sing the first song,
saying: Let us sing unto the Lord, for He is gloriously magnified
[Song of Moses: Exod.15]. But though you have uttered this first
song, you are still a long way from the Song of Songs. Pursue your
spiritual journey through the wilderness until you come to the well

---

[4] Origen has left us both a commentary (on *Cant.* 1:1–2:15) and two homilies (on
Cant. 1:1–12a and 1:12b-2:14). The latter are more popular in tone and in them the
ecclesiological interpretation is more prominent. All quotations are from R. P.
Lawson's translation, published in *Ancient Christian Writers* XXVI (London, 1957)
with very valuable annotations. There is also an edition, with translation, of the
homilies only, by O. Rousseau (*Sources Chrétiennes* XXXVII, 2nd edn. Paris, 1966).
Neither the homilies nor the commentary survive in the original Greek: the homilies
are preserved in Jerome's Latin, and the commentary in Rufinus' Latin. I have given
the page references to the edition in *Griechischen Christlichen Schriftsteller*.

which the kings dug so that there you may sing the second song
[Numbers 21:17-20]. After that, come to the threshold of the holy
land that, standing on the bank of Jordan, you may sing another
song of Moses, saying: Hear, O heaven, and I will speak, and let the
earth give ear to the words of my mouth [Deut. 32]. Again, you must
fight under Joshua and possess the holy land as your inheritance;
and a bee must prophesy for you and judge you — Deborah, you
understand, means 'bee' — in order that you may take that song
also on your lips, which is found in the Book of Judges [Judges 5: the
Song of Deborah]. Mount up hence to the Book of Kings, and come
to the song of David, when he fled out of the hand of all his enemies
and out of the hand of Saul, and said: The Lord is my stay and my
strength and my refuge and my saviour. [2 Sam. 22:2–end: the Song
of David]. You must go on next to Isaiah, so that with him you may
say: I will sing to the Beloved the song of my vineyard [Isa. 5]. And
when you have been through all the songs, then set your course for
greater heights, so that as a fair soul with her spouse you may sing
this Song of Songs too.   (*Hom.* I.1: *GCS*, 27 f)

It is not necessary here to draw out Origen's meaning in any
detail[5], it will be sufficient for us to note three points: first, the
ascent of the soul to God begins with her 'coming out of Egypt
and crossing the Red Sea', that is, with her conversion and
baptism. For, as we have already mentioned, the mystical
ascent for Origen begins in baptism and is a deepening and
bringing to fruition of baptismal grace. Secondly, the way of
the soul lies through deserts, and battles, while the soul finds
sustenance in wells. And in all this the soul discovers that God
is powerful and brings her to victory through His grace.
Aridity, moral struggle, consolations: all these are sufficiently
familiar in the spiritual life, as also victory through God's
grace — though not apart from human effort. Such is the way
Origen sees. In the absence, however, of any specific commentary by Origen, I think it would be hazardous to develop a
detailed account of the soul's ascent to God from this passage.
(In the prologue to the *Commentary* Origen suggests a similar
approach with a slightly different list of songs.) And, thirdly,
note the songs themselves. At every stage of the Christian life
the soul sings: it is full of joy. This is characteristic of Origen's

---

[5] Such a drawing-out can be found in the introduction to the *Sources Chrétiennes*
edition of the homilies.

spirituality, which knows nothing of the cloud, the dark night, found in the mysticism of others. His is a mysticism of light. It is optimistic — although balanced by a profound recognition of the necessity of grace. The Song of Songs is the song, then, the joyful song, of the summit of the spiritual life. As Origen puts it in his *Commentary*:

The soul is not made one with the Word of God and joined with Him until such time as all the winter of her personal disorders and the storm of her vices has passed so that she no longer vacillates and is carried about with every kind of doctrine. When, therefore, all these things have gone out of the soul, and the tempest of desires has fled from her, then the flowers of the virtues can begin to burgeon in her ... Then also will she hear 'the voice of the turtle-dove', which surely denotes that wisdom which the steward of the Word speaks among the perfect, the deep wisdom of God which is hidden in mystery.   (*Comm. on the Song* III (IV). 14: *GCS* 224)

That is one way in which Origen arrives at his understanding of the Song of Songs as being about the soul's intimate converse with God at the summit of the spiritual life. As far as I know, such a justification is peculiar to Origen. However, also in the *Commentary*, he suggests another way of arriving at this understanding of the Song which is more important, both as laying down a way of mapping out the ascent of the soul to God for later mystics, and also as giving commentaries on the Song of Songs a more specific context.

In the Prologue to the *Commentary* Origen remarks on the fact that philosophers divide their subject into three categories: ethics, physics, and enoptics[6] (enoptics means, roughly, metaphysics). The origin of some such division is Stoic, though Origen is actually referring to the sort of division found among Middle Platonists. He explains:

That study is called moral (*ethike*) which inculcates a seemly manner of life and gives a grounding in habits that incline to virtue. The study called natural (*physike*) is that in which the nature of each

[6] These terms are derived from the Greek words given with their Latin equivalents (*philosophia moralis, naturalis, inspectiva*) in the Latin version of the *Commentary* (*GCS*, 75, *ll.* 7–9). There is not absolute certainty, about them: see H. Crouzel, *Origène et la «connaissance mystique»* (Paris, 1961), 50 f., esp. 51 nn. 1 and 2, and Baehrens in *GCS*, ad loc.

single thing is considered; so that nothing in life may be done which
is contrary to nature, but everything is assigned to the uses for which
the Creator brought it into being. The study called inspective
(*enoptike*) is that by which we go beyond things seen and contemplate
somewhat of things divine and heavenly, beholding them with the
mind alone, for they are beyond the range of bodily sight.

(*GCS*, 75)

Origen then goes on to apply this distinction to the three
protocanonical books of Wisdom ascribed to Solomon:
Proverbs, Ecclesiastes, and the Song of Songs.

Wishing therefore to distinguish one from another these three
branches of learning, which we called general just now, that is, the
moral, the natural, and the inspective, and to differentiate between
then, Solomon issued them in three books, arranged in their proper
order. First, in Proverbs, he taught the moral science, putting rules
for living into the form of short and pithy maxims, as was fitting.
Secondly, he covered the science known as natural in Ecclesiastes.
In this, by discussing at length the things of nature, and by
distinguishing the useless and vain from the profitable and essential,
he counsels us to forsake vanity, and cultivate things useful and
upright. The inspective science likewise he has propounded in this
little book that we have now in hand, that is, the Song of Songs. In
this he instils into the soul the love of things divine and heavenly,
using for this purpose the figure of the Bride and Bridegroom, and
teaches us that communion with God must be attained by the paths
of charity and love. (*GCS*, 76)

So we have ethics assigned to Proverbs, physics assigned to
Ecclesiastes, and enoptics assigned to the Song. There are
three stages that the soul must pass through progressively:
first, learning virtue (*ethike*), next, adopting a right attitude to
natural things (*physike*), then ascending to contemplation of
God (*enoptike*). That Origen means a progression is clear when
he says, for instance:

If then a man has completed his course in the first subject, as taught
in Proverbs, by amending his behaviour and keeping the commandments, and thereafter, having seen how empty is the world and
realized the brittleness of transitory things, has come to renounce
the world and all that is therein, he will follow on from that point to
contemplate and to desire 'the things that are not seen', and 'that
are eternal'. To attain to these, however, we need God's mercy; so

that, having beheld the beauty of the Word of God, we may be kindled with a saving love for Him, and He Himself may deign to love the soul, whose longings for Himself He has perceived.

(*GCS*, 79)

The idea of the *successiveness* of the stages is often emphasized. For instance, speaking of Jesus as going before us through these stages, he says: 'We should speak of Him first as a beginner in Proverbs; then as advancing in Ecclesiastes; and lastly as more perfect in the Song of Songs.' We clearly have here the beginning of the idea of the three ways of the mystical life, and very nearly the later, familiar language of the way of purification (Origen's *ethike*), the way of illumination (*physike*) and the way of union (*enoptike*).

We have then a threefold division of the soul's ascent. The first, ethics, is concerned with the formation of the virtues. On this there is not much to comment, partly because Origen is here very Platonist and does not say anything we have not already come across, but partly too, because Origen himself does not dwell much on it. As Marguerite Harl remarks, 'Origen is an optimist for whom the struggle against the passions is a preliminary stage in one's interior development, to be passed through quickly.'[7]

Of natural contemplation we need to say a little more. It is clear from the passages already noted that for Origen this means basically not contemplation of the wonder of God in creation but a perception of the transience of the world and a desire to pass beyond it. However, we do sometimes find a more positive understanding of *physike*:

Since, then, it is impossible for a man living in the flesh to know anything of matters hidden and invisible unless he has apprehended some image and likeness thereto among things visible, I think that He who made all things in wisdom so created all the species of visible things upon earth that He placed in them some teaching and knowledge of things invisible and heavenly whereby the human mind might mount to spiritual understanding and seek the grounds of things in heaven; so that, taught by God's wisdom, it might say: The things that are hid and that are manifest have I learned.

(*Comm. on the Song* III. 12: *GCS*, 209 f.)

[7] *Origène et la fonction révélatrice du Verbe incarné* (Paris, 1958), 321.

This positive understanding of natural contemplation is more developed in the *Commentary on John*, where Origen discusses the idea that there are *logoi*, principles, implanted in the created order that can lead man to a conception of God's eternal wisdom:

> if anyone is capable of conceiving by thought an incorporeal existence, formed by all sorts of ideas, which embraces the principles of the universe, an existence living and, as it were, animated, he will know the Wisdom of God who is above every creature and who truly says of himself: God created me as the beginning of his ways for his works.   (*Comm. on John* I. xxxiv: *GCS*, 43)

So much for the first two ways. Origen's understanding of ethics and natural contemplation is deeply Platonic: the aim of these two ways is to subdue the body to the soul and then to free the soul from the body. Only when freed from the body can the soul enter on the way of *enoptike*, contemplation of God Himself, and on this way the soul passes beyond what it can achieve by its own efforts: it can only pass to this way, characterized by love, by reliance on God's mercy.[8] This is stated explicitly in the *Commentary on the Song of Songs* when, discussing the reference to 'midday' in the Song, Origen remarks:

> With regard to the time of vision, then, he 'sits at midday' who puts himself at leisure in order to see God. That is why Abraham is said to sit, not inside the tent but outside, at the door of the tent. For a man's mind also is out of doors and outside of the body, if it be far removed from carnal thoughts and desires; and therefore God visits him who is placed outside all these.   (II. 4: *GCS* 140)

This also suggests that *enoptike* is properly something the soul can look forward to after death. Released from the body by death, the soul becomes mind, and is free to contemplate invisible reality: the realm of the Platonic Forms. Sometimes Origen gives expression to this in a very explicit way, for instance in *De Principiis*:

> And so the rational being, growing at each successive stage, not as it grew when in this life in the flesh or body and in the soul, but

---

[8] See the passage from the Prologue to the *Commentary on the Song*, quoted above, p. 58 f.

increasing in mind and intelligence, advances as a mind already
perfect to perfect knowledge, no longer hindered by its former carnal
senses, but developing in intellectual power, ever approaching the
pure and gazing 'face to face', if I may so speak, on the causes of
things.   (II. xi. 7: *GCS* 191 f.)

Behind this Platonic distinction between mind and soul, *nous* and
psyche, lies Origen's whole understanding of the world of
spiritual beings and their destiny. Originally all spiritual
beings, *logikoi*, were minds, equal to one another, all contemplating the Father through the Word. Most of these minds (all
except the future mind of Christ) grew tired of this state of
bliss and fell. In falling their ardour cooled and they became
souls (*psyche*, supposedly derived from *psychesthai*, to cool). As
souls, they dwell in bodies which, as it were, arrest their fall
and provide them with the opportunity to ascend again to
contemplation of God by working themselves free from their
bodies and becoming minds, *noes*, again. As *nous*, the spiritual
being can contemplate the Ideas and realize its kinship with
this realm.[9] It is clear that this whole pattern is basically
Platonist. In particular, for Origen the 'real' world is the
realm of spiritual, non-material beings: the drama of Fall and
Redemption belongs essentially to this spiritual realm. Such a
presupposition consorts ill with faith in the Incarnate Word,
the Word incarnate in a physical, material world. We shall
soon see that this is a source of trouble for Origen.

But though this is Platonist, we must qualify. The notion of
the world of the Forms has undergone a change since Plato. In
some Middle Platonists, Albinus for example, the Forms or
Ideas are the *thoughts* of God, that is, they are the objects of
God's thought; we come, as it were, within the divine mind
when we contemplate them. They are not ultimate in themselves, as in Plato, but the eternal thoughts of the eternal and
ultimate God. With Origen this takes the precise form of
absorbing the world of the Ideas into the Logos. So Hans Urs
von Balthasar can say: 'The world of the Ideas is absorbed in
the unity of Christ. Their multiplicity is transformed into the
richness of the aspects of the concrete Unity [which is

[9] For all this see *De Principiis*, esp. I.v and II.viii; and also J. Daniélou, *Origène*
(Paris, 1948), 207–18.

Christ].'[10] The effect of this ought to make Origen's doctrine
of contemplation more Christocentric or, at least, Word-
centred, than would a merely Platonist theory. We must
examine to what extent this is true.

That Origen's doctrine of contemplation is centred on the
Word is easily seen. In the passage quoted earlier from the
Commentary on the Song of Songs about *enoptike* it is said that the
soul 'having beheld the beauty of the Word of God may be
kindled with a saving love for him': such language is characteristic of Origen. But is it *Word*-centred or *Christ*-centred? Is
this Word simply the eternal Word, or is it the *Word made flesh*?
How much does the distinctively Christian doctrine of the
Incarnation affect Origen's Platonist doctrine of contemplation?

In his writings on the Song of Songs we find plenty of
evidence that the Incarnation is important for Origen. Take
this passage from the second *Homily on the Song of Songs*:

After this the Bridegroom says: I am the flower of the field and the
lily of the valleys. For my sake, who was in the valley, he came down
to the valley; and coming to the valley, he became the lily of the
valleys in place of the tree of life that was planted in the paradise of
God, and was made the flower of the whole field, that is, of the whole
world and the entire earth. For what else can so truly be the flower of
the world as is the name of Christ?   (II. 6: *GCS*, 49 f.)

Or, in another passage from the same homily, commenting on
the passage where the Bridegroom is said to be 'behind our
wall, looking out through the windows, becoming visible
through the nets', we read:

The Bridegroom then appears through the nets: Jesus has made a
way for you, he has come down to earth and subjected himself to the
nets of the world. Seeing a great throng of mankind entangled in the
nets, seeing that nobody except himself could sunder them, he came
to the nets when he assumed a human body that was held in the
snares of the hostile powers. He broke those nets asunder for you,
and you say: 'Behold, he is at the back, behind our wall, looking out
through the windows, become visible through the nets.'
                                                        (II. 12: *GCS*, 58)

[10] *Parole et Mystère chez Origène* (Paris, 1957), 122, n. 26.

In the *Commentary*, in addition to this interpretation, the nets are made to refer to temptations that Jesus suffered 'before he could enter into union and alliance with his Church' (III. 13: *GCS*, 222). Another passage which yields an interpretation that involves the Incarnation is that where the Bride asks the Bridegroom: 'In the shelter of the rock by the outwork shew me thy face, and let me hear thy voice.' The rock is readily taken to refer to Christ (see I Cor. 10:4), and Origen says: 'Having therefore availed herself of the covering of this rock, the soul comes safely to the place on the outwork, that is, to the contemplation of things incorporeal and eternal.' Origen goes on:

Like to these is the saying of God to Moses: Lo, I have set thee in a cleft of the rock, and thou shalt see my back parts. That rock which is Christ is therefore not completely closed, but has clefts. But the cleft in the rock is he who reveals God to men and makes Him known to them; for no-one knoweth the Father save the Son. So no-one sees the back parts of God, that is to say, the things that are come to pass in the latter times, unless he be placed in the cleft of the rock, that is to say, when he is taught them by Christ's own revealing. (*Comm. on the Song* IV. 15: *GCS*, 231)

All these passages, in different ways, see the coming of Christ in the Incarnation as that to which the soul responds in its ascent to God. So, *per Christum* is strongly affirmed. Before we ask, how strongly? let us simply ask, how? How is the soul in its ascent to God coming to God through Christ? A full answer to that would have several strands. For instance, the idea that man is created after the image of God obviously has a part to play here, since, for Origen, the image of God is the Word himself, man being made after the fashion of the Word which became flesh. But what seems to be the dominant strand is hinted at in that last quotation about Christ as the rock in the cleft of which we can see God's back parts. God's back parts are here taken to mean (very unusually) prophecies about the last times. These can only be understood through Christ's revealing, which suggests that Christ is being seen as the key to the understanding of Scripture, where these prophecies are contained. If we think back to Philo we shall not, perhaps, be surprised to see this idea emerging here. As with Philo, the understanding of Scripture is the medium of union with the Word. Commenting on the passage: 'Behold, here he cometh leaping upon the mountains, skipping over the hills', Origen says:

> Now if at any time a soul who is constrained by love for the Word of God is in the thick of an argument about some passage — and everyone knows from his own experience how when one gets into a tight corner like this one gets shut up in the straits of propositions and enquiries — if at such a time some riddles or obscure sayings of the Law or the Prophets hang in the soul, and if then she should chance to perceive him to be present, and from afar should catch the sound of his voice, forthwith she is uplifted. And when he has begun more and more to draw near to her senses and to illuminate the things that are obscure, then she sees him 'leaping upon the mountains and the hills'; that is to say, he then suggests to her interpretations of a high and lofty sort, so that this soul can rightly say: 'Behold, he cometh leaping upon the mountains, skipping over the hills.'   (*Comm. on the Song* III. 11: *GCS* 202)

Understanding Scripture is not for Origen simply an academic exercise but a religious experience. The meaning found in Scripture is received from the Word, and the experience of *discovering* the meaning of Scripture is often expressed in 'mystical' language; he speaks of a 'sudden awakening', of inspiration, and of illumination. It seems to me that a large part of the content of *enoptike* is the discovery of 'spiritual', 'theological' meanings in Scripture through allegory. In this engagement with Scripture, Origen enters more and more deeply into communion with God — and leads others into this communion (something we learn from Gregory Thaumaturgus' *Address to Origen*).[11]

It is quite clear, then, that Origen's mysticism is centred on the Word, and that the Word is apprehended in Scripture. And insofar as Scripture contains the record of the Incarnation, and also prophetic witness to, and apostolic commentary on it, to that extent Origen clearly holds that contemplation of God is possible (in practice, not simply theoretically) only *per Christum*.

[11] On Origen's understanding of Scripture, see H. de Lubac, *Histoire et esprit: l'intelligence de l'écriture d'après Origène* (Paris, 1950), and also C. W. Macleod, 'Allegory and Mysticism', *Journal of Theological Studies* XXII (1971), 362–79.

But how strongly, how ultimately, does Origen hold to this *per Christum*? Let us start again with a passage from the *Commentary on the Song*. Discussing what is meant by the 'shadow of the apple tree' (*Cant.* 2:3), Origen says:

We must now come to the shadow of the apple tree, and, although one may avail oneself of another shadow, it seems that every soul, as long as she is in this present life, must needs have a shadow, by reason, I think, of that heat of the sun which, when it has arisen, immediately withers and destroys the seed that is not deeply rooted. The shadow of the Law indeed afforded but slight protection from this heat; but the shadow of Christ, under which we now live among the Gentiles, that is to say, the faith of his Incarnation, affords complete protection from it and extinguishes it. For he who used to burn up those who walked in the shadow of the Law was seen to fall as lightning from heaven at the time of the Passion of Christ. Yet the period of this shadow too is to be fulfilled at the end of the age; because, as we have said, after the consummation of the age we shall behold no longer through a glass and in a riddle, but face to face.

(*Comm. on the Song* III. 5: *GCS*, 183)

The period of the shadow, namely, of faith in the Incarnation, is temporary; it will pass away and then we shall see face to face. This idea is often found in Origen. In the *Homily on Exodus* he speaks of those 'who do not need to receive the Word of God according to the "it is made flesh", but according to the "Wisdom hidden in a mystery"' (XII. 4: *GCS*, 267) That way of putting it is characteristic: one of the passages quoted earlier about the summit of the soul's ascent spoke of 'that wisdom which the Word dispenses among the perfect, the deep wisdom of God which is hidden in mystery (*Comm.* IV. 14). So the soul, it seems, passes beyond faith in the Incarnation in its ascent to God. The Incarnation is only a stage. It would seem that Origen's Platonist presuppositions here are proof against the impact of the Christian doctrine of the Incarnation: the Incarnation is not really central, but simply a preliminary stage. That is evident in the *Commentary on John*, where Origen says: 'Christ said, I am the door. What then must we say of Wisdom, which God created as the beginning of his ways, for his works, in which her Father rejoices, delighting in her manifold intelligible beauty which is seen only by the eyes of the mind, and which arouses a heavenly love which perceives the divine beauty?' (I. ix: *GCS*, 14). At one place, however, in the *Commentary on John* this insistence that the Incarnation will be surpassed is tempered, though still substantially affirmed. Commenting on the mantle covered with blood that the Word wears in the Apocalypse, Origen says:

But he is not naked, the Word that John sees on the horse: he is wearing a robe covered with blood, since the Word made flesh, dying because he was made flesh, because of his blood which was poured on the ground when the soldier pierced his side, bears the marks of his passion. For, if we one day attain to a more elevated and more sublime contemplation of the Word and the Truth, without doubt we shall not entirely forget that we have been led there by his coming in our body.   (II. viii: *GCS*, 62)

We might conclude by saying that Origen's mysticism centred on Christ is ultimately transcended by a mysticism centred on the eternal Word.[12]

We have now seen something of the way in which Origen's Platonist presuppositions qualify and determine his understanding of *enoptike*. But what of the nature of *enoptike* itself? As we have seen, it is by means of love and reliance on God's mercy that the soul enters on this third and highest stage of her mystical ascent. Both these ideas — love, and the soul's reliance on something other than herself— are found in Plato, so there is a fundamental harmony between Plato and Origen here. But we shall see that Origen goes far beyond Plato in his development of these ideas.

Taking up Plato's distinction made in *Symposium* 180 E between common love and heavenly love (*eros pandemos* and *ouranios*), Origen develops from it a similar distinction, in the Prologue to the *Commentary on the Song*, between the inner, spiritual man, formed in the image and likeness of God, and the outer, material man, formed of the slime of the earth:

It follows that, just as there is one love, known as carnal and also known as Cupid [i.e. Eros] by the poets, according to which the

---

[12] For further discussion of the importance of the Incarnation in Origen's theology, see Harl, 191–218, and Koch, 62–78.

lover sows in the flesh; so also there is another, a spiritual love, by which the inner man who loves sows in the spirit . . . And the soul is moved by heavenly love and longing when, having clearly beheld the beauty and fairness of the Word of God, it falls deeply in love with his loveliness and receives from the Word himself a certain dart and wound of love . . . If then a man can so extend his thinking so to ponder and consider the beauty and grace of all the things that have been created in the Word, the very charm of them will so smite him, the grandeur of their brightness will so pierce him as with a chosen dart — as says the Prophet (Isaiah 49:2) — that he will suffer from the dart himself a saving wound and will be kindled with the blessed fire of his love.   (*Comm. on the Song*, Prologue: *GCS*, 66 f.)

Origen goes on to discuss the words for love, *agape* and *eros*, and argues that there is no real difference between them, except that *eros* can be misunderstood (in a carnal way), and so Scripture, as a rule, uses *agape* as being safer. The love that Origen is interested in as far as *enoptike* is concerned is a pure, spiritual longing for that which is invisible; and the two previous stages, ethics and natural contemplation, can be seen as purifying this love. Origen speaks eloquently of the soul's passionate longing for the Word of God, as when explaining the wound of love:

If there is anyone anywhere who has at some time burned with this faithful love of the Word of God; if there is anyone who has received the sweet wounds of him who is the chosen dart, as the prophet says; if there is anyone who has been pierced with the loveworthy spear of his knowledge, so that he yearns and longs for him by day and by night, can speak of nought but him, would hear of nought but him, can think of nothing else, and is disposed to no desire nor longing nor yet hope, except for him alone — if such there be, that soul then says in truth: 'I have been wounded by love.'
                         (*Comm. on the Song*, III. 8: *GCS*, 194)

This is the spiritual love of the inner man as opposed to the carnal love of the outer man, and Origen develops the contrast between them in his teaching that, as the outer man has five senses, so has the inner man five spiritual senses. This doctrine of the five spiritual senses has, it seems, its source in Origen and has great influence thereafter on later mysticism.

In an article,[13] Karl Rahner discusses its beginnings in Origen and gives a list of the important passages concerning it.[14] Briefly, this is Rahner's conclusion: Origen sees the biblical foundation for the five spiritual senses in Proverbs 2:5, where his text reads: 'And you will find a divine sense'; and in Hebrews 5:14 in the reference to the 'perfect who by reason of use have their senses exercised to discern good and evil', which, Origen goes on to point out, the bodily senses cannot do. Not all men have these spiritual senses. Some have none, and some have only one or two. It is vice that hinders the operation of these spiritual senses, and two things are necessary if one is to regain them: grace and practice. The Word is the cause of the right use of these senses, for he gives light to the eyes of the soul. The spiritual senses are awakened by grace, and by grace the Word is poured out into our senses. It is also the case that the spiritual senses become effective to the extent that the bodily senses are deadened. The spiritual senses belong properly to the *nous* rather than the soul (which, as we have seen, is fallen for Origen), although his language is by no means consistent on this point. It can be argued that the spiritual senses are not spiritual counterparts of the bodily senses, but are, rather, different figurative expressions for *nous*. In *De Principiis*, for example, Origen speaks of the 'powers of the soul' (I.i.9), which would support such an interpretation. (It must be pointed out, though, that not all references to spiritual senses in Origen's works suggest such a developed theory. Often they appear to be no more than an exegetical device, a way of interpreting such passages as that from the psalm: 'O *taste* and *see* how gracious the Lord is.' Obviously it is not bodily taste and sight that is in question, so there must be *spiritual* taste and sight.)

But what does it mean to talk of such spiritual senses? From Rahner we can see that it is a way of expounding the soul's experience of *enoptike*, contemplation of God. It is, as he puts it, 'the psychology of the doctrine of *theologia* conceived as the

[13] '*Le Début d'une doctrine des cinq sens spirituals chez Origène*', *Revue d'ascétique et de mystique* XIII (April 1932), 113–45: now available in an English translation in *Theological Investigations* XVI (London, 1979), 81–103.
[14] To which must be added *Conversation with Heraclides* 16 ff., discovered since Rahner wrote the article.

highest degree of the spiritual life' (though *theologia* is Evagrius' term, not Origen's). And there seem to be two elements in Origen's doctrine of the spiritual senses. As Rahner points out, and as can be verified by many of Origen's references to spiritual senses, they enable one to discern between good and evil, and are an expression of a kind of delicate spiritual sensitivity the soul learns under the influence of grace in *enoptike*, so that the soul no longer simply avoids breaking God's commandments, but has a feel for God's will, a kind of 'sixth sense' or insight (which is what 'enoptike' would seem to mean: in-sight). 'For that soul only is perfect who has her sense of smell so pure and purged that it can catch the fragrance of the spikenard and myrrh and cypress that proceed from the Word of God, and can inhale the grace of the divine odour' (*Comm. on the Song* II.11: *GCS*, 172). The spiritual senses are a faculty which, as Balthasar puts it, 'can be developed and improved to an infinite delicacy and precision, so as to report to the soul more and more unerringly what is the will of God in every situation'.[15] The other element in the doctrine of the spiritual senses is that it seems to be a way of representing the richness and variety of the soul's experience of God in contemplation: to speak in terms simply of vision or knowledge would be to give too 'flat' an impression of this experience. Both these elements are brought out in the following passage:

And perhaps, as the Apostle says, for those who have their senses exercised to the discerning of good and evil, Christ becomes each of these things in turn, to suit the several senses of the soul. He is called the true sight, therefore, that the soul's eyes may have something to lighten them. He is the Word, so that her ears may have something to hear. Again, he is the Bread of Life so that the soul's palate may have something to taste. And in the same way he is called spikenard or ointment, that the soul's sense of smell may apprehend the fragrance of the Word. For the same reason he is also said to be able to be felt and handled, and is called the Word made flesh so that the hand of the interior soul may touch concerning the Word of Life. But all these things are the One, Same Word of God, who adapts himself

---

[15] *Origenes: Geist und Feuer* (2nd edn. Salzburg, 1950), 307, quoted by Lawson in the notes to his translation of the *Commentary* and *Homilies*, 340, note 221. The whole note is of great interest.

to the sundry tempers of prayer according to these several guises, and so leaves none of the soul's faculties empty of his grace.

(*Comm. on the Song* II. 9: *GCS*, 167 f.)

The other strand in Origen's understanding of the soul's experience of this highest stage of her ascent is his emphasis on God's mercy. This, we have noted, links up with Plato's idea that at the summit of the mystic ascent the soul passes beyond what it can achieve by its own efforts. The final vision appears suddenly, *exaiphnes*, and this implies, as we saw in our first chapter,[16] both that the soul can do nothing to elicit this final *theoria*, and also that in this final vision the soul is immediately present to the Supreme Beauty. With Origen these two strands are developed in accordance with the modification of his Platonism that we have already noticed. The realm of the Ideas has become the divine *Logos* in all the diversity of its manifestations. So, kinship with the Ideas becomes union with Christ the *Logos*. We have in Origen something that is more like personal encounter than what we find in Plato. And even though, as we have seen, Origen remains too much of a Platonist to allow any final significance to the Incarnation of the Word — it is only a stage — yet the fact that the Word is thought of as meeting men as the Incarnate One (despite the qualifications with which Origen hedges this idea[17]) transforms his understanding of the Word. From being a principle mediating between the One and the many, the Word becomes a person mediating between God and the realm of spiritual beings. Even if the Word that Origen meets in his engagement with Scripture is, in some way, beyond the Incarnate Lord, his encounter with the Word is none the less a personal encounter.

Plato's idea that the soul attains the final vision *exaiphnes* is placed by Origen in a different, and much more fruitful, context, and thus transformed. We have seen something of what this means in the way Origen speaks of the sudden disclosures of the Word as he wrestles with Scripture. More generally, we can say that Plato's bare assertion about the suddenness and immediacy of the vision appears in Origen as the idea of the soul's dereliction and sense of abandonment by

[16] See above, 14.   [17] See above, 66, n. 12.

God, an abandonment which is suddenly relieved by the coming of the Word. One passage in the first *Homily on the Song* is particularly interesting, as it bears witness to Origen's own experience of dereliction:

The Bride then beholds the Bridegroom; and he, as soon as she has seen him, goes away. He does this frequently throughout the Song; and that is something nobody can understand who has not suffered it himself. God is my witness that I have often perceived the Bridegroom drawing near me and being most intensely present with me; then suddenly he has withdrawn and I could not find him, though I sought to do so. I long therefore for him to come again, and sometimes he does so. Then when he has appeared and I lay hold of him, he slips away once more. And when he has so slipped away my search for him begins anew. So does he act with me repeatedly, until in truth I hold him and go up, 'leaning on my Nephew's arm'.

(I. 7: *GCS*, 39)

Whether this is a 'mystical' experience of dereliction is not quite clear. Passages very similar to this occur elsewhere which quite clearly refer to Origen's experience as an exegete when sometimes he cannot see what a text means and is, in that sense, in difficulty; or when, on the contrary, the meaning 'just comes to him' (cf. *Comm*. III. 11, quoted above p. 64).I am unhappy about regarding these passages as directly mystical, as it seems to me quite likely that Origen is clothing in 'mystical' language an experience that is not directly an experience of God at all: namely, the experience one has when the meaning of something suddenly 'comes to one' (as we say, without any mystical metaphor). Even so, if we are to take Origen seriously, this is more than a figure of speech, for he sees his engagement with Scripture as an engagement with God. I suspect that these passages have a spectrum of meaning that ranges from the sort of thing I have mentioned to something which is a genuinely mystical experience of God. Certainly he can speak of these experiences in a way which makes it difficult not to regard the experience as mystical, and as Origen's own. For instance, in the *Comm. on the Song*, III. 13: '[The Word] does not always stay with her, however, for that for human nature is not possible: He may visit her from time to time, indeed, and yet from time to time she may be

forsaken too by Him, that she may long for Him the more'
(*GCS*, 218).

Origen understands this experience as the union of the
mind with the *Logos*, and only indirectly as contemplation of
God. In its union with the *Logos* through contemplation, the
soul shares in the Word's contemplation of God. From this
flow a number of consequences that are characteristic of
Origen's doctrine of contemplation. The soul's contemplation
of the *Logos* is natural; in contemplation of the *Logos* the soul
regains its proper state. Origen speaks neither of ecstasy, nor
of any ultimate unknowability of God or darkness in God. It is
possible that Origen dislikes the idea of ecstasy because of the
misuse of this idea among the Montanists.[18] Whatever the
reason, he develops a doctrine of contemplation where the
soul does not pass beyond itself. According to his understanding, the soul does not have to do with a God who is ultimately
unknowable. Darkness is only a phase we pass through: it is
not ultimate as in Philo, Gregory of Nyssa, or Denys the
Areopagite. Partly he sees this darkness as due to our lack of
effort. If we strive to know God, the darkness will vanish. But
he sometimes speaks of a more ultimate darkness which is the
mystery in which God is enveloped. Of this he says in the
Commentary on John:

If one reflects that the richness of what there is in God to
contemplate and know is incomprehensible to human nature and
perhaps to all beings which are born, apart from Christ and the
Spirit, one will understand how God is enveloped in darkness, for no
one can formulate any conception rich enough to do Him justice. It
is then in darkness that He has made His hiding-place; He has made
it thus because no one can know all concerning Him who is infinite.
(II. xxviii: *GCS*, 85)

But he says a few lines later:

In a manner more paradoxical, I would say also of the darkness
taken in a good sense that it hastens towards light, seizing it and
becoming light because, not being known, darkness changes its
value for him who now does not see, in such a way that, after
instruction, he declares that the darkness which was in him has
become light once it has become known.

[18] So Daniélou, *Origène*, 296.

Origen seems reluctant to entertain the notion of the ultimate unknowability of God. And unlike Philo and Gregory of Nyssa, for instance, for whom God *is* unknowable, Origen quite readily talks about 'knowing God' or 'seeing God'. Only rarely does he raise the question of the implications of God's infinity, while in *De Principiis* (II. iv. 1; IV. iv. 8) he definitely seems unhappy with such an idea.

What does Origen mean by 'knowing God', by contemplation of God? It is clear from the *Commentary on John* (XIX. iv) that Origen is aware that the biblical usage of 'know' means more than intellectual recognition. And he makes use of this in his explanation of what is meant by 'knowing God'. Knowing God is being known by God, and that means that God is united to those who know him, and gives them a share in his divinity. So, knowing God means divinization, *theopoiesis*. Knowing God is having the image of God, which we are, reformed after the likeness: the image is perfected so that we are like God. And contemplation is the means of this, for contemplation is, for Origen, a *transforming* vision. Speaking of the transfiguration of Moses' face when he went into the tabernacle, he says:

According to the literal meaning, something more divine than the manifestation that happened in the tabernacle and the temple was brought into effect in the face of Moses, who consorted with the divine nature. According to the spiritual meaning, those things which are known clearly about God and which are beheld by a mind made worthy by exceeding purity, are said to be the glory of God which is seen. So the mind, purified and passing beyond everything material, so that it perfects its contemplation of God, is made divine in what it contemplates.

(*Comm. on John* XXXII. xxvii: *GCS*, 472)

However, this idea of transforming contemplation is also applied to the Word himself, who, Origen says, would not remain divine (*theos* — without an article) unless he 'remained in unbroken contemplation of the Fatherly depths' (*Comm. on John* II. ii: *GCS*, 55). So we have a view of the world which is in some respects reminiscent of that of Plotinus. There is the ultimate God, *ho theos*, the One, the Father. There is the Word, who derives his divinity from contemplation of the Father (both the contemplation and the divinity that results from this being, in this case, indefectible). And then there is the realm of spiritual beings, the *logikoi*, who, through contemplation of the Word (and through him of God), are divinized.

We can see Origen as a founder of the tradition of intellectualist mysticism that was developed and bequeathed to the Eastern Church by Evagrius. In this tradition, contemplative union is the union of the *nous*, the highest point of the soul, with God through a transforming vision. And in such union the *nous* finds its true nature; it does not pass out of itself into the other; there is no ecstasy. Also the God with whom the soul is united is not unknowable. Consequently darkness is a stage which is left behind in the soul's ascent: there is no ultimate darkness in God. We have a mysticism of light. Origen, however, is not simply the precursor of one tradition, but of the whole of the Christian mystical tradition. Even if, as we shall see, later mystical theology developed emphases which are quite different from those we find in Origen, nevertheless they develop within the framework provided by him.

V. NICENE ORTHODOXY

THE Council of Nicaea, held in 325, marks a watershed in the history of Christian theology. The precise nature of the difference between the Orthodox and the Arians, between Alexander and Athanasius, on the one hand, and Arius, on the other, has been the subject of much scholarly debate. The point of difference is clear: for the Orthodox the Word or the Son was of one substance (*homoousios*) with the Father, for the Arians he was a creature, albeit a very exalted one. But as E. L. Mascall once wrote, 'the causes of Christian disunity are to be found in the agreements of Christians rather than in their disagreements'[1] — it is what we hold in common that leads to disagreement. Let us apply this insight to the Arian controversy: on what did Arius and Athanasius agree?

There is, we find, a striking agreement between them over the question of creation: both Athanasius and Arius have a very clearly articulated doctrine of *creatio ex nihilo*. This may not seem very surprising until it is realized that the doctrine was unknown to pagan philosophy, and emerged only slowly and uncertainly in early Christian theology. Even when it is verbally asserted, there can still be uncertainty as to whether a strict doctrine of creation out of nothing is implied.[2] With Athanasius and Arius there is no doubt, for they enumerate the alternatives and reject them.[3] Creation *ex nihilo* means for

---

[1] E. L. Mascall, *The Recovery of Unity* (London, 1958), 2.

[2] See G. C. Stead, 'The Platonism of Arius', *JTS* XV (1964), 25 f. More generally on the question of the Christian doctrine of creation *ex nihilo*, see R. M. Grant, *Miracle and Natural Law in Graeco-Roman and Early Christian Thought* (Amsterdam, 1952), 133–52.

[3] For Athanasius, see *De Incarnatione* 2, and for Arius, his letter to Eusebius of Nicomedia in H.-G. Opitz, *Urkunden zur Geschichte des Arianischen Streites* (*Athanasius Werke* III/1 (Berlin and Leipzig, 1934)), Urkunde 1 and his letter to Alexander of Alexandria (Urkunde 5).

them that there is a complete contrast between God and the
created order, between the uncreated and self-subsistent, and
that which is created out of nothing by the will of God. There
is no intermediate zone between God and the world. Early
attempts by Christians to formulate an understanding of
God's relation to the world had made use of such an intermediate zone, which they identified with the *Logos* of God (an
idea found in Middle Platonism[4]). The problem posed by the
Arian controversy was how to re-think the understanding of
God's relationship to the world, now that no such intermediate zone could be admitted, and the conclusions of such
rethinking were dramatic: Arius consigned the Word to the
created order; the Orthodox consigned him to the realm of the
(now strictly) divine. Nicaea can then be seen, as Friedo
Ricken has put it, as a 'crisis for early Christian Platonism'.[5]
The Orthodox freed themselves from an aspect of Platonism,
the implications of which they now fully understood, and
attained a new level of clarity in their understanding of the
revelation of the Christian God.

If the doctrine of creation *ex nihilo* had profound implications for dogmatic theology, it also, for the same reasons,
deeply affected mystical theology, for it raised fundamental
questions about the Platonist pattern of thought we have
found already in Christian mystical theology. The focus of this
questioning was the doctrine of *contemplation*. As we have seen,
contemplation was a unifying principle in Origen's cosmos: it
bound together the spiritual world from the Father down to
the lowest of the *logikoi*. As the Word held fast to divinity by
'unbroken contemplation of the paternal depths', so the *logikoi*
became divine through contemplation of the *Logos*. Behind
this was the Platonic idea of the soul's kinship with the divine:
it was this kinship that made contemplation possible and
which was realized in contemplation. But such an idea of the
soul's kinship with the divine was destroyed by the doctrine of
creation *ex nihilo*. Neither for Plato nor for Origen were souls
created: they were pre-existent and immortal. The most
fundamental ontological distinction in such a world was

---

[4] e.g. in Philo: see above 27.
[5] 'Nikaia als Krisis des altchristlichen Platonismus', *Theologie und Philosophie* 44
(1969), 321–41.

between the spiritual and the material. The soul belonged to the former realm in contrast to its body which was material: the soul belonged to the divine, spiritual realm and was only trapped in the material realm by its association with the body.[6] But the doctrine of creation *ex nihilo* implies that the most fundamental ontological divide is between God and the created order, to which latter both soul and body belong. The soul has nothing in common with God; there is no kinship between it and the divine. Its kinship is with its body, in virtue of their common creation, rather than with God. Contemplation can no longer realize a kinship with the divine, for there is no such kinship: and, once this is understood, this particular premiss of the doctrine of contemplation for such as Origen is removed.

It is clear, then, that the apprehension of the radical significance of the doctrine of *creatio ex nihilo*, which led to the Arian controversy and the Council of Nicaea, had equally profound implications for mystical theology. Indeed this 'crisis for early Christian Platonism' was most deeply felt in the realm of mystical theology and it was there that it found its most fundamental resolution.

Athanasius

The theologian whose name is most closely associated with Nicene Orthodoxy is Athanasius, who attended the Council as a deacon in the company of Alexander, Patriarch of Alexandria, whom he later (328) succeeded. The transformation wrought on the Origenist tradition by the appreciation of the radical significance of the doctrine of creation *ex nihilo* can be seen in his early treatise in two parts called *Contra Gentes* and *De Incarnatione*.[7] In *Contra Gentes* we see Athanasius, the young Origenist. The soul has fallen from the level of *nous* to the level of *psyche* — in straight Origenist fashion — and, as *psyche*, it is involved in the body. The soul can achieve union with God

---

[6] This is affirmed quite unmistakably by Plato in *Phaedo* 78 D-80 C.

[7] See J. Roldanus, *Le Christ et l'homme dans la théologie d'Athanase d'Alexandrie* (Leiden, 1968), 11–123, and also my article (for the evidence it adduces from Athanasius, though not for its conclusion), 'The Concept of the soul in Athanasius' *Contra Gentes - De Incarnatione*', *Texte and Untersuchungen*, 116, 227–31.

again by means of contemplation. Indeed, in his account of this, Athanasius is more Origenist than Origen, for the emphasis Origen puts on the soul's reliance on God's mercy in its return to God is lacking. But, if we turn to *De Incarnatione*, the picture changes radically. The soul in *De Incarnatione* is created *ex nihilo*, is frail, and depends on God's grace even for steadfastness before the fall. After the fall the soul's image-likeness to God is so damaged that the Incarnation of the very image of God — the *Logos* — after the pattern of which the soul was originally fashioned is necessary if man is to be saved. Contemplation is no longer a means of divinization: it is simply one of the activities of the divinized soul. No longer is the soul made divine by that which it contemplates, as in Origen. Rather, to quote Athanasius: 'The Word became man that we might become divine; he revealed himself through a body that we might receive an idea of the invisible Father' (*De Incarnatione*, 54).

This change from the Origenist *Contra Gentes* to the more characteristically Athanasian *De Incarnatione* is permanent: nowhere again in Athanasius' writings do we find the idea of divinizing contemplation. Indeed, in his *Life of St. Antony*, there is, surprisingly, scarcely any mention of *theoria*, contemplation, at all. One might say that there is in Athanasius a reaction against Origen that is at the same time anti-mystical. And the root of this reaction lies in the perception that the soul is not in any way connatural with God, and certainly not co-eternal with him. The clear assertion of the doctrine of *creatio ex nihilo* which, from Athanasius onwards becomes an accepted premise in patristic theology, has disclosed an ontological gulf between God and the creature and, *a fortiori*, between God and the soul. And this has led Athanasius to suspect any mysticism whereby the soul becomes divine through contemplation. So he has, at one level at any rate, made a complete break with the Platonist tradition. The premisses of the Platonist doctrine of contemplation are now systematically denied. The soul is not, after all, connatural with the divine, and contemplation, therefore, is not that activity by which it becomes divine. Divinization is a result of the Incarnation: it is an act of grace, in the fullest sense of the word. And divinization is not about some *direct* relationship

between the soul and God, as in Origen's theory of contemplation. The soul is divinized, or better, man is divinized, as he is
restored to conformity with the image of God, that is, the
Word, by the condescension of the Word himself to our fallen
state in the Incarnation.

But, in *Contra Gentes*, Athanasius introduces a metaphor for
the soul's resemblance to God which might have helped him
to bridge the gap between Origenist mystical theology and
one firmly based on the insights of Nicene orthodoxy. He
speaks of the soul 'being a mirror in which it can see the image
of the Father' (*Contra Gentes* 8). And later in the same work he
says: 'So when the soul has put off every stain of sin with
which it is tinged, and keeps pure only what is in the image,
then when this shines forth it can truly contemplate as in a
mirror the Word, the image of the Father, and in him
meditate on the Father, of whom the Saviour is the image'
(*C.G.* 34). This idea of the soul as a mirror which, when pure,
can reflect the image of God seems to be original to
Athanasius. (There are faint hints in Theophilus and
Plotinus, but nothing as clear and distinctive as we find in
Athanasius.)

To understand this metaphor we must first appreciate the
way in which the Greeks understood mirror images. According to Plato, who discusses the question in an appendix to the
Timaeus (46 A–C), what happens when we see an image in a
mirror is that the light from the eye meets the light from the
thing seen on the surface of the mirror, and these two sets of
rays of light mingle there, forming the mirror image that we
see. So the mirror image actually exists, it is formed on the
surface of the mirror; it is not, as in our modern understanding
of these phenomena, an illusion caused by rays of light being
reflected by the surface of the mirror. It is important to realize
this, for otherwise it is difficult to see that when the Fathers
spoke of the soul reflecting the image of God like a mirror they
were using an analogy to explain how the soul is the image of
God. So self-knowledge involves knowledge of God, because
God has made the soul to reflect His image. The idea of the
soul as a mirror reflecting God is thus for the Fathers (though
not for us with our different understanding of how mirrors
work) a metaphor that sees the soul as a real, though

dependent, image of God and also suggests that this image of
God in the soul is perceived in self-knowledge.

So Athanasius' metaphor of the soul as a mirror in which
God is reflected suggests that there is a real similarity between
the soul and God, and preserves the notion that self-knowledge is itself a way of knowing God. But it does this without
suggesting that there is a *natural* kinship between the soul and
God. There is no ontological continuity between the image in
the mirror and that of which it is the image; so, in the case of
the soul reflecting the image of God, this similarity discloses a
much deeper dissimilarity at the level of substance. On this
understanding, *theopoiesis*, divinization, will not mean the
rediscovery of any kinship between the soul and God, but
rather that, as it is purified, the soul more accurately reflects
the image of God, or becomes more truly that image. We
have, then, an adaptation of a familiar Platonist theme, while
the fundamental insight of Nicene orthodoxy into the radical
significance of the doctrine of *creatio ex nihilo* is not at all
blurred. Athanasius himself did not develop this idea, but he
bequeathed to his successors a metaphor to describe the soul's
resemblance to God of which they would make good use.

Gregory of Nyssa

In mystical theology, as in many aspects of dogmatic theology, it is Gregory of Nyssa who developed the Athanasian
heritage. One of the three Fathers known as the Cappadocian
Fathers (the other two being his brother, Basil the Great, and
Gregory Nazianzen), Gregory of Nyssa was an opponent of
the last representatives of the Arian tradition and thus
consolidated the achievement of Nicaea. As a speculative
theologian he was certainly the greatest of the three, though
inferior to the other two in rhetorical skill and organizing
ability.

Gregory's theology is deeply Nicene and, more precisely,
deeply Athanasian. For him, no less than for Athanasius, the
soul, along with all other creatures, is created out of nothing.
In his development of a hierarchical division of being, he
utilizes the Platonic distinction between intelligible and sensible reality, but, whereas within Platonism this distinction is

fundamental, for Gregory the realm of the intelligible is divided into the uncreated and creative on the one hand and, on the other, that which is created — and this is the fundamental divide. Thus, the distinction between the uncreated, intelligible reality, to which category belong only the members of the Blessed Trinity, and the created order, cuts across even the Platonic distinction between intelligible and sensible. The gulf between uncreated and created is such for Gregory that there is no possibility of the soul passing across it: there is no ecstasy, in which the soul leaves its nature as created and passes into the uncreated.

This rejection of the possibility of ecstasy marks Gregory of Nyssa off from the pagan mysticism of Platonism and neo-Platonism (though not from Origen or Philo). It is sometimes suggested that Gregory's fundamental position makes any real mysticism impossible.[8] But it seems to me that, on the contrary, his awareness of the unbridgeable gulf between the uncreated and the created implied by the radical doctrine of *creatio ex nihilo* gives to his mysticism its peculiar character and leads him to focus all the more clearly on the very heart of mysticism: an experience of immediacy with God Himself in love. His understanding of this doctrine of creation out of nothing means that there is no point of contact between the soul and God, and so God is totally unknowable to the soul, and the soul can have no experience of God except in so far as God makes such experience possible. It is the unknowability of God which leads to Gregory's insistence that it is only in virtue of the Incarnation, only because God has manifested Himself — and His love — among us, that we can know Him at all. As the soul responds to God's love, as it comes closer to the unknowable God, it enters into deeper and deeper darkness, and knows Him in a way that surpasses knowledge.

The pattern for Gregory's treatment of mystical theology is, inevitably, Origen. Many of the themes we discussed in the last chapter appear again in Gregory. But they are transformed, and this comes out in his treatment of the three ways, which Origen calls the ways of ethics, of natural contempla-

---

[8] On this see C. W. Macleod's two extremely interesting articles in *JTS*: 'Ἀνάλυσις: a study in Ancient Mysticism' (XXI (1970), 43–55) and art. cit., chapter 4, n. 11.

tion, and finally *enoptike*. Like Origen, Gregory relates this threefold way to the three books of Wisdom: Proverbs, Ecclesiastes, and the Song of Songs, and like Origen he sees these three stages as corresponding to man's spiritual growth, which passes from infancy (Proverbs), through youth (Eccles.) to maturity (Song of Songs). It is, however, less clear in Gregory that these three ways are strictly *successive*, as in Origen. For example, the first way is said to be the way of purification, but also of illumination, which is also characteristic of the second way. There is, then, at least overlapping between the three ways. But it seems that the true state of affairs is rather that these three ways are not so much three *stages* as three *moments* in the soul's approach to God.

That this is so can be seen if we notice a further striking contrast between Origen and Gregory in their understanding of the soul's ascent. For Origen, in the first way, the soul is prepared for contemplation, in the second the power of contemplation is gradually developed, and in the third the soul's contemplative powers come to fruition. The soul is learning to contemplate and, in that, it is discovering its true nature (Origen's doctrine here is further developed by Evagrius, as we shall see in the next chapter). But for Gregory contemplation, *theoria*, is not the goal of the soul's ascent. Rather there is both an active and a contemplative side to each moment of the soul's ascent. In the first way, the active side is found in the process of purification and the contemplative side in the soul's perception that God alone truly exists. If anything, it is the second way that is the true place of contemplation, for in the third way the soul passes beyond contemplation. In the third way, the Song of Songs 'initiates the understanding within the divine sanctuary' and gives us 'an account of the marriage, that is, of the union of the soul with God'. Because God is unknowable, contemplation is impossible in the third way, which is concerned with God in Himself: it is the way of union through love.[9]

We find another way of speaking of the three moments of the soul's approach to God in Gregory's *Homilies on the Song of*

---

[9] For the third way as the realm of union and love, see especially J. Daniélou, *Platonisme et Théologie Mystique* (2nd edn. Paris, 1953), 199–208. This is the most important work on Gregory's mystical theology.

Songs. He speaks of the soul's successive entry into light, cloud, and darkness: *phos*, *nephele*, and *gnophos*. This is the guiding metaphor for Gregory's understanding of the three ways:

> Moses' vision of God began with light; afterwards God spoke to him in a cloud. But when Moses rose higher and became more perfect he saw God in the darkness. Now the doctrine we are taught here is as follows. Our initial withdrawal from wrong and erroneous ideas of God is a transition from darkness to light. Next comes a closer awareness of hidden things, and by this the soul is guided through sense phenomena to the world of the invisible. And this awareness is a kind of cloud, which over-shadows all appearances, and slowly guides and accustoms the soul to look towards what is hidden. Next the soul makes progress through all these stages and goes on higher, and as she leaves below all that human nature can attain, she enters within the secret chamber of the divine knowledge, and here she is cut off on all sides by the divine darkness. Now she leaves outside all that can be grasped by sense or by reason, and the only thing left for her contemplation is the invisible and the incomprehensible. And here God is, as the Scriptures tell us in connection with Moses: 'But Moses went to the dark cloud wherein God was.' (Exod. 20:21)
> (*Comm. on the Song* XI: 1000–1)[10]

The progress is a progress from light to deeper and deeper darkness. The initial stage is the removal of the darkness (*skotos*) of error by the light of the truth. But, from then on, the further the soul progresses the deeper is the darkness into which it enters, until eventually the soul is cut off from all that can be grasped by sense and reason. The contrast with Origen is complete. Whereas for Origen the soul pursues a path of increasing light — the darkness it encounters is dissolved as it progresses further — with Gregory the soul travels deeper and deeper into darkness. The parallel with Philo is also apparent, the reason being the essential agreement of Philo and Gregory about the incomprehensibility of God over against Origen.

[10] Here, as in practically every long citation from Gregory, I have used Musurillo's excellent translation in J. Daniélou, *From Glory to Glory* (London, 1962), which contains a long series of extracts from Gregory's writings illustrating his mystical theology, as well as an excellent introduction by Daniélou. I have used the critical edition of Gregory's work by W. Jaeger (published by Brill of Leiden, 1960 ff.), except for the *Life of Moses*, for which I have used Daniélou's edition (*Sources Chrétiennes* I, 3rd edn., 1968). For clarity of reference, the column number of the relevant volume of Migne has often been given, which is printed in the margin of the modern critical editions.

Gregory, however, seems to me to go further than Philo in being able to give greater content to his idea of entering the divine darkness.

We find the same three stages of the Light, the Cloud, and the Darkness in Gregory's *Life of Moses*, where the connection between these stages and the events of the life of Moses is somewhat clearer than in the passage just quoted, the Light referring to God's revelation of Himself to Moses in the Burning Bush, and the Cloud and the Darkness referring to Moses' two ascents of Mount Sinai, in the second of which, in response to his request to see God's face, Moses is placed in a cleft in the rock and sees God's back parts as he passes by.

In the account of the burning bush in the second, allegorical part of the *Life of Moses*, Gregory says:

> From this light we learn what we must do to stand within the rays of the true light, for we cannot ascend to that height, where the light of truth is seen, with shoes on our feet, that is, unless the dead and earthly covering of skins is removed from the feet of the soul, that covering with which our nature was clothed in the beginning when we were made naked by our disobedience to the divine will. So when we have done these things the knowledge of truth will appear, manifesting itself. For the recognition of what is becomes a purification from opinion about what is not ... It seems to me, then, that the great Moses learnt in this theophany to know that none of the things the senses perceive or intelligence contemplates truly exist, but only the transcendent being and source of the universe on which all depend.   (*Life of Moses* II. 22, 24)

The first way, the way of Light, is the way in which the soul turns from false reality to God, the only true reality. The two sides, active and contemplative, of this way are clear: the active side is purification and the restoration within us of the divine image. Daniélou sums up the goal of the first way in two words, *apatheia* and *parresia*, serenity and boldness: thus prepared the soul is ready to approach God. The contemplative side of the first way is intimately bound up with the active side, for it is the recognition that God alone truly exists, that he is the only worthy object of the soul's love. Gregory also, following Origen, relates the first way, consisting as it does of purification and illumination, to the sacrament of Baptism, and indeed throughout his mystical theology there is a concern to relate it to the sacramental life of the Church.

The second way is the way of the Cloud. As with Origen, Gregory sees the second way — discussed by Solomon in Ecclesiastes — as the period when the soul learns the vanity of created things, and he also shares with Origen a more positive understanding of this way. The purified soul does not simply learn the vanity of all created things but also learns to see in them a manifestation of the glory of God. When Gregory speaks of this, he speaks of 'contemplation of true reality' and 'knowledge of intelligible reality'. The second way, then, is the realm of Platonic *theoria*: contemplation of the realm of genuine reality, of the Forms. First we note that Platonic *theoria* is not the end of the way according to Gregory, rather it belongs to the intermediate stage. In the final stage, as we shall see, we pass beyond *theoria*. There is here a striking contrast not just with Plato, but with Origen (and even more markedly with Evagrius). Contemplation is a stage on the way, not the end.

But Gregory's own treatment of *theoria* in the second way is itself interesting. It is not at all systematic; he frequently refers to it and makes it subserve a variety of ends. Sometimes we seem to have a simple transposition of a Platonic theme; more often Gregory's doctrine is that the purified soul can see the glory of God manifested in his creation. This is the interpretation he gives to the trumpets that Moses heard on his first ascent of Mount Sinai:

Now I think that the heavenly trumpet can be interpreted . . . as a guide in our progress towards the spiritual. In this sense it would refer to the splendid harmony of the world which proclaims the wisdom that shines forth in the universe and tells of the grandeur of God's glory reflected in things visible. Thus it is said: the heavens shew forth the glory of God. There is the loud-sounding trumpet that speaks the divine message in clear and ringing tones, as one of the prophets says: The heavens trumpeted from above. When the hearing of the heart has been purified, then will a man hear this sound — that is, the contemplation of the universe from which we derive our knowledge of the divine omnipotence — and by this he is led in spirit to penetrate to the realm where God exists. This realm the Scriptures call a dark cloud (*gnophos*). And by this is meant the invisibility and incomprehensibility of God. It is in this darkness that he sees the tabernacle not made by human hands, as I have said, later showing a material imitation to those below.

(*Life of Moses* II. 168-9)

In this passage several points are made about the nature of contemplation in the second way. The mention of darkness (*gnophos*) reminds us of a point we have already noticed, that in Gregory the three ways are not strictly successive but shade off one into another — the significance of natural contemplation only emerges as we pass beyond it and are precipitated into the darkness where God is, and where contemplation is impossible. But in this darkness, that is, as we move closer to God, we begin to discern there what Gregory, quoting Hebrews, calls the 'tabernacle not made with hands'. And in descrying this we find the deepest significance of natural contemplation. Gregory continues:

Taking a small clue from Paul, who has partially revealed the mystery involved here, we shall say that by this symbol Moses was instructed in anticipation of that Tabernacle which embraces the universe: and this is Christ, the Power and the Wisdom of God, Who being in His own nature not made by human hand, received a created existence when He was to build His tabernacle among us. Thus the same tabernacle is, in a certain sense, both created and uncreated: uncreated in His pre-existence, He receives a created subsistence precisely in this material tabernacle. This doctrine is not, of course, obscure to those who have received the authentic tradition of this mystery of our faith. For unique above all is He Who existed before all ages and came at the end of all ages. He needed no existence in time; for how would He Who existed before all time and all the ages need a birth in time? But it was for our sake that He accepted to be born among us who had lost existence by the abuse of our freedom, that He might restore to existence all that had gone astray from it. It is God, then, the Only-Begotten, Who encompasses in Himself the entire universe, Who has built His own tabernacle among us. (*Life of Moses* II. 174-7)

By this we are to understand that *theoria* has for its object not just the principles (*logoi*) which lie behind the world that God has created, but also the Word (*Logos*) through whom this world has been created; and not only the Word as Creator, but also as Incarnate. The object of *theoria* is not God as He is in Himself — for that is impossible since God is unknowable — but God as He has manifested Himself to us through His divine energies, in creating the world and in redeeming it. In this contemplation we keep company with the angels. As Daniélou puts it, this contemplation:

has for object human realities, but seen in their celestial perspective. Knowledge takes then a precise sense. It is neither knowledge of God, *theologia*, for God remains inaccessible; nor is it any longer ordinary knowledge of human things: it is supernatural knowledge of God's plan, the *oikonomia*, the history of spiritual creatures. And its own sphere is that of the angels.[11]

The third way is entry into darkness (*gnophos*). This is how Gregory describes Moses' entry into the Dark Cloud:

But what now is the meaning of Moses' entry into the darkness and of the vision of God that he enjoyed in it? The present text (Exod. 24:15) would seem to be somewhat contradictory to the divine apparition he has seen before. There he saw God in the light, whereas here he sees Him in the darkness. But we should not therefore think that this contradicts the entire sequence of spiritual lessons which we have been considering. For the sacred text is here teaching us that spiritual knowledge first occurs as an illumination in those who experience it. Indeed, all that is opposed to piety is conceived of as darkness; to shun the darkness is to share in the light. But as the soul makes progress, and by a greater and more perfect concentration comes to appreciate what the knowledge of truth is, the more it approaches this vision, and so much the more does it seem that the divine nature is invisible. It thus leaves all surface appearances, not only those that can be grasped by the senses but also those which the mind itself seems to see, and it keeps on going deeper until by the operation of the spirit it penetrates the invisible and the incomprehensible, and it is there that it sees God. The true vision and the true knowledge of what we seek consists precisely in not seeing, in an awareness that our goal transcends all knowledge and is everywhere cut off from us by the darkness of incomprehensibility. Thus that profound evangelist, John, who penetrated into this luminous darkness, tells us that 'no man hath seen God at any time' (John 1:18), teaching us by this negation that no man — indeed, no created intellect — can attain a knowledge of God.

(*Life of Moses* II. 162–4)

---

[11] Daniélou, *Platonisme*, 150.

To pass into darkness is to pass into the awareness of the incomprehensibility of God: here there is seeing by not seeing, knowing by unknowing. And the reason is the absolute unknowability of God. But Gregory goes further than simply saying that God is unknowable, and that to realize this is to pass into the divine darkness — which is possibly what Philo meant by that. This is how Gregory explains Moses' request to see God face to face:

What Moses was experiencing, I think, was a longing which filled his soul for the Supreme Good; and this longing was constantly being intensified by his hope in the Transcendent, arising from the beauty which he had already glimpsed; and this hope constantly inflamed his desire to see what was hidden because of all that he had attained at each stage. Thus it is that the ardent lover of beauty, constantly receiving an image, as it were, of what he longs for, wants to be filled with the very impression of the archetype. The bold demand of the soul that climbs the hills of desire tends towards the direct enjoyment of Beauty, and not merely through mirrors or reflections.

In refusing Moses' request, the voice of God in a sense grants it, by pointing out in a few words an infinite abyss of contemplation. For God in his bounty granted that his desire would be fulfilled; but He did not promise that his desire would ever cease or be fully satisfied. Indeed He would not have shown Himself to His servant if the vision would have been such as to terminate Moses' desire; for the true vision of God consists rather in this, that the soul that looks up to God never ceases to desire Him.

And a little later on he continues:

We can conceive then of no limitation in an infinite nature: and that which is limitless cannot by its nature be understood. And so every desire for the Beautiful which draws us on in this ascent is intensified by the soul's very progress towards it. And this is the real meaning of seeing God: never to have this desire satisfied. But fixing our eyes on those things which help us to see, we must ever keep alive in us the desire to see more and more. And so no limit can be set to our progress towards God: first of all, because no limitation can be put upon the beautiful, and secondly because the increase in our desire for the beautiful cannot be stopped by any sense of satisfaction.

(*Life of Moses* II. 231-3, 238-9)

Moses' desire to see God is constantly satisfied and yet never satisfied. 'Moses sought to see God', writes Gregory, 'and this is the instruction he receives on how he is to see Him: seeing God means following Him wherever He might lead' (*Comm. on the Song* VI (888 A)).

This is Gregory's doctrine of what Daniélou calls *epektasis*[12] (though the word only occurs once in Gregory in a mystical sense, as Daniélou himself acknowledges[13]). That is, the soul continually longs for God, continually reaches out for knowledge of Him. But there is no ultimate satisfaction, no final union, no ecstasy in which the soul is rapt up out of the temporal sequence and achieves union. There is simply a deeper and deeper penetration into darkness. Gregory develops this in his treatment of the bride's search for the bridegroom in the Song of Songs:

The soul, having gone out at the word of her Beloved, looks for Him but does not find Him. She calls on Him, though He cannot be reached by any verbal symbol, and she is told by the watchman that she is in love with the unattainable, and that the object of her longing cannot be apprehended. In this way she is, in a certain sense, wounded and beaten because of the frustration of what she desires, now that she thinks that her yearning for the Other cannot be fulfilled or satisfied. But the veil of her grief is removed when she learns that the true satisfaction of her desire consists in constantly going on with her quest and never ceasing in her ascent, seeing that every fulfilment of her desire continually generates further desire for the Transcendent.

Thus the veil of her despair is torn away and the bride realizes that she will always discover more and more of the incomprehensible and unhoped for beauty of her Spouse throughout all eternity. Then she is torn by an even more urgent longing, and through the daughters of Jerusalem she communicates to her Beloved the dispositions of her heart. For she has received within her God's special dart, she has been wounded in the heart by the point of faith, she has been mortally wounded by the arrow of love. And *God is love*.

(*Comm. on the Song* XII: 1037)

It is clear that this doctrine of *epektasis* springs out of Gregory's profound apprehension of the unbridgeable gulf between the soul and God implied by a radical doctrine of

---

[12] From *ep-ek-teinomai*, to reach out after, used by St. Paul in Phil. 3:13, 'reaching forth unto those things which are before', the verse that inspires Gregory's use of the word.   [13] *Platonisme*, 298 n.

creation out of nothing, and is for him an alternative to a doctrine of ecstasy. In his earlier writings, however (for instance, his *De Virginitate*), Gregory does speak of ecstasy. Should we then see something in Gregory's development analogous to that we have seen in Athanasius: a movement from a Platonic mystical premiss to a rejection of mysticism on the basis of the doctrine of *creatio ex nihilo*? Perhaps Gregory's doctrine of *epektasis* is a rejection of mysticism as such, and amounts to no more than the ideal of continual moral progress in the life of the Christian? Certainly it seems to be not just the rejection of ecstatic union with God, but of any idea that we can attain to God: 'Seeing God *means* following him . . . .'

Writing before Daniélou, Urs von Balthasar has this to say about Gregory's doctrine of epektasis, which he calls his philosophy of 'becoming and desire': 'It is a strange thing! We are dissatisfied by this metaphysic which absolutizes that which is most fundamental in us — dissatisfaction.'[14] And he goes on to suggest that where this metaphysic of becoming and desire is wrong is that it is based simply on an analysis of the nature of creaturely reality. But it is important to realize that Gregory has no such metaphysic: *epektasis* is a thread in his thought and cannot be disentangled from the rest of the fabric. Balthasar goes on to speak of Gregory's philosophy of the image and of love, and what he finds here qualifies his earlier conclusion. But, in Gregory's own work, the philosophy of becoming and desire never stood alone and is, indeed, only one way in which Gregory speaks of the soul's experience of the divine darkness. It expresses the fact that God cannot be comprehended, that the soul can come to no final knowledge of God, that its longing for God will never be finally satisfied: the soul will always be inspired by its experience of God to long for more. But this does not at all mean that God is remote from the soul and can never be attained. On the contrary, in the darkness God is present to the soul, and the soul is united with Him. The doctrine of *epektasis* expresses one side of the soul's experience of God: its inexhaustibility, the impossibility of any satiety. But Gregory has at least three themes that express the soul's experience of God's presence to

[14] *Présence et Pensée* (Paris, 1942), 76; see also J. Gaïth, *La Conception de la liberté chez Grégoire de Nysse* (Paris, 1953), 203 ff. for another view and criticism of Balthasar.

it in the darkness: the mirror of the soul, the spiritual senses, and the indwelling Word.

The idea that the soul can contemplate God in the mirror of the soul is expounded in Gregory's early work on the Beatitudes, and also frequently in his mature work, the *Homilies on the Song of Songs*. The sermon on the Sixth Beatitude ('Blessed are the pure in heart, for they shall see God') is exercised by the contradiction between the fact that in this Beatitude the vision of God is promised to the pure in heart, and yet elsewhere in Scripture it is clearly asserted that God cannot be seen. Gregory first suggests an answer by drawing on the distinction found in Philo and others between God's essence and his activities. God is unknown in his essence, yet makes himself known in his energies (Gregory uses the terms *ousia* and *energeiai*, and this passage is frequently quoted by Byzantine writers to provide support for the Palamite distinction between God's unknowable essence and his knowable energies): 'for He is invisible by nature, but becomes visible in His energies, for He may be contemplated in the things that are referred to Him' (*Hom.* VI: 1269 A).[15] This provides a straightforward resolution of the paradox that God seems to be both unknowable and yet can be known. But Gregory is not satisfied, because knowing God through the activity of his energies is to infer the existence of God from his operations, and this is something that the 'wise of this world' might be able to achieve. But 'the Lord does not say it is blessed to know something about God, but to have God present within oneself' (1269 C),[16] for, to know God is to possess Him, not to be informed about Him. So what the Beatitude means is that 'if a man's heart has been purified from every creature and all unruly affections, he will see the Image of the Divine Nature in his own beauty.' Because the soul is a mirror reflecting the divine image, the soul can contemplate God by contemplating the divine image present within itself. The soul must purify itself, otherwise the image will be blurred and distorted, but the grace of being in the image is a *grace*, a gift from God, enabling man to reflect the divine Nature: 'For He who made

---

[15] H. Graefs translation in: *St. Gregory of Nyssa: The Lord's Prayer, The Beatitudes* (*Ancient Christian Writers* XVIII, London, 1954), 147.

[16] Trans. ibid., 148.

you did at the same time endow your nature with this wonderful quality. For God imprinted on it the likeness of the glories of His own Nature, as if moulding the form of a carving into wax' (1271 A).

In the darkness of unknowability the soul contemplates God in the mirror that it is. Gabriel Horn has contrasted the 'Mirror' and the 'Cloud' as Gregory's 'two ways of seeing God',[17] and Balthasar has followed him in understanding knowledge of God gained through the mirror of the soul as a compensation for the impossibility of seeing the unknowable God, a compensation the soul accepts with resignation.[18] But Leys would seem to be right in rejecting this suggestion[19] and understanding by the soul's knowledge of God through the mirror another way of describing the soul's experience in the darkness, a way that suggests the positive side of the experience. He points out that the soul does not see anything in the mirror: there is no reflected image (*ou . . . antiprosopon theama*). The mirror of the soul enables the soul to contemplate by possessing in itself in a created mode what God is in an uncreated mode: it makes possible real participation in God, but God remains incomprehensible.

The simile of the mirror is based on the fact that the soul becomes like God as it is purified by increasing in virtue, something brought out very clearly in the following quotation from the *Commentary on the Song*:

There are many different perfumes, not all equally fragrant, from which a certain harmonious and artistic blend produces a very special kind of unguent called spikenard, taking its name from one of the fragrant herbs that are compounded in it. It is the result of many different perfumes coalescing into a single fragrance; and this is the sweet scent which the Bridegroom perceives with pure senses. In this text I think that the Word teaches us that by His very nature He transcends the entire order and structure of the created universe, that He is inaccessible, intangible, and incomprehensible. But in His stead we have this perfume within us distilled from the perfection of our virtues; and this imitates in its purity His essential incorruptibil-

[17] 'Le "Miroir", la "Nuée", deux manières de voir Dieu d'après S. Grégoire de Nysse', *Revue d'ascétique et de mystique*, VIII (1927), 113–31.

[18] *Présence*, 99.

[19] R. Leys, *L'Image de Dieu chez Saint Grégoire de Nysse* (Brussels and Paris, 1951), 41 f.

ity, in its goodness His goodness, in its immortality His immortality, in its stability His immutability, and in all the virtues we possess we represent His true virtue, which as the prophet Habakkuk says, covers all the heavens (Hab.3:3).

And so when the bride says to the friends of the Bridegroom, 'My spikenard sent forth the odour of him' (Cant. 1:11), this is the profound lesson I think she is teaching us. It is that even though one may gather from all the different meadows of virtue every perfume and every flower of fragrance, and should make his whole life fragrant with the good odour of all these virtuous actions, and become perfect in this way, even he would not be able to look steadily upon the Word of God, no more than he could the sun. But he can look upon this Sun within himself as in a mirror. For the all-perfect virtue of God sends forth rays of sinlessness to illuminate the lives of those who are pure; and these rays make the invisible visible, and allow us to comprehend the inaccessible by impressing an image of the Sun upon the mirror of our souls. Now as far as our interpretation goes, it is much the same thing to speak of the sun's rays, or the emanations of virtue, or the fragrance of perfume. For no matter which of these analogies we use for the purpose of our discourse, the underlying idea is one and the same: that it is through our virtues that we derive a knowledge of the Good that surpasses all understanding, in the same way that we may infer the beauty of an archetype from its image.   (*Comm. on the Song* III: 824 A–C)

The soul, by its virtues, participates in God's perfect virtue, its fragrance is derived from Him; and the Bridegroom delights in the fragrance and beauty of the soul.

This leads to the second theme by which Gregory explores the soul's experience of God in the Darkness: that of the spiritual senses. Elsewhere in the *Commentary on the Song*, instead of the virtues of the soul giving it a fragrance that delights the Bridegroom, the Word, the virtues reawaken the senses of the soul so that the soul itself can sense the Bridegroom. Gregory draws these together in one place where he compares the soul to a lily and the Word to an apple: we delight the Bridegroom with our fragrance, but the Word (the apple) does more than delight the senses, it offers nourishment:

The bride then rightly recognizes the difference between herself and her Lord. As Light, He is an object of beauty for our eyes; He is a sweet odour for our sense of smell; and Life for those who partake of

Him. He that eateth Him, as the Gospel says, shall live. Our human nature, matured by virtue, becomes a flower — but it does not offer nourishment to the Husbandman but simply adorns itself. For He has no need of our goods, but rather we have need of His . . .

(Comm. on the Song IV: 844 B)

It seems to me that Gregory goes beyond Origen in his understanding of the spiritual senses (though he is clearly indebted to him). Whereas Origen is more interested in the idea that there *are* spiritual senses, Gregory uses the idea to explore more deeply the nature of the soul's experience of the divine darkness:

She is encompassed by a divine night, during which her Spouse approaches, but does not reveal Himself. But how can that which is invisible reveal itself in the night? By the fact that He gives the soul some sense of His presence, even while He eludes her clear apprehension, concealed as He is by the invisibility of His nature.

(Comm. on the Song XI: 1001 B–C)

In the dark night, the soul cannot *see*, but she can *feel* the presence of the Word: the Word 'gives the soul some sense of his presence' (*aisthesin tina . . . tes parousias*). And the senses that Gregory shows most interest in are precisely those that are concerned with presence: smell, taste, and touch or feeling. We have seen examples of feeling and smell; Gregory also makes frequent reference to the 'sweetness' (*glukus*) of the soul's experience of God in the Darkness. Gregory is emphasizing, it seems, that in the Darkness the soul is given an experience of God's presence to it. It is important to note too that this presence is something which comes upon the soul: the soul does not find God, but rather is found by him. Gregory's thought here is based on the coming of God among us in the Incarnation: the soul's longing for God is a response to God's love for us in becoming one with us in the Incarnation.

This leads us into the third facet, mentioned earlier, of Gregory's understanding of the soul's experience in the Darkness: the indwelling of the Word in the soul. We have already seen that the development of the virtues in the soul manifest within the soul the image of God: the soul knows God by possessing Him in herself. Gregory often speaks more directly of the presence of the Word within the soul; for instance, he sees in the soul's progress Jesus advancing in wisdom and stature within the soul

Now Jesus, who is born as a child in us, advances in wisdom and age and grace, in different ways in the hearts of those who receive Him. He is not the same in everyone, but only according to the measure of those in whom He dwells, adapting Himself to the capacity of each one who receives Him. To some He comes as a babe, to others as one advancing, to others in full maturity . . .

(Comm. on the Song III: 828 D)

In the continuation of the passage Gregory uses a variety of words to describe that part of the soul where the Word dwells: the heart (*kardia*), the directing part of the soul (*hegemonikon*, a Stoic term), the conscience (*syneidesis*), the mind's depths (*batheia dianoias*). As Daniélou remarks,[20] Gregory seems to be searching for some term to describe the deepest, most inward part of the soul, that which Tauler called the Ground of the Soul, and St. Francis de Sales 'la fine pointe de l'âme'. It is interesting to note too that there are several places (especially in *Homily XI on the Song*) where Gregory contrasts the discursive reason (*zetetike dianoia*), which is baffled as it seeks to understand God as He is in Himself, with the heart (*kardia*), which recognizes with wonder and excitement the presence of the Word. This makes more explicit something conveyed by each of these ways in which Gregory speaks of the soul's mystical experience: that in striving to do justice to it he passes beyond the intellectualism of Origen and the intellectual categories of any Platonic mystical thought and, using the language of the Bible, which speaks of man responding to God with his heart, develops a mysticism that knows God beyond knowledge, that feels the presence of God in the darkness of unknowing. This mysticism of feeling radically transcends what we have found so far in the history of mystical thought.

What these three facets of mystical experience — the mirror of the soul, the spiritual senses, and the indwelling Word — add up to is a very varied and sensitive account of the soul's experience of God in the divine darkness. It is an experience beyond the senses and beyond the intellect; it is a feeling

[20] *Platonisme*, 255.

awareness of a fragrance that delights and enraptures the soul. The doctrine of *epektasis* must be seen in this light. It is not after all the substitution of moralism for mysticism: it is an understanding of mystical experience in which the soul is drawn on more and more to deeper and deeper experience. For the experience of God is inexhaustible; He can never be finally known or comprehended. This continually being drawn onwards is sometimes compared by Gregory to ecstasy, and it may be that he thought there were moments when the soul was rapt in God. But, when he speaks of ecstasy, his language is usually metaphorical and seems to mean that the soul is constantly being drawn out of itself in the sense of longing for deeper and deeper knowledge of God. So, there is a paradox in the soul's deep delight in her experience of God, while yet longing for more. To describe these experiences Gregory uses such oxymorons as 'watchful sleep' and 'sober drunkenness'.

If there is properly an ecstatic element in Gregory's doctrine, it is in the ecstatic nature of love, which continually seeks to draw the soul out of itself to union with God as He is in Himself. Gregory uses both *eros* and *agape* to describe this love, a love which is essentially a desire for union with the beloved. As we noted above, the third way is defined as the stage where the soul finds union (*anakrasis*) with God. And it is this desire for union which is the principle of the soul's entry into darkness, of the highest stage of the soul's mystical ascent. It is a desire for what is impossible — union with the unknowable God, fed by what is actual — union with God in the soul. Daniélou[21] sees this paradox implied in Gregory's use of both *eros* and *agape* to describe the soul's love for God. The longing that stretches the soul out towards God as He is in Himself, this *ecstatic* longing, is *eros*; and *eros* is the *ecstatic* aspect of *agape*:

The bride then puts the veil from her eyes and with pure vision sees the ineffable beauty of her Spouse. And thus she is wounded by a spiritual and fiery dart of *eros*. For *agape* that is strained to intensity is called *eros*. And no one should be ashamed of this, whenever the arrow comes from God and not from the flesh. But the bride rather

[21] Ibid., 206.

glories in her wound, for the point of this spiritual yearning has pierced to the depths of her heart. And this she makes clear when she says to the other maidens: I am wounded with love.

(Comm. on the Song XIII: 1048 CD)

Ecstasy is, then, not an experience in which the soul is rapt up out of the temporal sequence into some eternal state — even momentarily. There is no state of final rest for the soul: it is continually drawn out of itself in its love for God. This is what Gregory means by ecstasy: the intense experience of longing, desire, and love of which *epektasis* — following after God — is the fruit. Desire for God is continually satisfied and yet never satisfied, for the satisfaction of the desire leads to an even greater desire for God. The soul continually reaches out after God. There is no final vision, for the soul's experience in the darkness is not — cannot be — *theoria*, for there is no possibility of sight in this darkness. God's presence cannot be seen or comprehended, but only felt and accepted. This denial of the ultimacy of *theoria*, of contemplation, is what marks Gregory off most sharply from Origen and Evagrius. The Platonic doctrine of contemplation is left behind; it is beyond *theoria*, in the darkness of unknowing, that the soul penetrates more and more deeply into the knowledge and presence of God through love.

VI. THE MONASTIC CONTRIBUTION

IT would be a great mistake if, in discussing mystical theology, we confined our attention to theologians. Prayer is something done, rather than something thought about, and while all theology should relate to prayer, mystical theology does so directly in being reflection on the way of prayer, the way to union of the soul with God. Hence it is that we find monasticism — a life devoted above all to prayer — making a special contribution to mystical theology in the patristic period. Nevertheless, it is precisely in the monastic tradition itself that we find a pronounced anti-mystical strand: an insistence that man is utterly remote from God, and in this world must live a life of repentance and ceaseless struggle against the powers of evil.

The rise of monasticism in the fourth century is a sudden and startling phenomenon with few real antecedents. This dramatic flight to the desert is generally attributed to the desire of Christians for martyrdom when martyrdom, after Constantine's final defeat of Licinius in 323, had ceased to be a possibility. 'White' martyrdom was exchanged for 'red' martyrdom, and thus continuity with Christ himself was preserved at a time when, as the Church became acceptable in the Roman world, and thus no longer stood in contrast to the world, that continuity might otherwise have been imperilled. But how was this 'white martyrdom' understood? Martyrdom had become, during the early centuries of the Church's existence, the ideal of sanctity: the martyrs were the 'athletes' of the Christian life, those who had achieved a mighty victory in a great combat (*agon*). This combat was with the forces of evil, represented by the State and its idolatrous demands: it is often represented as a combat with demons. All this was carried over into monasticism. Compare, for instance, the account of Pionius' body after he had been burnt alive, with Athanasius' account of Antony's body in his *Life of Antony*. Pionius' body was 'like that of an athlete in full array at the height of his powers. His ears were not distorted; his hair lay in order on the surface of his head; and his beard was full as though with the first blossom of hair. His face shone once again . . .'[1] Of Antony we read that when he emerged from his first period of solitary asceticism, those who saw him were 'astonished to see that his body had kept its former appearance, that it was neither obese from want of exercise, nor emaciated from his fastings and struggles with the demons'; we learn too that 'the joy in his soul expressed itself in the cheerfulness of his face' and he is called a 'martyr . . . ever fighting the battles of the Faith'.[2] The monk, like the martyr, is in the front line of the battle against the powers of evil. This is how Athanasius understood the monastic life, as we can see from his *Life of Antony*, but it also very closely parallels his understanding of the Incarnation: for, in the Incarnation, God the Word takes a body so as to be able to meet the powers of evil on their own ground and defeat them.

Athanasius marks an important step forward in the Christian understanding of the soul's way to God. In contrast to earlier forms of mystical theology based on the Platonist premiss of the soul's natural kinship with God, Athanasius posits a great ontological gulf between God and all else — souls included. This gulf can only be crossed by God: man can only know God if God comes to him, comes *down* into the realm of corruption and death that man inhabits. And this he does in the Incarnation. Athanasius' understanding of the Incarnation and his understanding of the monastic life thus link up with each other. In the light of the Incarnation, those who desire to identify themselves with this God who comes down must follow the same movement. No longer will they be drawn upwards to holiness in ever greater likeness to the

---

[1] *Martyrdom of Pionius the Presbyter and his companions*, 22; in *Acts of the Christian Martyrs* (Oxford, 1972), ed. H. Musurillo, 165.
[2] *Life of St. Antony*, 14, 67, 47: R. T. Meyer's translation in *Ancient Christian Writers X* (Longmans, 1950).

invisible God; now they will find themselves being drawn down into the material world with the Word made flesh. So, in the *Life of Antony*, we read nothing of the soul's ascent to God in contemplation, but rather of its descent into the world given over to sin, a descent to the place of the demons there to do battle with them. And two centuries later, when the greatest of the monastic rules came to be written, that of St. Benedict, we find no word in it about contemplation.

And yet this anti-mystical strand in monasticism is only part of the story. The life of contemplation, the search for a sense of kinship with God, continues to call men, and so the two strands, what we might call mystical and anti-mystical, are woven together in the history of Christian monasticism and are the source of endless tensions. But, at the outset of this history, we find them both embodied in a state of perfect development in one man, Evagrius of Pontus.

Evagrius of Pontus

The tradition that finds expression in Evagrius' writings is an intellectualist tradition that owes a great deal to Origen. Evagrius was a friend of Basil and Gregory Nazianzen, who had themselves published a collection of extracts from Origen's writings called the *Philocalia*,[3] though their enthusiasm for Origen was tempered by a recognition of the more doubtful aspects of his theology. Evagrius himself was a thoroughgoing devotee of Origen's theology and his own work represents a development of that of Origen. On the doctrinal side he seems to have accepted all the more dubious parts of Origenism and developed them: indeed it seems that it was Evagrius' own understanding of Origenism that was condemned at the Fifth Ecumenical Council in 553, which also condemned Evagrius personally.[4] Because of his heresy, much of Evagrius' work has survived not in Greek, but in the languages of the non-Chalcedonian churches (which, of course, did not accept the authority of subsequent councils) —

[3] Not to be confused with the *Philocalia* of Nicodemus of the Holy Mountain to which reference will be made later.

[4] See A. Guillaumont, *Les 'Kephalaia Gnostica' d'Évagre le Pontique et l'histoire de l'origénisme chez les Grecs et chez les Syriens* (*Patristica Sorbonensia* 5, Paris, 1962).

mainly Syriac — while some important works (in particular his *Treatise on Prayer*) survived in Greek because of their being attributed to St. Nilus.

Our knowledge of the facts of Evagrius' life depends on Palladius, the historian of early monasticism and author of the *Lausiac History*, who spent several years with the monks of Egypt, during which time he was a disciple of Evagrius. According to his account, Evagrius came from Ibora in Pontus (more precisely, Helenopontus), a town in Cappadocia, not far from St. Basil's monastery, under whose influence Evagrius came while still quite young and by whom he was ordained lector. But he seems to have rejected the kind of monastic life organized by Basil and was drawn instead to the intellectual life of the capital, Constantinople, where his own brilliance had full scope among the many acute theological debates of the time. In Palladius' words, 'he flourished in the great city, confuting every heresy with youthful exuberance' (*Lausiac History*, 38.2).

It was during this time that Evagrius had a vision, or perhaps a dream, in which he swore to leave Constantinople and the temptations which were besetting him there. On coming to himself he reflected that 'even if this oath were made in my vision, nevertheless did I swear it'. The next day he left for Jerusalem where the remarkable Melania eventually helped him to embrace the life of a monk without further prevarications. And so, in 383, he went first to Nitria and then, after a couple of years, even deeper into the Egyptian desert, to Kellia, where he stayed until his death in 399 at the age of fifty-five. Evagrius, therefore, was in the Egyptian desert at the high point in its monastic history, and there he lived as a hermit for sixteen years. It is out of this experience that he writes.

His great works that have survived in Greek are the *Praktikos*,[5] also called *The Monk*, and the *Treatise on Prayer* (the latter ascribed to Nilus).[6] In Syriac the most important work

[5] Edition by A. and C. Guillaumont in *Sources Chrétiennes* 170–1 (Paris, 1971); abbreviated as P.

[6] Text in the *Philocalia* of Nicodemus of the Holy Mountain (Venice, 1782), 155–65; the enumeration of the chapters in *PG* 79 is slightly different. Abbreviated as O.

is his *Kephalaia Gnostica* (Gnostic Chapters):[7] this is a treatise of esoteric doctrine, one of the manuscripts of which contains, more or less unadulterated, the Origenist doctrines that were condemned in 553.[8] The form of these works is striking. Each consists of a collection of short 'chapters', as they are usually called, though they are often no more than sentences: 100 in P, 153 in O, and 90 in each of the Gnostic 'Centuries'. The idea of brief chapters recalls earlier examples of 'gnomic' wisdom, for example, the book of Proverbs, or the sayings of such a one as Heraclitus, but much more significantly, it reminds one of the sayings of the Desert Fathers — pithy sentences, or sometimes very brief stories, which were collected together. The last ten chapters of the *Praktikos*, indeed, consist of ten such sayings.

It is, however, not only in such a matter of style that Evagrius makes contact with the Desert Fathers: his whole understanding of mystical theology belongs to that tradition. For the Desert Fathers life was a continual combat with the demons tempting one to sin, and it is a life which Evagrius endeavours to understand and elucidate. This will become apparent as we follow his account of the spiritual progress of the soul.

Like Origen, Evagrius divides the way of the soul into three stages. But instead of *ethike*, *physike*, and *enoptike*, he uses the terms which through his influence have become familiar: *praktike*, *physike*, and *theologia*. *Praktike* is the stage during which the soul develops the practice of the virtues. This use of the word *praktikos* is a new departure. It usually means 'concerned with business, with activity'; Aristotle had spoken of the *bios praktikos*, the active life, in contradistinction to the contemplative life, *bios theoretikos*.[9] This is what *praktikos* means for Evagrius' friend, Gregory Nazianzen, who contrasts the active life, *bios praktikos*, with that of the monk.[10] For Evagrius, however, far from *praktike* having anything to do with the active life, it presupposes *hesychia*, the life of quiet of the monk (or contemplative, we would say). *Praktike* is the life of

[7] *Patrologia Orientalis* XXVIII 1 (Paris, 1958), ed. with trans. by A. Guillaumont: refs. to this edition, and to the second MS (S_2) judged by Guillaumont to be more authentic. Abbreviated as G.

[8] See Guillaumont, *Les 'Kephalaia Gnostica'*.

[9] *Nicomachean Ethics*, 1095b10–15, 1098a3, 1176a30–1179a32.

[10] See discussion in Guillaumont, *Traité Pratique* (*SC* 170), Introduction 38–63.

struggle with the demons, a struggle to overcome temptation and subdue the passions. *Physike* is, as with Origen, the stage of natural contemplation — seeing created reality in God, as it were. *Theologia* is knowledge (*gnosis*) of the Holy Trinity, contemplation of God as He is in Himself. Evagrius, however, sometimes divides the spiritual life in another way into two: *praktike* and *theoretike* or *gnostike* — the level of activity or effort, and the level of contemplation, knowledge, or prayer. With this division, however, there is an area of overlap, when the soul is still engaged in active struggle against the demons, and yet has already begun to contemplate. This area of overlap, as we shall see, corresponds to the middle section of the threefold division, namely, *physike*.

In *praktike*, the soul acquires the virtues. More precisely, in the course of this stage the soul attains the state of *apatheia*, which literally means impassibility, freedom from passions. Bousset, in his book on the Fathers of the Desert, remarks that Evagrius' ability lay especially 'in the field of practical piety':[11] it is certainly true that Evagrius' ideas on *praktike* were treasured among the monks, and it is the works dealing with this that are preserved in Greek. So, although hitherto we have given little space to the early stages of the mystical life, with Evagrius it will be better, if we are to appreciate his genius, to devote some space to *praktike*.

What does Evagrius mean by *apatheia*? For the moment let us simply state that Evagrius does not mean a state of insensibility in which the soul is like a stone, as Jerome alleged.[12] Rather *apatheia* means a state of tranquillity, a state in which the soul is no longer disturbed by its passions. It is the goal of *praktike*, or 'the flower of *praktike*' (P 81), but it is not an end in itself. As Evagrius puts it in the prologue to the *Praktikos*, '*apatheia* gives birth to love, love is the door of natural knowledge [that is, *physike*] which leads to *theologia* and final bliss.' *Apatheia* is a necessary condition for *agape*, which is the true 'goal of *praktike*' (p 84). *Apatheia* is indeed for Evagrius the most natural, the most healthy, state of the soul; a soul subject to impulses and passions is disordered, dis-

[11] W. Bousset, *Apophthegmata* (Tübingen, 1923), 304; quoted by P. Sherwood, *Maximus the Confessor: Ascetic Life and Four Centuries on Charity* (London, 1955), 235.
[12] *Ep.* 133; see Guillaumont, *Traité Pratique*, 99.

eased. And health, of course, is not an end in itself, but enables one to act most effectively.

Praktike, then, is the way of *apatheia*. The way begins with faith, *pistis*. In the prologue to the *Praktikos* Evagrius states that this fundamental attitude of faith is made secure by the fear of God and continence and rendered unshakeable by endurance and hope, and from these virtues is born *apatheia*.[13] Evagrius is, however, only interested in the monastic or eremitical way of *praktike* (and it is not clear that he thinks any other is possible) — the way that begins with faith but also with withdrawal into silence and solitude, *hesychia*. It is a way of struggle with the demons, and according to Evagrius it is only the hermits who engage in open, or direct, warfare with them: 'The demons fight hand to hand with the hermits, but in their battle against those who live a life of virtue in a monastery or a community they fight only indirectly — through the more negligent brethren. The latter battle is a much slighter affair than the former, since never will you find on earth men as spiteful as the demons or able to work all wickedness so quickly' (P 5). The first stage of *praktike* is, then, for Evagrius withdrawal into solitude and silence there to fight the demons hand to hand.

This is a battle not against actual sinning so much as against temptation to sin, against thoughts, imaginations, considerations — all comprehended in the Greek word, *logismos*. It is a much harder battle. 'You have heard that it was said, "You shall not commit adultery." But I say unto you that everyone who looks at a woman lustfully has already committed adultery with her in his heart.' This saying of Jesus is taken quite literally by Evagrius — sinning in the heart, sinning with the *logismoi*, this is what *praktike* is concerned with. And in this Evagrius is in agreement with one of Antony the Great's recorded sayings: 'He who wishes to live in solitude in the desert is delivered from three conflicts: hearing, speech and sight; there is only one conflict for him and that is with the heart.'[14] It is the way of the demons to stir up the

---

[13] *Prologue* 8; cf. P 81, which again speaks of faith as the foundation of *praktike*, and says that it is an indwelling good which naturally exists even in those who do not yet believe in God.

[14] Alphabetical Series, Antony 11, according to the Latin version of Pelagius.

imagination, the *logismoi*, not directly — for the demons cannot know the heart, only God can (O 63 f.) — but through the lower part of the soul, the passionate and desiring part. Although they cannot see the heart, they can see from the monk's behaviour what sort of a state he is in, depressed or self-satisfied or whatever, and attack accordingly.

Evagrius divides the *logismoi* into eight types, eight kinds of evil thoughts. His list is the precursor of the Western list of seven deadly sins, though it is more a diagnostic device than a topic of moral theology. These are gluttony, fornication, avarice, grief, anger, accidie or listlessness, vainglory, and pride.[15] What Evagrius means by these is not so much the grand sins they call to mind, as temptations that play on the particular tendency of the soul thus indicated. So *gastrimargia*, gluttony, is not a temptation to eat more than necessary, but the temptation to mitigate one's ascetic discipline because of fears about one's health. Similarly, fornication is not exactly the temptation literally to fornicate, but rather is concerned with the continual recurrence of sexual fantasies which afflict the hermit and remind him of the sexual side of his nature. The temptation is to give up the ascetic life altogether as pointless. If you still feel like that, why bother? Evagrius discusses all the types of *logismos* and how to deal with them (P 6–14). His discussion is very shrewd and displays great psychological subtlety and insight.

It is important to notice the single-mindedness of Evagrius here. He is not so much concerned about the virtues for their own sakes: for instance, he is not concerned with love and the avoidance of anger because this is better for those with whom we have to do. Love and the avoidance of anger are for him important because they calm the soul, bring it to a state of *apatheia* and so make prayer possible.

The first stage of *praktike* is struggle with the desiring part of the soul: this afflicts the soul in prayer by causing distraction. When the soul has attained the stage at which it can pray without distraction (P 63), then the struggle goes on day and night with the passionate part of the soul. Evagrius has a great deal to say about this. Whereas the desiring part only distracts

[15] Using the usual English equivalents — not always quite appropriate. The Greek words are: *gastrimargia, porneia, philarguria, lupe, orge, akedia, kenodoxia, hyperephania.*

the mind in prayer, the passionate part darkens the mind (P 74) and makes prayer impossible. It is a recurrent theme in the treatise *On Prayer* that anger — even apparently justified anger — 'troubles the eye of the mind and causes ruin to the state of prayer' (O 27, cf 20–6). The remedy lies in patience, avoiding any judging of others, and psalm singing which 'calms the passions and brings tranquillity to the unruliness of the body' (O 83).

When the soul has calmed the irrational part (that is, the desiring and the passionate part), it enjoys undistracted and untroubled prayer, and then is wide open to the attacks of the demons of vainglory and pride. Vainglory here means being pleased with oneself, and pride means self-sufficiency, principally in relation to God. The demon of vainglory attacks the soul by causing it to see visions, to have the sense that it is actually apprehending God. So we read:

When the mind prays purely and impassibly, then the demons no longer come from the left [the irrational side of the soul?] but from the right. And they represent to him the glory of God as a certain form which delights the senses so that he thinks he has attained perfectly the end of his prayer. It was told me by a certain contemplative, that this comes from the passion of vainglory. And the place which is touched by the demon is the brain.

(O 73)[16]

The remedy against this is in the realization that images have no place in prayer, that 'undistracted prayer is the highest activity of the mind' (O 35), and that images and shapes belong to the lower reaches of mental activity (cf. O 83–5).

Praktike leads to *apatheia*. That the soul is on the verge of reaching *apatheia* becomes manifest when the soul can pray without distraction, when it is unconcerned about the things of the world in the time of prayer (O 63, 65, 67). Another proof that the soul has attained the state of *apatheia* is when the *nous* begins to see its own light, and remains still and unmoved before the dreams of the night, and serene when it beholds things going on outside itself (*ta pragmata* in Evagrius' ter-

---

[16] Cf. 116. The last sentence refers to Evagrius' theory, expounded in O 74, that the demons cause these visions by interfering 'in a very shrewd way' with the part of the brain that controls sight.

minology — P 64). '*Nous* begins to see its own light': what
Evagrius seems to mean is that when the soul has attained
impassibility then the mind is free to contemplate, to pray. It
becomes aware of its powers of contemplation, of its spiritual
senses (G II.35), of its own glory and light, which is *gnosis* (G
I.87). So, as the soul attains *apatheia*, the *nous* becomes aware
of itself, its own light, its own powers: it enters into *theoria*. In
fact the mind enters on the second stage of the way, that of
natural contemplation, the stage he calls *physike*.

In *Praktikos* 60, Evagrius distinguishes between perfect and
imperfect *apatheia* and it would seem that *physike* is the stage in
between, when the soul has begun to attain *apatheia*, but has
not yet reached perfection. In this stage the soul struggles
against the demons (so it is still in *praktike*) but has also begun
to contemplate, and what it has begun to contemplate is the
'*logoi* of the things that have come to be' (O 80), the principles
which lie behind the created order. This is natural contemplation, seeing the world in God (for those principles, or *logoi*,
exist in God, in His Word, or *Logos*). Evagrius does not dwell
on this natural contemplation, except in so far as it is
important for the soul's progress (we see again his single-
minded concentration on the soul's way) and that through it
the soul can now oppose the demons, not just by struggling
but by its own ability to understand them and their ways.
When the mind gets to this stage, it becomes its own physician
and can discern 'the healing command' (P 82) which can heal
those powers that impede its own contemplation. It can use
the fruits of its own contemplation to advance its contemplation. Now, having attained in some degree *apatheia*, so that it is
no longer bound up in the passions, the soul can see the
principles of the war with the demons, and easily comprehend
their manœuvres. At this stage the soul becomes not only a
physician for itself, but one who can help others.

In the *Gnostic Chapters* Evagrius distinguishes two stages of
natural contemplation. Second natural contemplation, the
lower stage, is the contemplation of beings (G I.74); in this
second natural contemplation we see the manifold wisdom of
Christ (G II.2). Above this there is first natural contemplation
which is concerned with the incorporeal *logoi* that lie behind
everything that is. The details of Evagrius' doctrine here are

not clear (treatises which consist of brief, gnomic utterances are not conducive to clarity), but the general idea seems clear enough. A soul which has attained *apatheia* is sufficiently detached to be able to contemplate. It begins by contemplating the natural order itself, then it rises beyond this and discerns the principles which lie behind it. Since the universe is created by the Word of God, this is to enter into the mind of the Word. There is, then, a movement within natural contemplation from the material to the immaterial, from the world of embodied existence to the realm of immaterial (naked, *gymnos*) existence, of the angels who continually behold the face of God. In second natural contemplation we are still in the realm of the manifold; in first contemplation there is greater unity or collectedness. The soul first learns to contemplate, and then learns through its experience of contemplation to be aware of her nature as a mind, a *nous*. In second natural contemplation what is important is contemplation itself, the act of contemplating; in first contemplation the soul realizes itself as *nous*, as one of the company of minds. Beyond this there is *theologia*. So we have the following three beatitudes:

Blessed is he who has loved nothing of second natural contemplation, except the contemplation.
Blessed is he who has hated nothing of first natural contemplation of natures, except their wickedness.
Blessed is he who has reached the ignorance that is inexhaustible.
(G III.86–8)

The 'ignorance that is inexhaustible':[17] this is the realm of *theologia*, contemplation of the Holy Trinity. In this state the soul returns to its original state of being without a body, of being naked (a state presumably only possible after death). Contemplation is here absolutely simple, absolutely imageless. The mind *is* what it contemplates in *theologia*, contemplation of the Trinity. So, in one place (G IV.77), Evagrius explains that the objects which the mind contemplates are outside of it and yet contemplation of them is constituted within the mind itself, but that in contemplation of the Holy

---

[17] Or, according to S₂, the 'knowledge that is inexhaustible'. See I. Hausherr, 'Ignorance infinie ou science infinie', in *Hesychasme et prière* (Rome, 1966), 238–46, who argues that both readings could be regarded as Evagrian.

Trinity this is not so, for here this distinction is overcome, here there is essential knowledge, knowledge, that is, which is not knowledge of something *else*, but knowledge in which knower and known are one. Elsewhere (G IV.87) he says that in all contemplation the object of contemplation is over against the mind, except in contemplation of the Holy Trinity. This is none the less a state of *knowledge*. God is knowable (see, e.g., G I.3) and when the mind is stripped and naked it can know Him. There is no entry into the divine darkness in Evagrius' theology, no apophatic theology. Nor is there any idea that the final state of the soul is ecstatic (Evagrius, like Origen, only speaks of ecstasy disparagingly). Evagrius understood the darkness of Exod. 20:21, which Gregory of Nyssa and Denys the Areopagite interpret as the divine darkness, as the 'spiritual contemplation concerning the *logoi* of the providence and judgement of those who are on earth' (G V.16), by which he seems to mean that in contemplation things that are remote from God appear obscure to one who is approaching close to Him.[18] But, whatever he means, this intelligible *gnophos* appears to be a passing phenomenon: it is not the experience of being close to God, as in Gregory and Denys. There is indeed *progress* in *theologia*, there is always more to know of the infinity of God, there is an unlimited ignorance:[19] but it is an ignorance that is continually yielding to knowledge — such as we have already seen in Origen — not the radical unknowability of Gregory and Denys. In this Evagrius follows not just Origen, but his immediate contemporaries and admirers of Origen, Gregory of Nazianzus and Basil the Great.[20]

Theologia is the realm of prayer (*proseuche*). For Evagrius prayer is not so much an activity as a state (*katastasis*), not so much something that you do as something that you are.[21] He

---

[18] See the accompanying chapters in G.

[19] G I.88; cf. 87, and see Hausherr in Orientalis Christiana Periodica II (1936), 351 ff. (also in *Hesychasme*, 38–49).

[20] See Hausherr, art.cit., and also Greg. Naz. *Oratio* XXXVIII.7 (*PG* 37.1434).

[21] Here is perhaps a suitable place to explain a rather recondite point about the form of Evagrius' works. It is evident that the number of chapters in each work is no matter of chance. In the introduction to O, Evagrius explains at great length the significance of 153 (among other things the number of fishes in the miraculous catch recorded in John 21). 100 is clearly a number of perfection, and Evagrius was followed in the idea that apparently originates with him of a treatise on the spiritual

says of the mind that it is its nature to pray (P 49). In prayer the soul regains its primordial state as *nous*. *Apatheia* is the prerequisite for prayer understood in this way. 'The state of prayer is an impassible habit which snatches up the soul that loves wisdom to the intellectual heights by a most sublime love.'[22] For this state the soul must have perfect control over the irrational parts of the soul and be beyond any thought that is involved with the passions (any image — though Evagrius means more than that: O 54): in other words the soul must have attained perfect *apatheia*. For a soul to attempt such prayer without having attained such a state is to put itself in great danger:

As it serves nothing except to injure the eyes to look on the sun intently and without a veil at high noon when it is hottest; so for an impure mind, still bound to the passions, to counterfeit the awesome and transcendent prayer which is in spirit and in truth avails absolutely nothing, but rather the opposite, for it arouses the divine to vexation. (O146; cf. 145)

But such prayer, for the soul who has attained to it, is an advance beyond *apatheia*; *apatheia* is not the same thing as this state of pure prayer, or prayer in truth. If the impassible soul wishes to know true prayer, it must avoid *psila noemata* — mere thoughts, 'mere', that is, in contrast to *theologia*, contemplation of the Holy Trinity. Such 'mere thoughts' keep the soul far from God and distract it. They also keep the soul at the level of multiplicity.[23] Pure prayer is beyond this, and it is beyond

---

life of 100 chapters by Diadochus of Photicē and Maximus the Confessor — cf. too Thomas Traherne's *Centuries of Meditations*. The form of G is odd: 6 centuries (as they are called) of only 90 chapters each. These are probably best understood as an incomplete set of 7 genuine centuries: but the incompleteness is not due to chance, it represents the incompleteness of the unlimited ignorance of *theologia*. *Gnosis* can only be indicated, not explained; it is more a *state* of knowing, than any amount of knowledge. Such an interpretation perhaps gains support from the fact that P is a treatise of only 90 chapters, the last 10 being drawn from the oral tradition of sayings of the Desert Fathers: *praktike* is something done, explanation can only take one part of the way, example is indispensable. On this see Guillaumont, *Les 'Kephalaia Gnostica'*, 20–2.

[22] O 53; cf. O 14, where prayer is said to be the offspring of gentleness and lack of anger, and O 82, about praying gently.

[23] See O 56–8; cf. G IV.90: *gnosis* does not need a soul apt at dialectics, but a soul that can *see*; for dialectics can be found in souls that are impure, but vision is found in pure souls only.

in the sense that it is of grace, given by God and received by the soul. 'If you wish to pray, you have need of God who gives prayer to him who prays . . .' (O 59). It is not by chance, then, that two chapters very close to those we have just referred to concern God's direct action within the soul (in contrast to the operation of demons, and even angels, who can work only indirectly by inspiring *logismoi* in us):

The Holy Spirit sympathizes with our weakness and visits us even when we are unclean. If he finds a mind single and full of love for true prayer, he comes upon it, and all the reasonings that beset it and the phalanx of thoughts he drives away, and turns it to love of spiritual prayer. (O 63)

Others [i.e. angels and demons] through changes in the body reach the mind through reasonings and thoughts and contemplations; but the Lord Himself does the opposite, coming to the mind itself and imparting to it knowledge of what is wished. And through the mind he calms the incontinence of the body. (O 64)

Prayer is a communing of the mind with God (O 3) and is effected by God's own condescension to the soul. Such a soul becomes *theologos*, a theologian, one who can speak about God, one who knows God. 'If you are a theologian, you pray in truth; if you pray in truth, you are a theologian' (O 61).

Behind this idea of prayer as a state — the natural, pure (O 84) state of the *nous* — lies Evagrius' Origenist metaphysics. Souls are fallen minds and it is in prayer that the soul regains its proper activity as *nous* (G III.28). In this life its experience of such a state will be transient, for only the mind separated from the body (naked mind) can sustain this state of pure, immaterial prayer (cf. G III.15). The angels are such pure minds who enjoy contemplation of pure reality continually (G III.4), who continually behold the face of God (cf. Matt. 18:10). So the mind that attains the state of pure prayer becomes equal to the angels. 'The monk becomes equal to the angels (*isangelos*) through his prayer, as he longs to see the face of the Father who is in heaven' (O 113). Clearly there is Platonic or neo-Platonic influence behind the idea of angels as pure minds, men and demons being fallen minds. But we would be mistaken in supposing that that is all there is to

Evagrius' understanding of the angels. As the demons attack the soul, so the angels defend the soul against them:

The holy angels urge us to prayer and stand by us rejoicing, and pray for us.   (O 81)

The angel of God stands by, and by a word only can dispel any power that operates against us, and cause the light of the intellect to shine unerringly.   (O 75)[24]

The monk, in becoming equal to the angels, becomes one who through his prayer helps others: 'it is right to pray not only for your own purification, but also for the whole race, that you may imitate the way of the angels' (O 40; cf. 122).

From this point of view we can understand the two series of beatitudes in the treatise *On Prayer*; the first of the mind in prayer and the second of the monk. The first series expound this state of pure, immaterial prayer, a state in which the mind becomes purely mind, like the angels:

Blessed the mind which in time of prayer has attained perfect formlessness.
Blessed the mind which in undistracted prayer receives an ever-growing desire for God.
Blessed the mind which in time of prayer becomes immaterial and stripped of everything.
Blessed the mind which in time of prayer possesses perfect insensibility.   (O 117–20)

It is the monk who pursues this way of prayer, who flees desire and the passions,[25] who attains the angelic state and thus finds himself *close to the world*, able to help it more effectively than one who is bound to it:

Blessed the monk who regards all men as God, after God.
Blessed the monk who regards the salvation and progress of all with great joy, as if it were his own.
Blessed the monk who thinks himself the offscouring of all.
The monk is separated from all and united to all.

---

[24] Cf. G V.7. According to VI.88 it is not only the angels but the stars too that work with us for our salvation.

[25] Especially anger or aggressiveness — cf. the similar emphasis in Buddhism: see, e.g., the texts quoted in E. Conze, *Buddhist Meditation* (London, Unwin Books, 1972), 118–25.

The monk is one who regards himself as one with all because he sees himself appearing continually in each person. (O 121–5)

Evagrius' achievement is to have worked out, within a devoutly Origenist framework, a subtle and penetrating understanding of the monastic way of mystical prayer. In this he owes of course a great deal to Origen, and also to Clement of Alexandria. Like them he is an intellectualist, both in the sense that he moves within a framework of ideas that belongs to an intellectual tradition, namely, Platonism, but also because the goal of the mystical life is conceived of as the supreme activity of the mind or intellect. This is the significance of his rejection of any understanding of union with God as ecstasy: the mind does not go out of itself at the summit of the mystical ascent, rather it realizes its true activity and, functioning purely and effectively as mind, it contemplates God and knows Him, for which purpose it was fashioned. This intellectual side of Evagrius was condemned by the later Church: it was felt to be less mystical *theology* than mystical *philosophy*. But what Evagrius added to the Origenist tradition, what is really original about his mystical theology, was his intense practical concern, and this clearly arose out of his own participation in the lived tradition of the Desert Fathers, out of his own experience of the eremitical life. This was gratefully accepted by Eastern monasticism and his most important works on the monastic way of prayer (as opposed to speculation about the metaphysical presuppositions of that way) — the *Praktikos* and *On Prayer* — were preserved in Greek, and exercised an enormous influence on Eastern Orthodox spiritual and mystical theology.

The Macarian Homilies

Evagrius speaks to us from the Egyptian Desert, from the world of the Desert Fathers, but he also speaks to us as an intellectual, familiar with Origen and the concepts and ideas of late classical philosophy. In the Macarian *Homilies*[26] we are

---

[26] The textual problems of these homilies are very complicated and have by no means been cleared up. See H. Dörries, *Symeon von Mesopotamien* (*Texte und Untersuchungen* 55, 1, Leipzig, 1941). A Greek text — the most influential one — is

in a different world: actually geographically different, for, though they are ascribed to Macarius the Egyptian, they come from Syria. But different in spirituality too: whereas Evagrius is intellectualist, the spirituality of the Macarian *Homilies* is deeply experiential, sometimes even crudely so. These are monks who, in their prayer, see God with their very eyes. Great store is set by this experience. Evagrianism, we have seen, was condemned as a heresy, and so too was the doctrine preached in the Macarian *Homilies*. For, though the Macarian *Homilies* were (and are) read and valued in orthodox circles, they are the product of a sect called the Messalians, and the ascription of these homilies to Macarius was a device to keep them circulating among the orthodox.

What is Messalianism?[27] It was a monastic movement in Syria at the end of the fourth century. Its message is simple: the only thing that matters is prayer. Fasting, asceticism (even morality), baptism, the Eucharist, the institution of the Church — all this is beside the point, the only thing that matters is prayer. Hence their name: Euchites, from the Greek *euche*, prayer; or Messalians, from the Syriac *mṣallyane*, the praying ones. We hear about them first from Epiphanius, who talks entirely about their behaviour, not at all about their beliefs. Theodoret[28] gives us a more interesting account, telling us about the answers of an old man who was a Messalian. According to this old man, the sacrament of baptism is of no value; only assiduous prayer can drive away the demon who dwells in each one of us. From the fall of Adam, all those descended from him are by nature in the servitude of the demons. It is only prayer that can drive the demon out, the Holy Spirit in answer to this prayer filling the

---

published as vol. 4 of *Patristische Texte und Studien: Die 50 Geistlichen Homilien des Makarios*, edited by Dörries, Klostermann, and Kroeger (Berlin, 1964). The text of a MS in the Vatican library, which includes both homilies and letters (and which is richer in chapters condemned by Timothy of Constantinople and John Damascene than the more well-known text — see below) has been published as two volumes of *Die Griechischen Christlichen Schriftsteller* (Berlin, 1973) by H. Berthold. There is a translation of the 50 homilies, based mainly on the text in Migne (*PG* 34) by A. J. Mason (London, SPCK, 1921) of which I have made use.

[27] For this paragraph see the introduction to the edition of the *Liber Graduum*, published in *Patrologia Syriaca* III (ed. M. Kmosko), which gives all the ancient witnesses to Messalianism (apart from the Macarian *Homilies*).

[28] *Historia Ecclesiastica* IV.10.

soul and making his presence felt in a sensible and visible way, freeing the body from the movement of the passions and the soul from the inclination to do evil. Fasting is not necessary, nor doctrine to bridle the soul, nor any sort of training or asceticism. Not only is the body freed from evil motions, but it plainly sees things to come, and beholds the Trinity with its eyes. In the next chapter of his Church History, Theodoret gives another account of Messalianism which adds to the words of the old man only the idea that the demon is expelled in sweat and spit, and that the Messalians sleep a great deal. From this we see that the characteristics of Messalianism are a great stress on the serious effect of the Fall on man, sin becoming more or less natural to man after the Fall, and the idea that only prayer can have any effect. Alongside this there is a stress on *experience*, real physical experience of the effect of grace and the presence of the Spirit. These are the doctrines that are condemned as Messalian in the series of chapters excerpted from the writings of the Messalians by Timothy of Constantinople (late sixth or early seventh century) and John of Damascus. It is the fact that most of these chapters come from the Macarian *Homilies* which makes unavoidable the judgement that the *Homilies* are of Messalian provenance. The only particular point from these chapters we need to add is that the state of the soul after the expelling of the demon and the indwelling of the Spirit is called *apatheia*. Such is a summary of most of the evidence for the Messalian heresy between the fourth and the eighth century, from which it appears that Messalianism was a coherent and identifiable type of spirituality which was opposed by the Church. It was first condemned at the third Ecumenical Council in 431 — and often thereafter.

But there is more to Messalianism than this: the fifty *Homilies* of Macarius are a moving and profound account of the soul's experience of God in prayer, and it was for this that the Macarian *Homilies* were preserved and valued in the Church. None the less their framework is undoubtedly that of Messalianism, though in the most widely circulated text of the *Homilies* the extremes of Messalianism have been softened.[29]

---

[29] For example, the Macarian *Homilies* set great store by asceticism. It should be mentioned that the categorical tone of the text would be disputed by some scholars,

The spirituality of the Macarian *Homilies* is a spirituality of the *heart*. Here we find a certain contrast with Evagrius, whose spirituality might be characterized as a spirituality of the mind or *nous*.[30] A spirituality of the heart, of longing for God in the depth of one's being, of feeling that is deeper than thought, a spirituality that seeks to penetrate the depths of the soul: this is what we find in these homilies. The soul, they say, is like a tree with many limbs and branches: it is very difficult for us to grasp all these parts of the soul. A man's soul is vast and unfathomable to himself.[31] It is from this that there stems the importance of prayer. By himself a man can only do anything with but a part of himself. The self that he thinks he is but a part. It is only God who can draw all these many parts of the soul together, and all we can do is to long for this operation of the grace of God, to pray constantly.

Before a man is penetrated by grace he is bound by Adam's sin. Macarius (let us call him that for convenience, though it is possible, even likely, that the author of these homilies was a Messalian mentioned by Theodoret called Symeon of Mesopotamia[32]) has a strong doctrine of the Fall:

When man transgressed the commandment and was exiled from Paradise, he was bound down in two ways and with two different chains. One was in this life, in the affairs of this life and in the love of the world ... But besides this, in the hidden region, the soul is hedged and hemmed in and walled round, and bound with chains of darkness by the spirits of wickedness, unable to love the Lord as it would, or to believe as it would, or pray as it would. Contrariety has

---

who are not convinced by the evidence of the Messalianism of the *Homilies*. This feeling has gained particular strength from the argument that the Macarian writings are dependent on Gregory of Nyssa, an argument put forward by W. Jaeger in *Two Rediscovered Works of Ancient Christian Literature: Gregory of Nyssa and Macarius* (Leiden, 1954). It does not seem to me that this position can be sustained: see R. Staats, *Gregor von Nyssa und die Messalianer* (Berlin, 1968), and H. Chadwick's review of it in the *Journal of Ecclesiastical History* XX (1969), 319 f. For the teaching of the Macarian *Homilies* see: E. A. David, *Das Bild vom neuen Menschen* (Salzburg, and Munich, 1968), and also H. Chadwick, 'Messalianerne — en evangelisk bevegelse i det 4. århundre', *Tidsskrift for Teologi og Kirke* 3/1979, 161–72.

[30] Though we should not exaggerate this. Evagrius too speaks of the heart, and the importance of feeling in prayer: see O 42f. and P 4.

[31] See XXVI.9, XII.11, XV.32 (*Homilies* cited by number and section as in Dörries-Klostermann-Kroeger and Mason).

[32] Some MSS of the *Homilies* (including all the Arabic versions) ascribe them to one 'Symeon'.

come upon everyone both in visible things and in those hidden, from the transgression of the first man. (XXI.2)[33]

Fallen man has lost his image and likeness to God (XII.1), and sin has entered into his heart (XV.12). Sin is mixed, or mingled, in the heart (I.8 — Macarius is very fond of the analogy of mingling, both in relation to grace in the heart and in relation to sin). The soul is completely enslaved to sin, no member of it is free from sin — neither thoughts, nor mind, nor body: 'it is impossible to separate between the soul and sin, unless God should stop and repress this evil wind, which dwells in the soul and body' (II.3). The soul is so completely bound up with sin that it becomes natural to it.

Natural — but not pleasant:

After falling from the commandment and entering the sinful state, the race of Adam has acquired that likeness [to Cain] in secret; it is tossed about with shifting thoughts of fear and terror and every kind of commotion; the prince of this world keeps each soul on the waves of all sorts and varieties of pleasure and lust, unless it be begotten of God; as corn is turned incessantly in the sieve, he keeps men's thoughts rocking about in various directions, and shakes and entices them all by worldly lusts, and pleasures of the flesh, and fears, and commotions. (V.2)[34]

Timothy of Constantinople says that the Messalians hold that each man is possessed by a demon that leads him to actions that are *atopos* — absurd, literally displaced or out of place. The word *atopos* is not used in the passage just quoted (nor can I find an example elsewhere in the Macarian *Homilies*) but it expresses very well Macarius' understanding of the effect of sin and the demons on man. The demons dwell in the soul of man, in all its many members, and a man can gain possession, as it were, of only a part of his soul. Many of his actions are not 'his own', or rather are due to a part of him possessed not by himself but by the demons. Man's soul is torn apart by the demons, he is rocked about, tossed by the demons: thus many

---

[33] Cf. St. Bernard's idea of *regio dissimilitudinis*, in *Sermo de Diversis* XLII.2 f., an idea probably derived from Augustine, *Confessions* VII.x.16. The similarities and contrasts between Messalianism and Augustine are worth noting.

[34] Similar metaphors for the demons' attacks on the soul are also found in Evagrius: O III, 140.

of his actions are *atopos*, 'displaced', absurd. The effect of grace on the soul is quite different. A soul who has received the grace of God finds stillness.[35] The heart, with all its depths, becomes calm and unified and still. And this state can only be possessed by single-mindedness and complete detachment (see *Homily* V).

How does this change come about? We have already seen that for Macarius only God can effect it; and, further, only by grace in answer to prayer. Baptism has no effect here, though it is true that this point is not pressed in the Macarian *Homilies*.[36] The effect of the grace of God is inward: what matters is feeling the presence of grace in the depths of the heart. External rites like baptism, external promises such as are written in Scripture, are irrelevant; what matters is inner experience, inner assurance.[37]

In order to be free from sin, the soul needs the grace of God. But its life in sin has penetrated so deeply into the soul that the grace of God appears foreign, strange to it. The grace of the Holy Spirit is 'something foreign to our nature' (IV.6). It is something we must *receive* — for it comes to us from above, from outside. The soul cannot of itself acquire grace, it cannot of itself escape from the power of sin:

It is of no use for the heavenly places, it is of no use for the kingdom — that soul which supposes that it can achieve perfect purity of itself, and by itself alone, without the Spirit. Unless the man who is under the influence of passions will come to God, denying the world, and will believe with patience and hope to receive a good thing foreign to his own nature, namely the power of the Holy Spirit, and unless the Lord shall drop upon the soul from on high the life of the Godhead, such a man will never experience true life, will never recover from the drunkenness of matter; the enlightenment of the Spirit will never shine in that benighted soul, or kindle in it a holy daytime; it will never awake out of that deepest sleep of ignorance, and so come to know God of a truth, through God's power and the efficacy of grace.   (XXIV.5)

---

[35] 'rest and stability and calm and a settled disposition': XV.14.
[36] It is mentioned two or three times, e.g. ibid.
[37] *peira, plerophoria* — see XV.20.

Not that there is nothing the soul can do. Macarius has a great deal to say about how the soul can *force itself* to do what eventually God will grant it:

A man must force himself to that which is good, even against the inclination of his heart, continually expecting God's mercy with no doubtful faith, and force himself to charity, when he has no charity; force himself to meekness, when he has no meekness; force himself to pity, and to have a merciful heart; force himself to be looked down upon, and when he is made light of or put to shame, not to be angry, as is said, Beloved, avenge not yourselves; to force himself to prayer, when he has not spiritual prayer; and thus God, beholding him thus striving, and compelling himself by force, in spite of an unwilling heart, gives him true prayer of the Spirit, gives him true charity, meekness, bowels of mercy, true kindness, and in short fills him with the fruits of the Spirit. (XIX.3)

Obviously there is a correlation between the foreignness of the gift one is seeking and the force one has to use on oneself in the search. What the soul seeks is no longer natural to it since the Fall, and so it must force itself to it. Nevertheless there is a great difference between the results of our forced efforts and what we receive as a result of God's gift:

The things you do of yourself are all very well, and acceptable to God, but they are not quite pure. For instance, you love God but not perfectly. The Lord comes, and gives a love which is unchangeable, the heavenly love. You pray in a natural manner with wandering and doubt; God gives you the pure prayer in spirit and in truth. (XXVI.21)

But the chief thing the soul can do, that without which all else is worthless, is to pray, or persevere in prayer. 'Perseverance in prayer: that is the greatest of all good exertions and the chief of good actions' (XL.2; cf. III.3 and frequently).

The coming of grace, the presence of the Spirit, the coming of the Lord to the soul: Macarius does not isolate these from the Incarnation. They are all possible because of the Incarnation. This comes out chiefly in *Homily* XI, though it is mentioned elsewhere (e.g. XXVIII.3). Here Macarius speaks of the Lord as Him who comes in person, who fashioned body and soul, and undoes the whole business of the wicked one, and his works accomplished in man's thoughts, and renews and forms a heavenly image, and makes a new thing of the soul, that Adam may again be king over death and lord of the creature. (XI.6)

He speaks of Moses' lifting up the serpent in the wilderness as a symbol of the Incarnation. The serpent is

a figure of the body of the Lord. The body which He took of the ever-Virgin Mary, He offered it up upon the cross and hung it there, and fastened it upon the tree; and the dead body overcame and slew the live serpent creeping in the heart . . . (XI.9)

The understanding of the Incarnation here echoes Athanasius' classic treatment of it in his *De Incarnatione*. But Macarius is more interested in what the Incarnation makes possible now than in what happened in the past.[38]

But when you hear that at that time the Lord delivered the souls from hell and darkness, and went down into hell, and did a glorious work, do not imagine that these things are so very far from your own soul . . . When the prince of wickedness and his angels burrow there, and make paths and thoroughfares there, on which the powers of Satan walk into your mind and thoughts, are you not a hell, a tomb, a sepulchre, a dead man towards God? . . . Well, then, the Lord comes into souls that seek after him, into the deep of the hell of the heart . . . He breaks through the heavy stones that lie on the soul, opens the sepulchres, raises up the man that is dead indeed, brings out of the dark jail the imprisoned soul. (XI.11)

And when this happens, the soul *feels* this inpouring of grace, this coming of the Lord. The advent of grace is an experience, and an experience that brings assurance. Experience, assurance (*peira, plerophoria*): these are central words in the Macarian vocabulary. Macarius speaks of this in several ways. He speaks of fire,[39] and of testing.[40] He speaks of the spiritual senses awakened in the soul by the advent of grace:

---

[38] Cf. Angelus Silesius, *Cherubinischer Wandersmann* I.61:
    Wird Christus tausendmal zu Bethlehem geboren
    Und nicht in dir, du bleibst doch ewiglich verloren.
[39] VIII.9, XI.1, and frequently.   [40] e.g. XV.20.

This is a thing which everyone ought to know, that there are eyes that are more inward than these eyes and hearing more inward than this hearing. As the eyes sensibly behold and recognize the face of a friend or beloved one, so the eyes of the worthy and faithful soul, being spiritually enlightened by the light of God, behold and recognize the true friend, the sweetest and greatly longed-for bridegroom, the Lord, while the soul is shone upon by the adorable Spirit; and thus beholding with the mind the desirable and only inexpressible beauty, it is smitten with a passionate love of God, and is directed into all virtues of the Spirit, and thus possesses an unbounded, unfailing love for the Lord it longs for.

(XXVIII.5; cf. IV.7)

This experience of grace is, then, a beginning. It gives the soul a taste for the true beauty and glory and richness of God (cf. V.5) and fills it with a great longing to enjoy this true beauty yet more fully. And this longing expresses itself in prayer, and it is through prayer, through attention to God,[41] that the soul is restored to the image and likeness of God. Macarius uses the analogy (perhaps taken from Athanasius, *De Incarnatione* 14, though there the analogy is treated quite differently) of a portrait painter. As a portrait painter can only paint a good portrait if the sitter looks at him,

in like manner Christ, the good artist, for those who believe Him and gaze continually at Him, straightway portrays after His own image a heavenly man. Out of His own Spirit, out of the substance of light itself, the ineffable light, He paints a heavenly image, and bestows upon it its good and gracious Spouse. If a man does not gaze constantly at Him, overlooking everything else, the Lord will not paint His image with His own light. We must therefore gaze upon Him, believing and loving Him, throwing away all else, and attending to Him, in order that He may paint His own heavenly image and send it into our souls, and thus, wearing Christ, we may receive eternal life, and even here may have full assurance and be at rest.

(XXX.4)

This experience of grace must be felt (in one way or another: Macarius is very sensitive to the variety of ways in which souls can experience the grace of God.[42]) On this

---

[41] *prosoche* — by chance similar to *proseuche*.
[42] See, e.g., *Hom.* VIII.

Macarius is insistent.[43] In *Homily* I, after having described various ways in which the soul can experience the presence of grace, he concludes:

But if thou art conscious that thou hast none of these things, then weep and lament, because even yet thou hast not found the eternal heavenly riches. Be in trouble therefore for thy penury, beseeching the Lord night and day, because thou hast stopped short in the dreadful poverty of sin.   (I.12)

The way to seek the experience of grace is through prayer, perseverance in prayer, night and day lamenting one's sinful state and beseeching God.

This perseverance in prayer is still essential even after the coming of grace to the soul, for, as Macarius makes clear, sin still dwells in the soul. Even 'when a man is deep in, and is rich in grace, there is still a remnant of evil with him' (XVI.4), until he reaches perfection, and the author of the *Homilies* confesses that he has never known one 'perfect and free' (VIII.4). The soul has many members, as Macarius often iterates, but

sin has come in and taken possession of all its members and of the ranges of the heart. Then, when man seeks, grace comes to him, and takes possession, it may be, of two members of the soul. So the inexperienced man, being comforted by grace, imagines that grace has taken possession of all the members of his soul, and that sin is rooted out. But the greatest part is still under the power of sin, and only one part under grace; and he is cheated and knows it not.
                                                                                         (L.4)

The chief way in which Macarius speaks of the soul's experience of grace is in terms of *light*. The soul becomes penetrated and suffused with the light of the Godhead:

The soul who has been perfectly illuminated by the ineffable beauty of the glory of the light of the face of Christ, and has perfect participation in the Holy Spirit and become worthy to be a dwelling-place and throne of God, becomes wholly eye and wholly light and wholly face and wholly glory and wholly Spirit, being so made by

---

[43] This seems to me the nub of the heretical nature of Messalianism, and therefore a decisive justification for regarding the Macarian *Homilies* as Messalian. See Hausherr, 'L'erreur fondamentale et la logique de la Messalianisme', *OCP*, I (1935), 328–60, esp. 337.

Christ who drives and guides and carries and bears her about, and graces and adorns her with spiritual beauty. (I.2)

In this light the soul is able to contemplate itself,[44] and also see visions with full assurance (VII.5). 'With full assurance' — what the soul sees when suffused with the divine light is not an illusion, it is real. Some places in the Macarian *Homilies* suggest that these visions are seen by the *nous*, the mind, the eye of the soul, the spiritual eye (e.g. VIII.8). But, in other places, one is given the impression that it is with these very eyes, these bodily eyes, that the soul sees visions. Clearly it is easy to move from insisting (as the *Homilies* do) on the reality of what is seen to saying that it is seen 'with these very eyes', so to speak. So, in *Homily* IV, Macarius develops the theory that God, out of His great goodness, changes Himself into material form so that He can be perceived by man:

And how much more cannot He, who is as He will and what He will, through His unspeakable kindness and inconceivable goodness, change and diminish and assimilate Himself, embodying Himself according to their capacity in holy and faithful souls, that He, the invisible, might be seen by them, He, the impalpable, be felt, after the subtilty of the soul's nature — and that they might feel His sweetness, and enjoy in real experience the goodness of the light of that ineffable enjoyment? (IV.11)

Rather more important, though, is the way Macarius associates this idea that the soul is penetrated by the divine light with the Transfiguration of our Lord on Mount Tabor when the light penetrated not just his soul but his body too:

As the body of the Lord was glorified, when He went up into the mountain, and was transfigured into the divine glory and into the infinite light, so are the bodies of the saints glorified and shine like lightning. The glory that was within Christ was outspread upon his body and shone; and in like manner in the saints, the power of Christ within them shall in that day be poured outwardly upon their bodies. (XV.38; cf. XX.3, I.3)

Macarius seems to restrict this transfiguration of the body to the resurrection on the last day, but there is no doubt that

---

[44] Cf. Evagrius, above 127 f.

here in one of the sources of the Palamite idea of transfiguration in the Uncreated Light.[45]

Perfection, we have seen, is rarely reached in this life;
indeed the author of these homilies knows not a single
example, though he occasionally speaks of it. When the soul
reaches perfection, all traces of evil in the soul will be
excluded, the soul will be wholly penetrated by the divine
light and become wholly diaphanous to the Spirit. It will
become God,[46] and all this unalterably.[47] This state of perfection is a state of rapture:

It comes to pass that being all day engaged he gives himself to prayer
for an hour, and the inward man is rapt in prayer into this
unfathomable deep of that other world in great sweetness, so that his
whole mind is up aloft, rapt away thither, and estranged from things
below. For the time being forgetfulness comes upon him with regard
to the interests of the earthly mind, because his thoughts are filled
and taken captive to divine and heavenly things, to things infinite
and past comprehension, to wonderful things which no human lips
can express, so that for that hour he prays and says, 'Would God
that my soul might pass along with my prayer!'   (VIII.1)

Macarius describes the man in this state as one 'free and
perfect'; he also suggests that 'the perfect measure has not
been given, in order that he may be free to take an interest in
his brethren, and in the ministry of the word' (VIII.4). He
speaks too of a kinship between the soul and God (XLV.3),
and says that this is realized in the state of perfection in union
between the soul and God:

When the soul cleaves to the Lord, and the Lord pities and loves it,
coming to it and cleaving to it, and the intention from that time
remains continually faithful to the grace of the Lord, they become
one spirit, one composite thing, one intention, the soul and the Lord,
and while the body belonging to it is prostrate upon earth, the
intention of the soul has its conversation wholly in the heavenly
Jerusalem, mounting even to the third heaven, and cleaving to
the Lord, and ministering to Him there.

(XLVI.3; cf. XLV.7, XLIX.3 f.)

---

[45] As Hausherr points out, *OCP* XII (1946), 22 (reprinted in *Hésychasme*, 105).
[46] *apotheoutai*: XXVI.2.
[47] *atreptos*. On this cf. Basil, *De Spiritu Sancto*, 9.

This kinship between the soul and God, realized in the state of union, is not something natural to the soul, but something granted to it by the grace of God. This Macarius makes clear when he says:

Consider here, and discern, and understand how. Listen. He is God; the soul is not God. He is the Lord; it is a servant. He is Creator; it is a creature. He is the Maker; it is the thing made. There is nothing common to His nature and to that of the soul. But by reason of His infinite, unspeakable, inconceivable love and compassion, it pleased Him to dwell in this thing of His making, this intelligent creature, this precious and extraordinary work, as the Scripture says, 'that we should be a kind of first-fruits of His creatures', for His wisdom and fellowship, for His own habitation, for His own precious and pure bride. (XLIX.4)

Such is a brief sketch of the main points of the extraordinarily interesting and intensely practical homilies attributed to Macarius the Egyptian. They were writings essentially for monks and were intended for monks as they pursued their life of solitude and prayer, a life which is, for Macarius, a descent into the depths — the depths of sin, the depths of one's own heart:

As men in the trade go down naked into the depths of the sea, into the watery death, to find those pearls that will do for a royal crown, and purple dye, so those who live the monastic life go naked out of the world, and go down into the deep of the sea of evil and into the gulf of darkness, and from these depths they take and bring up precious stones suitable for the crown of Christ, for the heavenly Church, for a new world, and a city of light, and people of angels. (XV.51)

Diadochus of Photicē

Diadochus is important to us for the way in which the apparently diverse traditions of Evagrianism and Messalianism converge in his thought and, without expounding his doctrine in any detail, it is this at which we shall briefly look.

We know virtually nothing about Diadochus, except that he was bishop of Photicē in Epirus in the middle of the fifth century. He is mentioned by Photius as among the opponents of the monophysites contemporary with the Council of

Chalcedon.[48] The writings of his that survive are a *Century of Gnostic Chapters*[49] on the spiritual life, a sermon on the Ascension,[50] and a work called the *Vision of St. Diadochus*,[51] which takes the form of a series of questions and answers. His *Century of Gnostic Chapters* was very influential in the Greek East: it is quoted by, among others, Maximus the Confessor and appears in the *Philocalia* of Nicodemus of the Holy Mountain.[52] It was also translated into Latin.

Diadochus is very aware of the heresy of the Messalians (though he does not mention them by name): much of his writing is directed against their opinions. *Century* 3 is directed against the idea, constantly attributed to the Messalians, of the substantiality of evil, and though this idea does not occur in the Macarian *Homilies* (or not directly), Diadochus' concluding remarks in this chapter, that the 'nature of good' is more powerful than the 'habit of evil', strikes a distinctly un-Macarian note. He frequently attacks the idea of the Messalians that God is apprehended through the senses.[53] An idea mentioned by Timothy of Constantinople as Messalian, that the souls of the departed know the hearts of men on this earth, is dealt with too[54]. But the main thrust of his anti-Messalian polemic is directed against their disbelief in the efficacy of baptism and their idea that even after baptism both grace and the demons dwell in the soul of man.

Diadochus' opposition to the fundamental position of Messalianism is, then, clear. But, none the less, his own position bears many marks of Messalian influence. Take his vocabulary, for example. He speaks much of feeling, and central to his spiritual doctrine is the idea of the spiritual sense of the soul. He speaks often of the soul's being 'in all feeling and assurance' — very Messalian language. He speaks of the

---

[48] See: Diadoque de Photicē, *Œuvres Spirituelles* (Sources Chrétiennes 5, 3rd edn., E. des Places, SJ), Introduction, 9. This contains all the surviving works of Diadochus, and is the edition I have used. On Diadochus and his relation to Messalianism, see F. Dörr, *Diadochus von Photike und die Messalianer* (Freiburg im Breisgau, 1937).

[49] Pages 84–163 in des Places's edition. Reference is made to this work simply by number of chapter. [50] pp. 164–8.

[51] pp. 169–79. There is also a brief *Catechesis* (pp. 180–3), the authorship of which is disputed as between Diadochus and Symeon the New Theologian.

[52] pp. 205–37 in the *Editio Princeps* (Venice, 1782).

[53] 35, and in the *Vision*. [54] *Vision*, pp. 176 f.

heart, and of entering into the heart. He speaks of the importance of constant 'recollection of God', which is one of the ways in which the Macarian *Homilies* speak of constant prayer;[55] Evagrius, in contrast, is discouraging on the place of memory in prayer.[56]. And yet, his Evagrianism is no less marked. He has the same understanding of the progressive purification of the soul, beginning with the desiring part and advancing to the passionate part, the same doctrine that visions for one who has attained *apatheia* are the work of the demon of vainglory, the same understanding of the way in which the demons attack the soul (which doctrine he uses to explain why the Messalians mistakenly imagine that the demons still dwell in the souls of the baptized), and much else. But his most important similarity to Evagrius is his understanding of the spiritual nature of prayer: he has none of the materialism of the Messalians. What he does, indeed, is to draw together what is right in the spirituality of the heart and the spirituality of the mind; his is a spirituality that is of the heart, but not crudely materialistic, of the mind, yet not intellectualist.

The centre of Diadochus' spiritual theology is perhaps his clear grasp of the significance of baptism. Neither of the monastic traditions we have discussed in this chapter gives any place to baptism. Evagrius does not mention baptism, and even his understanding of the basic significance of faith cannot be related to baptism, as he regards faith as an innate capacity.[57] The Messalian position explicitly rejects any place in the spiritual life for baptism. In rejecting this tenet of the Messalians, Diadochus is led to develop an understanding of the spiritual life that sees God's work in the soul through the sacrament of baptism as the foundation of that life. In baptism we are born again, and the power that the devil had over us as a result of the Fall is overthrown:

From that very hour in which we were born again the devil is outside and grace within. (76)

Grace is hidden in the depth of the mind from the moment of baptism, its presence being hidden even from the spiritual sense. But

[55] See Macarius, *Hom.* XLIII.3; XIX.2.
[56] See Evagrius, O 45-7. [57] See P 81, and above 104, n.13.

when anyone begins to love God with all his resolution, then by an
ineffable communication through the feeling of the mind it communicates part of its benefits to the soul.   (77)

Diadochus thus restores to its fundamental place in the
spiritual life God's working in the soul through the sacrament
of baptism.

For the rest he combines what was good, as we have said,
both in Evagrius and Messalianism. Central to this work of
assimilation is his idea of the soul's spiritual sense — *aisthesis
noos*, feeling of the mind, *aisthesis noera*, intellectual feeling (or
intellectual — or spiritual — sense). The very word indicates
his bold conjunction of feeling and the mind, the heart and the
intellect, Macarius and Evagrius. This is a spiritual or
intellectual sense by which 'love quests after the invisible' (1):
it is love, *agape*, which uses this spiritual sense. Several
passages contrast the single spiritual sense with the five bodily
senses (24, 29) and state that the multiplicity to which the
spiritual sense is subjected as a result of its being bound to the
five bodily senses is a result of the sin of Adam (25). The Fall
has fragmented and dissipated this single spiritual sense, and
the way of return is by entry into the heart, a collecting of the
powers of the soul in the singleness of the heart:

That sight, taste and the other senses dissipate the heart's recollection, when we use them beyond their measure, is taught us by the
first Eve. For as long as she did not look with pleasure on the
forbidden tree, she preserved carefully her recollection of the divine
precept. Because she was still shielded by the wings of divine love,
she remained unaware of her nakedness. But when she looked at the
tree with pleasure, and touched it with great desire, and tasted the
fruit of it with delight, immediately she was aware of the embrace of
her body and felt that she was naked. She gave all her desire to the
enjoyment of what was present to her, joining Adam to her own fault
through the pleasant appearance of the fruit. From then on the
human mind could only with difficulty call to mind either God or his
commands. We must, therefore, fix our gaze eternally on the depths
of the heart with an unbroken recollection of God, and live as though
we were blind to this deceitful life. For it is proper to the true
spiritual philosophy never to give wing to any desire for visible
things.   (76)

Here the Fall is explained solely in terms of the decline and dissipation of the spiritual sense from the invisible to the visible. It is an emphasis which fits well with a spirituality of the heart which yet clearly sees true reality as invisible and immaterial. There is great stress on inwardness, and a sharp contrast between recollection of God by concentrating all one's powers on the heart, and dissipation of the powers of the soul through the multiplicity of the bodily senses.

But it is not possible for man by his own efforts to counteract the effect of the Fall: 'the mind's purification can only come about through the Holy Spirit' (28). This is made possible through the Incarnation and we lay hold on what Christ has effected for us in his Incarnation and Death through the rebirth of baptism (78). After baptism grace dwells in the heart of man and the demons can only attack from outside (79). The presence of grace in the soul is often hidden, as we have seen; we only become conscious of it, as we co-operate with it. But the Messalians spoke of the experience of sin dwelling in our hearts even after baptism, of the experience of a struggle in the depth of the heart between indwelling grace and indwelling evil. Diadochus rejects this Messalian position at two levels. On the one hand, he refuses to accept the Messalian equation of the presence of grace and conscious awareness of this power within us.[58] On the other hand, he makes use of Evagrius' explanation of how the demons attack the soul — by unleashing *logismoi* within us that we can turn to sin by giving them our consent — to explain how the Messalians misinterpret their inner experience. There are, indeed, both good and bad *logismoi* in the heart, and it does feel as if the bad *logismoi* have come from the heart. But, in reality, such *logismoi* are inspired in us by the demons working on the body or the temperament or the lower part of the soul, or sometimes by a habitual recollection of evil from the first deceit of all (this is Diadochus' idea of original sin).[59]

In baptism, according to Diadochus, two gifts are given. The first, given at once, is restoration in the image of God. The second, which far surpasses the first, is restoration

---

[58] Cf. 77 (quoted above), which speaks of grace in the soul hidden even from the spiritual sense itself.　　　　　[59] For all this see 83.

according to the likeness of God, and this is not given at once but depends upon our co-operation. All this is explained in *Century* 89:

When therefore the mind begins with great feeling to taste the goodness of the Holy Spirit, then we ought to know that grace begins to paint, as it were, in accordance with the likeness, on that which is according to the image.

Diadochus uses, as Macarius has done, the analogy of a painter, who, in this case, first traces the outline and then applies the colours. The grace of God first traces on man in baptism the form of the image that he had in the beginning, and as he begins

with all his will to desire the beauty of the likeness and stands naked and undaunted in this work, then grace causes virtue upon virtue to blossom in us and it raises the form of the soul from glory to glory and bestows on the soul the form of the likeness. So the spiritual sense reveals to us that we are being fashioned after the likeness, but the perfection of the likeness we know through being illuminated.

The spiritual sense, then, is that by means of which we progress in the spiritual life. It is by discovering it and using it that we cause the image (*eikon*) in ourselves, which has been restored in baptism, to take on the full glory of the likeness (*homoiosis*). Through it we acquire virtues (one point that Diadochus stresses is that one of the chief functions of the spiritual sense is discernment: see 26–34) and thus adorn the soul with spiritual beauty. But beyond all that our spiritual sense can do there lies perfection. This is to receive 'spiritual love' and it can only be received when the soul is enlightened in complete assurance by the Holy Spirit. The final perfection of the likeness can only be accomplished through love: 'no other virtue can acquire impassibility for the soul, but only love.'

That is perhaps enough to indicate how in Diadochus we find a uniting of the two traditions that come from the fourth century monastic milieu, that of Evagrius and that ascribed to Macarius. It is not being claimed that Diadochus is typical of the East. There is a constant tension in Eastern mystical theology between Evagrianism and Messalianism, a tension that will be complicated, not lessened, by the later influence of Denys the Areopagite, and this tension is resolved in various ways. Diadochus simply provides us with an example of how these two, apparently so diverse, traditions could converge.

It is the traditions that developed within monasticism that are the basic traditions for later mystical theology, for this was something that especially concerned those who led the monastic life. In the West the monastic tradition is represented chiefly by Cassian, who introduced the Evagrian tradition in a modified form: the heretical elements were elided, the teaching about contemplative prayer very much modified, so it was the practical wisdom of Evagrius the monk which was made known to the West.[60] So for the tradition of Western mystical *theology* it is perhaps to Augustine, and his influence within monastic circles, that we should look. In the East the tradition is an uneasy, but potentially immensely fruitful, symbiosis of Evagrianism and Messalianism, later fertilized by the influence of Denys the Areopagite.

[60] For Cassian and the West, see O. Chadwick, *John Cassian* (CUP, 1968²), and also the volume edited by him called *Western Asceticism* (*Library of Christian Classics*, XIII, London, 1958). Also on Cassian, see C. Butler, *Benedictine Monachism* (London, 1919), esp. 78–82 for his teaching on contemplative prayer.

VII. AUGUSTINE

THE rest of this book is concerned with the Greek-speaking world, but in this chapter we shall discuss the thought of a Latin writer, Augustine. This may give a false impression for two reasons: it may suggest that there is no one else in the West of interest to us in the Patristic period other than Augustine; and, because Augustine's thought is so personal, it may suggest a greater cleavage between Greek East and Latin West than is in fact the case. But such an impression would be misleading. There are many other Latin writers we might have discussed: Ambrose, Marius Victorinus, and Cassian, to name but three. All these three were important, and yet their importance is not so much intrinsic as that they were instrumental in transmitting to the West the treasures of the East. All three knew Greek, and either translated the works of the Greeks (as Victorinus did some of the works of Plato, Plotinus, and Porphyry, in which translations Augustine himself presumably read the 'Platonists') or incorporated much translated Greek theology and philosophy in their own works either openly (as with Cassian, the disciple of the Fathers of the Egyptian Desert, and in particular of Evagrius) or surreptitiously (as Jerome accused Ambrose of having done[1]). From the writings of these, and others like them, the West learned the theology of the Greek East. Augustine's importance does not lie here: his knowledge of Greek theology was not profound, rather with him we have a theologian formed by Latin philosophical and theological traditions. As such, he is uniquely important for the West. The bulk of his writings and the range of his interests is far greater than that of any of the

---

[1] See J. N. D. Kelly, *Jerome* (London, 1975), 143 f.

Greek Fathers (except possibly Origen, most of whose works
are in any case lost) and all this is infused by a tremendously
personal vision of God, man, and the world. The most
immediately obvious contrast between Augustine and the
Greek Fathers is one of *feeling*. The mystical theology of the
Eastern Fathers has an atmosphere of objectivity. We do not
hear about their own experiences, rather we have an interpretation of scripture and the light it sheds on the soul's quest. It
is not personal experience that convinces, but appeal to
Sacred Revelation. (The same is true *mutatis mutandis* for
Plotinus: we only rarely hear of his personal experience of the
One.) Yet, the contrast between Augustine and the Greek
Fathers is not complete, it is true, since for him, no less than
for the Greeks, truth is to be found in what God has revealed,
not in human experience. But his *Confessions* are unparalleled
in the ancient world for introspective self-scrutiny. A whole
new dimension is opened up of introversion and a searching,
psychological self-probing. Nor is this an isolated phenomenon in the writings of Saint Augustine: in practically all his
works we find not just Augustine's thought but the man
himself. This gives to his mystical thought a dimension of
inwardness that is often lacking in the writings of the Eastern
Fathers.

This distinctive, and very seductive, tenor that we find in
Augustine's writings, combined with the range and breadth of
his interests, and the fact that they focus on those theological
themes — grace, the Church, the sacraments — that were to
be the centre of theological interest in the West: all this means
that Augustine stamps subsequent Western theology with a
distinctive character. The West becomes Augustinian, either
directly, when it seeks to develop the insights of the 'Doctor of
Grace', or indirectly, when, trying to free itself from a
dominant Augustinianism, it none the less concerns itself with
the problems that engaged Augustine. So his importance for
us, as we attempt to trace the development of mystical
theology in the formative period of the Church's history, is
twofold: for he was both an original and an influential
thinker.

'Thou hast made us for thyself and our hearts are restless
till they rest in thee' — there, right at the beginning of the

Confessions, we find the guiding principle of Augustine's mystical theology. The soul's longing for God: a longing that is a longing to *return*, to return to the One who made it, a longing that is experienced as restlessness, inability to settle and rest anywhere, a pressing sense that in all created things there lies something beyond, something that calls us to God. This sense of not being at home in the world is fundamental to Augustine's mystical thought, but it is not something new in Augustine. It is not even new in Christianity. Plato had this longing — a longing to escape from the shadows of the cave to the pure light of the sun of the intelligible world. To an even greater degree we find it in Plotinus: a longing for the Fatherland, a longing for whence we have come — 'The Fatherland to us is There whence we have come, and There is the Father' (*Ennead* I. 6.8). Augustine, as we shall see, is deeply indebted to Plotinus, but we shall see too that in his hands this longing for God is transformed from a human restlessness to our response to the incredible love and condescension of God, indeed is the movement of the Holy Spirit Himself in our hearts.

But let us begin by looking at one of the more famous passages from the *Confessions*, the account of the mystical vision Augustine experienced at Ostia with his mother, Monica:

When the day was approaching on which she was to depart this life — a day that you knew though we did not — it came about, as I believe by your secret arrangement, that she and I stood alone leaning in a window, which looked inwards to the garden within the house where we were staying, at Ostia on the Tiber; for there we were away from everybody, resting for the sea-voyage from the weariness of our long journey by land. There we talked together, she and I alone, in deep joy; and 'forgetting the things that were behind and looking forward to those that were before,' we were discussing in the presence of Truth, which You are, what the eternal life of the saints could be like, 'which eye has not seen nor ear heard, nor has it entered into the heart of man.' But with the mouth of our heart we panted for the high waters of your fountain, the fountain of the life which is with You: that being sprinkled from that fountain according to our capacity, we might in some sense meditate upon so great a matter.

And our conversation had brought us to the point that any pleasure whatsoever of the bodily senses, in any brightness whatsoever of corporeal light, seemed to us not worthy of comparison with the pleasure of that eternal light, not worthy even of mention. Rising as our love flamed upward towards that Self-same, we passed in review the various levels of bodily things, up to the heavens themselves, whence sun and moon and stars shine upon this earth. And higher still we soared, thinking in our minds and speaking and marvelling at Your works. And so we came to our own souls, and went beyond them to come at last to that region of richness unending, where You feed Israel forever with the food of truth; and there life is that Wisdom by which all things are made, both the things that have been and the things that are yet to be. But this Wisdom itself is not made: it is as it has ever been, and so it shall be forever: indeed 'has ever been' and 'shall be forever' have no place in it, but it simply is, for it is eternal; whereas 'to have been' and 'to be going to be' are not eternal. And while we were thus talking of His Wisdom and panting for it, with all the effort of our heart we did for one instant attain to touch it; then sighing, and leaving the first fruits of our spirit bound to it, we returned to the sound of our own tongue, in which a word has both beginning and ending. For what is like to your Word, Our Lord, who abides in Himself forever, yet grows not old and makes all things new!

So we said: if to any man the tumult of the flesh grew silent, silent the images of earth and sea and air; and if the heavens grew silent, and the very soul grew silent to herself and by not thinking of self mounted beyond self: if all dreams and imagined visions grew silent, and every tongue and every sign and whatsoever is transient — for indeed if any man could hear them, he should hear them saying with one voice: We did not make ourselves, but He made us who abides forever: but if, having uttered this and so set us to listening to Him who made them, they all grew silent, and in their silence He alone spoke to us, not by them but by Himself: so that we should hear His word, not by any tongue of flesh nor the voice of any angel nor the sound of thunder nor in the darkness of a parable, but that we should hear Himself whom in all these things we love, should hear Himself and not them: just as we too had but now reached forth and in a flash of the mind attained to touch the eternal Wisdom which abides over all: and if this should continue, and all other visions so different be quite taken away, and this one should so ravish and absorb and wrap the beholder in inward joys that his life should eternally be such as that one moment of understanding for which we had been sighing — would this not be: 'Enter thou into the joy of

Thy Lord'? But when shall it be? Shall it be when 'we shall all rise again' and 'shall not all be changed'?

(*Confessions* IX. x. 23–5)[2]

There are three things to note about this passage by way of introduction to Augustine's mystical theology.

First, the nature of the account. It is at once an account of a personal experience, and yet not a purely solitary one. The experience grows out of his conversation with his mother. This makes one wonder to what extent friendship, companionship, communion with other human beings, is important for Augustine in his ascent to God, or whether — as with Plotinus — it is a flight of the 'alone to the Alone'. I do not think one can be clear on this as far as Augustine is concerned, but there is a strand — and an important strand — in Augustine's thought that stresses the social nature of final beatitude. In *The City of God* (XIX. 5) he says: 'For how could the City of God, about which we are already engaged in writing the nineteenth book, begin at the start or progress in its course or reach its appointed goal, if the life of the saints were not social (*si non esset socialis vita sanctorum*)?' Ladner, in his little-known but immensely important book, *The Idea of Reform*, remarks:

Would Augustine find on earth those *perfecti*, those *sancti*, of whose life in a *vita socialis*, in communion with the saints and angels of heaven he speaks in *De Civitate Dei*? If there had ever been such a society, how could it be restored? Through Saint Augustine's whole life there runs the search for a perfect communal and societal way of Christian life. In the days of his conversion he believed to have found it in the group of intellectually and religiously inclined friends who lived together in the country house of Verecundus at Cassiciacum; later he found it more fully in a type of monasticism which was modelled after the common life of the Apostles in Jerusalem, described in the Acts of the Apostles. (5: 12–14)[3]

I think there is here a new note in monasticism, though it strikes a chord that echoes back through the Hellenic —

---

[2] All quotations from the *Confessions* are from F. J. Sheed's translation (Sheed and Ward, first printed 1944 and frequently thereafter). The Latin edition used is that of M. Skutella, revised by H. Juergens and W. Schaub, in *Bibliotheca Teubneriana* (Stuttgart, 1969).

[3] G. B. Ladner, *The Idea of Reform: its Impact on Christian thought and action in the Age of the Fathers* (Cambridge, Mass., Harvard University Press, 1959), 282 f.

particularly the Platonist — tradition, to the group that gathered round Socrates at the end of the fifth century B.C. It is important for us as growing out of the observation that the vision was not a solitary experience.

The second point to notice is the nature of the summit of this experience. 'And while we were thus talking . . . with all the effort of our heart did we for one instant attain to touch it (*attingimus eam modice toto ictu cordis*); then sighing, and leaving the first fruits of our spirit bound to it, we returned to the sound of our own tongue. . . .' We have, it would seem, a transitory experience of rapture or ecstasy. It corresponds closely with Augustine's definition of ecstasy in the so-called literal commentary on Genesis: 'When the attention of the mind is wholly turned away and withdrawn (*penitus avertitur atque abripitur*) from the bodily senses, it is called ecstasy. Then whatever bodies may be present are not seen with the open eyes, nor any voices heard at all' (*De Genesi ad litteram* XII. xii. 25). As in his other descriptions, this ecstasy is sudden and fleeting, and draws out the whole force of the soul (*toto ictu cordis*) with, it would seem, a certain violence. (*Ictus* means 'blow' and is a favourite word of Augustine's in this context. In *Conf.* VII. xvii. 23 he speaks of arriving at that which is *in ictu trepidantis aspectus* — in the thrust, or the blow, of a trembling glance.) But, he goes on, in this passage from the ninth book of the *Confessions*, to say of this experience of ecstasy or rapture: 'If this should continue . . . and this [vision] should so ravish and absorb and wrap the beholder in inward joys that this life should eternally be such as that one moment of understanding . . . would this not be: "Enter thou into the joy of the Lord"?' The experience of rapture is, for Augustine, a foretaste of the joys of heaven. This is an idea he often expresses: for instance, 'Sometimes You admit me to a state of mind that I am not ordinarily in, a kind of delight which could it ever be made permanent in me would be hard to distinguish from the life to come' (*Conf.* X. xl. 65).

This parallel and contrast between ecstasy and the beatific vision is something that is very unusual with the Greek Fathers, but absolutely commonplace in Augustine. For Augustine, ecstasy is something which *if it went on forever* would be indistinguishable from the joys of heaven. But it does not, it is fleeting. Ecstasy is something that brings to Augustine's mind the thought of the beatific vision, but it is other than it. In Gregory of Nyssa, for instance, we are rarely aware that death will make much difference to what he is describing of the soul's experience of God; and even in Origen, where sometimes quite clearly the mystic ascent is something that can only be properly undertaken after death, often enough the whole contrast between this life and the next recedes into the background. The idea that man is mortal, destined to die, and that this is a fundamental qualification of the life he is living now is much more prominent with Augustine than with the Greeks. For Augustine, ecstasy is a breach of that qualification, and its very fleetingness emphasizes the fact. I think there can be discerned here a fundamental difference of temper between Augustine and the Greek apophatic tradition. As Ladner puts it:

Without limiting the essential vision of God on earth in principle, Augustine never names anyone except Moses and Paul as having possessed it, whereas for the Greeks it was the great goal of all mystical experience, though according to them it could be had, even in heaven, not in final attainment, but only in never-ending pursuit . . . The Greeks could not imagine any vision of God as 'satisfying' because the essential vision to them meant comprehensive union, whereas in the Western tradition there can be a true, though not a full, vision of God in this life, with fulfilment in the beatific vision in heaven.[4]

The third point to note about this passage from *Confessions* IX is the way of ascent:

Rising as our love flamed upward towards that Self-same, we passed in review the various levels of bodily things, up to the heavens themselves, whence sun and moon and stars shine upon this earth. And higher still we soared, thinking in our minds and speaking and marvelling at Your works: and so we came to our own souls, and went beyond them to come at last to that region of richness unending . . .

It is a way of ascent, upwards and inwards, passing beyond material things into the depths of the soul.

[4] 191, n. 18

Admiring the world of sense as we look out upon its vastness and beauty and the order of its eternal march, thinking of the gods within it, seen and hidden, and the celestial spirits and all the life of animal and plant, let us mount to its archetype, to the yet more authentic sphere . . .   (*Ennead* V.1.4)

That is Plotinus. The parallel with Augustine is remarkable, The alteration of the gods in Plotinus into *sol et luna et stellae* in Augustine is striking and natural. Later on in the same passage from the *Confessions*, there is another close parallel with a passage from the same treatise of the *Enneads*.

So we said: if to any man the tumult of the flesh grew silent, silent the images of earth and sea and air; and if the heavens grew silent, and the very soul grew silent to herself and by not thinking of self mounted beyond self . . .

clearly echoes this:

Quiet must the imprisoning body be for her, and the wave of the body's passion; let all things likewise be quiet that lie about her. Quiet let the earth be, quiet the sea and the air, and the heaven itself pausing the while. Then into that unmoving firmament let her conceive soul flowing in, poured in like a tide from without, from all sides invading it and filling it with light.   (*Ennead* V.1.2)

Even in translation the parallel is striking. But, in the original texts, the parallel between the repeated *sileat* of Augustine and Plotinus' *hesychon* is even more marked. There is a difference of feel, however, between Plotinus' soul being flooded with light, and Augustine's soul passing out of itself to touch the Eternal Wisdom.

So, in Augustine's account of his (and his mother's) vision at Ostia, we have close parallels with passages in one of Plotinus' *Enneads*. And they are not simply verbal parallels: there is a fundamental sympathy. Augustine has learnt from Plotinus. This is again another contrast with what we find in Greek mystical theology. There the influence of Plotinus is not deep — a turn of phrase, a metaphor, no more (though this judgement will need modification when we come to Denys the Areopagite). But Augustine has drunk deep of Plotinus, and found much in common between Plotinus' soul and his own. What he takes from Plotinus is not the odd idea, but much of the same spirit: there is a deep sympathy between them. Paul Henry says of Augustine's debt to Plotinus:

What seduced Augustine was the familiar and the known, the 'déjà vu', or at least something anticipated. In the realm of the sensible, it was the feeling of Plotinus for all that is beautiful, a feeling deeply shared, in however different a way, by the young African aesthete; it was the 'desire for God in the philosophy of Plotinus', the echo in the Enneads of the *fecisti nos ad te* — 'thou hast made us for thyself' — which caught the heart of the son of Monica; it was the conformity of the Platonist doctrine of the Logos with the teaching of the Church on the Word, preached by Ambrose.[5]

Augustine's debt to Plotinus was, then, a very personal debt: as he read Plotinus he found a movement of thought that echoed in his own soul. But how did he read Plotinus? It does not seem that Augustine's command of Greek was very great, and so it seems likely that he read him in translation. It is very likely that the translation he knew was that of Marius Victorinus, a fellow African and professor of rhetoric, the example of whose conversion made such an impact on Augustine. Victorinus was deeply indebted to Porphyry in his understanding of Plotinus, and it seems probable that Augustine shared in that debt. What exactly this amounted to in detail is still far from clear, but this much seems to be true: that Plotinus, seen through the eyes of Porphyry and Victorinus, was the mystic, the master of the mysteries of the interior life, as opposed to the hierophant and source of a metaphysical justification of a form of occult paganism that we find in the writings of Porphyry's own pupil, Iamblichus, and his school. That Augustine found one so congenial in Plotinus is then, in part, to the credit of Porphyry and Victorinus.

From our initial quotation from the *Confessions*, then, we have noticed three points: that the experience was not solitary, Augustine's eschatological interpretation of ecstasy as a fore-taste of heaven, and his debt to Plotinus. On the first of these points we can say little further. Augustine's estimate of the importance of companionship is complex; it perplexed Augustine, and he perplexes his readers. He is ambivalent, drawn

[5] *La Vision d'Ostie* (Paris, 1938), 77.

both to the Plotinian aloneness and to the importance and indeed necessity of companionship. It is an unresolved tension. The second and third of these points, however, lead us further into Augustine's thought. For, in his understanding of mysticism he goes beyond Plotinus, and does so by gradually deepening his understanding of the Christian interpretation of eschatology.

The end — the goal of human life — can either be seen as the natural culmination of our human longing for God, or as something that God gives us. The former is the line taken by Platonism, and it is reinforced by the Platonic idea that the soul is *returning* to the divine realm in its ascent, that it is going back home. The latter is characteristically Christian and is something that Augustine progressively makes his own in his understanding of the soul's way to God. As we take this further, it will be better, because of the personal nature of Augustine's thought, not simply to attempt to summarize his thought and reduce it to some system, but to follow his own accounts of the soul's ascent to God. We shall take two accounts: the tenth book of the *Confessions* and his somewhat later *De Trinitate*, one of the greatest works of his maturity.

The soul's ascent to God in Confessions

We have already seen something of Augustine's understanding of the mystic ascent in the *Confessions*, and there are other places where a similarly Plotinian exercise is engaged in. But Book X is somewhat different: in this Augustine is beginning to develop his own characteristic thought and we can see how he reaches beyond Plotinus, and even fundamentally breaks with him. *Confessions* X is Augustine's account of his search for God through the memory. He begins — as always — with the soul's love for God, longing for God. 'But', he asks,

what is it that I love when I love You? Not the beauty of any bodily thing, nor the order of the seasons, not the brightness of light that rejoices the eye, nor the sweet melodies of all songs, nor the sweet fragrance of flowers and ointments and spices; not manna or honey, not the limbs that carnal love embraces. None of these things do I love in loving my God. Yet in a sense I do love light and melody and fragrance and food and embrace when I love my God — the light and the voice and the fragrance and the food and embrace in the soul, when that light shines upon my soul which no place can contain, that voice sounds which no time can take from me, I breathe that fragrance which no wind scatters, I eat the food which is not lessened by eating, and I lie in the embrace which satiety never comes to sunder. This it is that I love, when I love my God.

(X.vi)

And yet — 'what is this God?' There follows the famous passage in which Augustine interrogates creation which all points beyond itself, saying it is not God. So he ascends above the material creation by entering into himself, into his soul which gives life and sense to his body and which has made possible the very seeing and interrogating that he is engaged in. Augustine enters into his soul. 'I ask again what it is that I love when I love my God? Who is He that is above the topmost point of my soul? By that same soul I shall ascend to Him' (X.vii). 'I shall mount beyond this power of my nature, still rising by degrees towards Him who made me. And so I come to the fields and vast palaces of *memory* . . .' (X.viii).

Memory — *memoria* — is that into which Augustine enters. It means for him more than just a faculty of recollection: it really means the whole mind, both conscious and unconscious, in contrast to mind — *mens* — which refers only to the conscious mind. Augustine is fascinated by this vast cavern of memory that contains everything he has experienced or can imagine. The whole universe is embraced by his memory. And so he exclaims:

Great is the power of memory, exceedingly great, O my God, a spreading limitless room within me. Who can reach its uttermost depth? Yet it is a faculty of my soul and belongs to my nature. In fact I cannot totally grasp all that I am. Thus the mind is not large enough to contain itself: but . . . how can it not contain itself? How can there be any of itself that is not *in* itself? As this question struck me, I was overcome with wonder and almost with stupor.

(X.viii)

It is important to grasp what Augustine is doing in this. Memory, for Augustine, is the whole mind — it is potentially the whole spiritual world, for, to know anything is to have it in mind, to hold it in my memory. Augustine is, in fact, developing something from Plotinus here. Plato had distinguished between the changing world that we experience through the senses, and the real world, the spiritual world, that we apprehend with the mind. Plotinus sees this real world as the interior world: 'We are each of us the spiritual world' (*Enneads* III. 4.3). I enter into myself, withdraw from the sensible world in order to apprehend — to be in — the real world. And this movement of withdrawal, introversion, concentration is something that requires practice and effort. It is a way of meditation more than anything else. This Augustine takes up. The first step to God is discovery of self, discovery of the self as a spiritual being that contains and transcends the material order. It is something like what we find in Pascal when he contemplates man as a 'roseau pensant', a thinking reed. 'It is not in space that I should search for my dignity, but in the ordering of my thought. There is no advantage to me in the possession of land. As space, the universe encloses me and swallows me up like a little speck: *par la pensée je le comprends* — by thought I understand (or embrace) it.'[6]

The first step to knowledge of God is true knowledge of the self. But though the self, the memory, is a vast and wonderful thing, it is not God, nor does it contain God. And yet, in a way it touches God, it strains beyond itself to God. For the mind longs for the truth, for reality, for true joy, joy that endures, that abides in the truth; and in this it is reaching beyond itself. Truth is not something that man possesses: it is like a light that shines in his mind and that he apprehends, even if only dimly. 'You are not the mind itself' — Augustine exclaims — 'because you are the Lord God of the mind, and all these things suffer change, but You remain unchangeable over all; and yet You deign to dwell in my memory ever since the time I first learned of You' (X.xxv. 36). 'You *deign* to dwell in my memory' — Augustine has perceived God's condescension to himself. And so he exclaims:

Late have I loved thee, O Beauty so ancient and so new; late have I loved thee! For behold Thou wert within me, and I outside; and I sought thee outside and in my perversity fell upon those lovely things that thou has made. Thou wert with me and I was not with thee. I was kept from Thee by those things, yet had they not been in

[6] *Pensées* (Lafuma's edition), 113; cf. 200.

Thee, they would not have been at all. Thou didst call and cry to me
and break open my deafness: and Thou didst send forth Thy beams
and shine upon me and chase away my blindness: Thou didst
breathe fragrance upon me, and I drew in my breath and do now
pant for Thee: I tasted Thee, and now hunger and thirst for Thee:
Thou didst touch me, and I have burned for Thy peace.

(X.xxvii)

The end of Augustine's quest is to have his longing satisfied,
to find the Truth — but to find it as something disclosed, to
receive it as grace. So a chapter later he says: 'All my hope is
naught save in Thy great mercy. Grant what Thou com-
mandest, and command what Thou wilt — *da quod iubes, et iube
quod vis.*'

Thus we have Augustine's way of the soul's ascent. It is
deeply Plotinian, and he feels free to cite Plotinus as he
develops it. The soul desires God; a desire that may be
aroused by created things. Its search is a search for the object
of its love. It passes through creation and rises above it —
above and within — into the soul. There it finds a vast and
wonderful thing, which Augustine calls memory, and driven
by its desire for God, it at last recognizes God, not as one who
can be found, but as one who discloses himself in the soul, that
soul which depends on him for its very existence. It is, as I
have said, deeply Plotinian. Even the final disclosure of God
finds parallels in Plotinus.

But only parallels. Plotinus' One is immutable and insens-
ible. It is the object of the soul's quest — but cares nothing for
the soul, or its quest. Not so with Augustine's God: 'Thou
didst call and cry to me, and break open my deafness.'
Augustine's emphasis on grace and on God's own activity
towards the soul vastly transcends Plotinus' notion of the
soul's dependence on the One. We have just noted that,
immediately after Augustine's conclusion of the search for
God in the memory, there comes that quintessential statement
of the Augustinian doctrine of grace: '*da quod iubes, et iube quod
vis* — give what you command, and command what you will.'
He continues:

Thou dost command continence . . . For by continence we are all
collected and bound up into unity within ourself, whereas we had
been scattered abroad in multiplicity. Too little does any man love

Thee, who loves some other thing together with Thee, loving it not on account of Thee, O Thou Love, who art ever burning and never extinguished! O Charity, my God, enkindle me! Thou dost command continence: grant what Thou dost command and command what Thou wilt. (X.xxix)

And Augustine goes on for the rest of Book X to examine himself and see how far he is from this continence — which means essentially, for Augustine, a single-minded devotion to God. This leads him at length to the doctrine of the Mediator: only through the Incarnation of the Word is the possibility of union with God opened to us. This is very important, for here Augustine cuts himself off completely from his neo-Platonist background. It is important to notice, too, that his doctrine of the Mediator is integral to his understanding of man's response to God. What God requires of man, we have seen, is continence, single-minded devotion to Himself, purity of heart. But without God's condescension to us in the Incarnation to respond to, we will either — in Augustine's view — be provoked to despair by our awareness of sin, or seek to ascend to God under the inspiration of pride. Man can only find purity of heart through humility, and he can only come to humility and avoid despair, if this humility is awakened in his heart by the love of God in the Incarnation:

But the true Mediator, whom in the secret of Your mercy You have shown to men and sent to men, that by His example they might learn humility — the Mediator between God and man, the man Christ Jesus, appeared between sinful mortals and the immortal Just One . . . Rightly is my hope strong in Him, who sits at Thy right hand and intercedes for us; otherwise I should despair. For many and great are my infirmities, many and great; but Thy medicine is of more power. We might well have thought Thy Word remote from union with man and so despaired of ourselves, if He had not been made flesh and dwelt among us. (X.xliii)

So, in Augustine's treatment of the soul's ascent to God in the *Confessions*, we find that, though he owes a very great deal to neo-Platonism, yet, in his fundamental appreciation of the soul's way, his understanding of the Incarnation is more important. Grace becomes more than our dependence on God (an idea that we can find in various forms in Platonism and neo-Platonism): rather, to speak of grace is to speak of God's self-emptying and His coming down to us. Grace means God's humility and the awakening of our response in humility.

The soul's ascent in De Trinitate

If we now turn to *De Trinitate*,[7] we see how Augustine takes all this much further, and at the same time begins to develop his own trinitarian mystical theology. The whole context has now changed. We no longer have Plotinian exercises by which the soul seeks to assuage her restlessness by finding a deep enough satisfaction for her longing. Rather we start with God's revelation of Himself in Scripture and the Church. The first seven books of *De Trinitate* attempt to establish from Scripture what God has revealed of Himself. And God has revealed Himself as Trinity. Augustine then seeks to understand what he believes. In this he moves from an attempt to illustrate his belief — 'understand' in that sense — to an outline of how the soul can come to contemplate the God in whom she believes. The latter half of *De Trinitate* concerns, then, the soul's ascent to God. All this is informed by Augustine's understanding of the doctrine of the Trinity, drawn from Scripture and Tradition.

The key to his understanding of the soul's ascent to God is his doctrine that the soul is created in the image and likeness of God. Augustine's understanding of this marks a new departure in the history of theology. According to Greek theology — and Ambrose and the early Augustine — it is the Son, the Word of God, who is the image of God; man is only created *according to* the image of God: he is therefore a copy of the Word, the true image of God, an image of the Image. For the later Augustine, such an understanding of the doctrine of the image of God is subordinationist: the Son is God, co-equal with the Father, not the image of the Father. The image must be something other than God. For Augustine the image of God is man, or to be precise, man's rational soul. And since

---

[7] In the edition in the *Bibliothèque Augustinienne* (vol. 15 edited by M. Mellet and Th. Camelot, vol. 16 by P. Agaësse and J. Moingt, Paris 1955). There is an English translation of books VIII–X, XIV, and XV by J. Burnaby in *Augustine: Later Writings, Library of Christian Classics* VIII (SCM Press, 1955), which I have usually used, where available.

God is the Trinity, the image of God in man's soul is trinitarian. That is why in Genesis God says, 'Let *us* make man after *our* image, in *our* likeness.' The reason why Scripture speaks of man being created *after* the image is not because man is not actually the image of God (as earlier theology had argued) but because man is not a perfect, or equal, image of God. So Augustine says,

For why the 'our', if the Son is the image of the Father alone? But it is on account of the imperfect likeness, as we have said, that man is spoken of as 'after the image', and so 'our', that man might be an image of the Trinity; not equal to the Trinity, as the Son is to the Father, but approaching it, as is said, by a certain likeness; as in things distinct there can be closeness, not however in this case spatially, but by imitation. (VII.vi.12)

Behind Augustine's use of the idea of the image lies the influence of Plotinus. For Plotinus the notion of the image is important in his understanding of the movement of procession and return: what proceeds is an image of that from which it proceeds: Intelligence is an image of the One, and Soul an image of Intelligence. An image is like that of which it is the image, but less than it; and more importantly, the image *derives immediately* — without any intermediary — from that of which it is the image. Further, the image seeks to return to that of which it is the image — it longs for its archetype. In virtue of the likeness that exists between image and archetype, the image can know the archetype — like is known by like — and by contemplating the archetype can come to know the archetype more deeply, and so become more like the archetype. In fact the act of contemplation *is* the act of return. Now the act of contemplation is an act of introversion, since to ascend in the scale of being is to enter more deeply into oneself, into the centre of one's being.

It is this understanding of the image that Augustine adopts and explores. For him the starting-point is that man is the image of God. This is his starting-point, not something that he discovers: it is something revealed in the Scriptures. But the meaning of man's image-likeness to God is found in what we have just discussed: Plotinus' doctrine of the image. Man is the image of God because he is the immediate creation of God, because there is no nature interposed between man and God:

Not everything that among creatures bears some likeness to God is rightly called his image, but only that than which God alone is more exalted. That is directly drawn from Him, if between Himself and it there is no interposed nature.   (XI.v.8)

With this understanding of the relationship of the soul to God, Augustine seeks to show in *De Trinitate* how the soul can return to God. This *itinerarium mentis ad deum* — to borrow the phrase of the deeply Augustinian Bonaventure — begins in earnest in Book VIII. The quest falls into two parts. In books VIII-X Augustine seeks to discover the true nature of man: the first step in the search of God is to seek to discover one's self.[8] Without true self-knowledge man has only a distorted idea of the image of God in himself, and so the way to God is flawed from the start. In this section of *De Trinitate* we see clearly something that is often overlooked: that Augustine is less concerned to illustrate the doctrine of the Trinity from his understanding of man, than to discover the true nature of man by means of the doctrine of the Trinity that he believes by faith. In the second section Augustine seeks to show how this image of God in man can be turned to God so that it can truly reflect Him and man know Him most deeply.

In Book VIII Augustine begins, in a way by now familiar to us, by discussing the soul's search for the truth:

Behold and see, if you can, O soul encumbered with a body that is corrupted, and weighed down by many and varied thoughts, behold and see, if you can: God is Truth. For this is written: 'God is light': not the light these eyes see, but what the heart hears when you hear these words: 'He is Truth'. Do not seek what that truth is; for at once the darkness of bodily images and the clouds of imagination crowd in and disturb that serenity which illuminated you in a sudden flash (*primu ictu*), when I said: 'Truth'. Behold: in that first flash by which you were seized as by a blinding light when there is said 'Truth', remain if you can. But you cannot, you fall back into things accustomed and earthly. By what weight are you at last dragged back, I ask, unless conquered by the desire for what is tawdry and by the errors of our wandering?   (VIII.ii.3)

The language here (in particular the use of the word *ictus*) recalls Augustine's reflections on ecstasy and accounts of it

---

[8] Cf. 143 above.

(see above). In these accounts though, the ecstasy, the rapture, the flash of vision, is represented as the summit of the mystic quest, even though it is fleeting, something that allows men a glimpse, but no more than a glimpse, of the joys of heaven. In *De Trinitate*, however, its context is quite different. It is not the summit of anything: it is rather the beginning. The flash of vision that discloses a fleeting glimpse of truth in itself opens up the possibility of the quest, it is not at all the goal of the quest. Here we have an extraordinary break with Plotinus: what for Plotinus is the culmination of the soul's experience is for the mature Augustine only the beginning of the way. That this is a settled conviction of the mature Augustine can be seen from his *Homilies on John*. There too we have the idea of a dimly perceived significance that dawns upon the soul when it thinks of God (I.8), so that it is as if we were looking from afar towards our homeland, and the sea lay in between. We can see where we would be and yet the sea of this world lies in between, which we cannot cross in our own strength. It is only Christ, who comes from our homeland to us in this world, who can enable us to pass from hence to there. He does this by making available a wooden vessel which can traverse the sea. 'For no one can cross the sea of this world unless he is carried by the cross of Christ' (II.2).

The soul, awakened by the flash of vision, longs for the truth, longs to be able to contemplate the truth not just fleetingly, but in an abiding way. So it is a longing that cannot be satisfied with any particular goods, any particular truths, but only with the Good Itself, the Truth Itself — God Himself. The soul longs for God; it loves the God whom it hopes ultimately to see. But how can anyone love that which he does not know? How can one love anything one does not know? It is this puzzle, which is more than an intellectual conundrum, that Augustine uses to 'open up', as it were, the soul's experience. For he sees this love, this longing for the true, and thus ultimately for God, as a sort of principle of cohesion in the soul. It is what draws the soul together into unity and draws the soul into the realm of eternal reality — or rather discovers *within* the soul that realm of eternal reality (the higher is the more inward).

In Augustine's analysis of the soul's experience here, we

can, I think, discern two strands. First, the love of the soul for
God is the return of the image to God, and so, if God is
trinitarian, it ought to be possible to discern a trinity in the
soul's experience of love. But secondly, and more importantly,
the love that draws the soul into the eternal realm reveals the
soul to itself as it really is: it leads the soul to true self-
knowledge. The soul will only come to God through loving the
image of God it finds in itself, if this image is a true image, the
result of true self-knowledge. The first step in the soul's
coming to know God will be knowledge of self: so it is that
books VIII-X are concerned with the search for the true
image of God in man.

It is the first concern, that the soul's love for God should
disclose a trinity, that leads to the trinity of love at the end of
book VIII: the trinity of the lover, the beloved, and the love
that binds them together. But, though there is a certain trinity
here, there is not any real unity, for lover and beloved are
distinct persons:

A further ascent still remains for us, a higher realm in which our
search is to be pursued, so far as men may. We have found, not the
thing itself, but where it is to be sought; and that will suffice to give
us a point from which a fresh start may be undertaken.

(VIII.x.14)

Augustine now proceeds by looking at man himself and
attempts to discern an image of the Trinity there.

Let us not speak yet of the highest, not yet of the Father, the Son and
the Holy Spirit; but of this unequal image, yet still an image, that is
man; for it is familiar to us, and perhaps easier for the frailty of our
mind to behold.   (IX.ii.2)

Augustine begins by considering the mind loving itself. There
is now identity between the lover and the beloved, but the
trinity of love has vanished, and we have only two terms: the
mind and its love. Augustine, however, recalls the interpenetration of love and knowledge: the mind cannot love itself, if it
does not know itself. The trinity has now reappeared, and we
have found a trinity in man himself: the trinity of *mens, notitia,*
and *amor*: mind, knowledge, and love:

And in these three, when the mind knows itself and loves itself, there
remains a trinity, mind, love and knowledge; and it is confused by

no mingling; although each is singly in itself, and all are wholly in one another, whether one in both or both in one, and so all in all.
(IX.v.8)

The way Augustine treats this image of the trinity he has now discovered in man is guided by his principle that this image will only reflect God truly, if it is a true image. And it will only be a true image if the third element of the image — self-knowledge — is genuine. If, say, the mind mistakes its own nature and thinks of itself as material, then the trinity in the soul will be imperfect. If, on the other hand, the soul thinks of itself as divine there will be a corresponding imperfection in the image. But, when the mind knows itself as it truly is, and loves itself, then there will be a genuine image in the soul. You could say (though Augustine does not put it like this directly) that a soul which fails to know itself will still manifest a trinitarian image, but a heretical one rather than an orthodox one. A mind that thinks itself material, say, will form a material idea of itself in its self-knowledge, and its self-love will be still further debased, since it will be a love of what is material. Mind, which *is* spiritual, whatever one thinks, will be higher than its self-knowledge or self-love, and so the trinity of mind, self-knowledge, and self-love in the soul will be subordinationist — Arian in fact.

In Book X Augustine seeks to refine the image in the soul so that a genuinely orthodox trinity is discerned in the soul. Although self-knowledge may be very mistaken, it can never be entirely lost, for the mind is always present to itself. Self-knowledge as such, as opposed to speculation as to what mind (including my own) consists of, is certain:

Who doubts that he is alive, and remembers, and understands, and wills, and thinks, and knows and judges? If one doubts, one lives; if one doubts whether one doubts, one remembers; if one doubts, one understands that one doubts; if one doubts, it is certain that one wills to; if one doubts, one thinks; if one doubts, one knows that one does not know; if one doubts, one judges that one ought not to consent rashly. Whatever anyone doubts, he ought not to doubt these: if it were not so, it would be impossible to doubt anything.
(X.x.14)

Augustine deduces from this that the mind is spiritual, for all these spiritual properties (doubting, thinking, willing, etc.)

are certain, whereas theories as to whether the mind is air or fire or whatever are not. What is immediate to the mind are its spiritual properties: it is therefore in these spiritual properties that the trinity in the mind, the image of God, is to be sought. And Augustine finds it in three of these spiritual properties of which the mind is certain: memory, understanding, and will:

Now this triad of memory, understanding and will, are not three lives, but one; nor three minds, but one. It follows that they are not three substances but one substance . . . they are three inasmuch as they are related to each other . . . I remember that I possess memory and understanding and will: I understand that I understand and will and remember; I will my own willing and remembering and understanding . . . Since all are created by one another singly and as whole, the whole of each is equal to the whole of each, and the whole of each to the whole of all together. And these three constitute one thing, one life, one mind, one essence.   (X.xi.18)

There is a completely co-equal trinity in the mind, each member of the trinity entirely co-penetrates the others, there is complete co-inherence. So we have arrived at the true image of God in the mind — a truly spiritual trinity, which therefore safeguards true self-knowledge in the formal sense as knowledge of the mind as a spiritual and not a material being:

We might now attempt to raise our thoughts, with such power of concentration as is at our disposal, towards that supreme and most exalted essence of which the human mind is an image — inadequate indeed, but still an image.   (X.xii.19)

We have reached the end of the first stage in the soul's ascent to God: we have found the true image of God in man. The next stage now begins: the return of this image to its archetype, God. This is a process, and not simply an act: the soul must learn what it means to be the image of God in its memory, understanding, and will, and learning that, learn how to pass beyond the image to God Himself in contemplation of Him. The method Augustine pursues is a familiar one: the method of withdrawal and introversion. Augustine begins in Book XI by drawing attention to the trinity manifest in man's perception of the external world: the thing seen, the process of seeing, and our intention of seeing. From this external trinity, in which there is a certain likeness to God, Augustine derives a more internal trinity which is manifest when the soul *remembers* what it has seen: a trinity of memory, internal vision, and the will that effects this. By these considerations Augustine is seeking to bring home to the soul what it means for it to be a spiritual image of the spiritual Trinity. But how can the mind attain to a trinity that realizes its spiritual nature? Even the trinity of memory, internal vision, and will is derived from the external world and depends on it. How can the soul rise from being tied to the external world and the change and corruption bound up with it?

In Book XII Augustine introduces a distinction between knowledge and wisdom, *scientia* and *sapientia*. The distinction is that between knowledge which is concerned with the external world perceived through the senses, knowledge therefore concerned with action in the world (*scientia*), and that knowledge, or wisdom, which is concerned with eternal reality and contemplation of it (*sapientia*). The question we have asked in the last paragraph can now be paraphrased as: how can the soul move from *scientia* to *sapientia*? Clearly this distinction, and the idea that *sapientia* is the aim of the soul, is derived from Augustine's Platonic roots: but we shall see that his treatment of it goes beyond neo-Platonism.

That the soul now only knows *scientia* is a result of the Fall: before the Fall the soul knew *sapientia*. As a result of the Fall the soul has turned from eternal truths to involvement in corporeal realities. But the Fall is manifested not simply in involvement in the senses, but in what the senses provide much opportunity for: selfish, or private, involvement in the senses. The world we perceive through the senses is, inevitably, a world perceived from our own point of view. That can be an indifferent fact, but it can become a principle of action, so that everything in the world is referred back to ourselves: 'the soul loving its own power, slips from what is universal and common to what is private and partial.' This is, in fact, the beginning of pride, *superbia*, the root of sin. Augustine therefore interprets the account of the Fall in Genesis by saying that the serpent's achievement was to persuade the woman to grasp a personal and private good, rather than the common and public good which is unchangeable. So *scientia*, which is concerned with the things of sense, belongs to the fallen world, but it has both a good and a bad use: it is not something to be relinquished, but rather rightly used:

Bodily things are perceived by the bodily senses : eternal, unchangeable and spiritual things are understood by reason of wisdom. Desire is close to the reason which belongs to *scientia*, since it is about bodily things perceived by the senses that we are reasoning when it is a matter of *scientia* which is concerned with action: this is well done, when that knowledge (*notitia*) is referred to the goal of the highest good, but badly if we enjoy bodily things and so rest in a false happiness.   (XII.xii.17)

So it is that Scripture distinguishes between *sapientia* and *scientia* in Job 28:28, where it says: 'Behold piety is wisdom (*sapientia*), and to abstain from evil is knowledge (*scientia*)' (according to Augustine's text, which is not that of the Vulgate). *Scientia*, then, is concerned with governing our conduct in this world and directing us to the *summum bonum*; *sapientia* is concerned with contemplation. It might have been expected that Augustine, having established this distinction between *scientia* and *sapientia*, would now pass immediately to a consideration of *sapientia* and the return of the soul to God in contemplation. But Book XIII which follows is concerned with the trinity of *faith*, because man cannot of his own efforts free himself from the effects of the Fall and turn to God in contemplation. That is only possible as a result of faith in the Incarnation.

Perhaps the key to this is to be found in a remark much earlier in *De Trinitate*. In Book IV Augustine says that the mind must be purified if it is to attain the eternal, but because its impurity is the result of its attachment to the temporal, it must be purified by means of the temporal·

It is only through temporal things that we can be purified so that we become accustomed to eternal realities, through temporal things to which we are now accustomed and to which we cling . . . Just as the rational mind, when purified, ought to contemplate eternal reality, so that mind, when being purified, ought to have faith in temporal things.   (IV.xviii.24)

Man cannot, through his own powers, move the centre of his concern from the temporal to the eternal, from *scientia* to *sapientia*. The eternal must be given to him within the temporal. And this is achieved in the Incarnation, for in Christ, the Incarnate Lord, are hidden 'all the treasures of wisdom and knowledge', as St. Paul says (Col. 2:3). So in God Incarnate there are the treasures both of *scientia* (which we can reach) and *sapientia* (which we want to reach):

All these things that the Word made flesh did and suffered for us in space and time, pertain to *scientia*, not to *sapientia* (in accordance with the distinction we have already demonstrated). That the Word is beyond time and space, and is co-eternal with the Father and wholly everywhere: concerning that, if anyone could, and inasmuch as he could, make a true judgement, that judgement would belong to *sapientia*: and in the Word made flesh, who is Jesus Christ, he possesses the treasures of *sapientia* and *scientia* . . . Our *scientia* is Christ, our *sapientia* is the same Christ. He introduces among us faith concerning temporal things, he shows truth concerning eternal things. Through him we rise to him, we pass through *scientia* to *sapientia*: we do not however move away from the one and the same Christ, 'in which are hid all the treasures of wisdom and knowledge.' (XIII.xix.24)

The truths of faith, the truths concerning the Incarnate Word, are the means whereby we pass from the temporal to the eternal. And there is to be discerned here a trinity of faith, the holding in the mind of the truths about the Incarnation, contemplating them, and delighting in them: a trinity of *retentio*, *contemplatio*, and *dilectio* (or *memoria*, *contuitus*, *dilectio*). It is only through the trinity of faith, which belongs to *scientia*, that we can pass to *sapientia*, contemplation of the eternal. We must submit to the way of faith, we must accept what the Incarnate Word has done for us, if we are to attain to contemplation. We must submit to being purified through temporal things. And that requires humility: only the humble mind can submit to the Incarnate One, who himself teaches us the way of humility:

Because it is pride that is the cause of all our sickness which the Son of God came to heal, he descended and was made humble. How can man continue in his pride? God has been made humble for him. It shames you perhaps to imitate a humble man; imitate then the humble God. The Son of God came in a man and was made humble: that teaches you to be humble, it does not teach you to make man a

beast. God Himself was made man; you, man, know that you are
man: that is the whole of humility, to know that. Therefore because
God teaches humility, he says: I am not come to do my own will, but
the will of him that sent me. For this is a commendation of humility.
Pride indeed does its own will, humility does the will of God. Thus
he who comes to me, I will not cast out. Why? Because I have not
come to do my will, but the will of him who sent me. Humble I am
come, I am come to teach humility, I am come the master of
humility: he who comes to me, is incorporated in me; he who comes
to me is made humble; he who cleaves to me will be humble; because
he does not his own will but God's will; and therefore he is not cast
out . . .   (*Tractatus in Joannem*, XXV.16)

Augustine passes in Book XIV to consider how the image
of God is perfected in man when man contemplates God.
He now considers what it is in man that can be the image of
God. He argues that it must be something that is eternal in
man:

But if the soul's nature is immortal, so that after its original creation
it can never cease to be, God forbid that the soul's most precious
possession should not endure with its own immortality; and what
can be more precious in its created nature than its making in the
image of its Creator?   (XIV.iii.4)

It cannot therefore be the trinity of faith itself that is the image
of God in man, for, in the beatific vision in heaven, faith is
superseded by vision. Neither can it be the trinity that will
then be discerned in vision, for that does not yet exist: neither
the trinity of faith, nor the trinity of vision can then be the
image of God. But the trinity of memory, understanding, and
will manifested in the mind's remembering itself, understanding itself, and loving itself, is something that is as eternal as
the soul. This trinity has been in the mind since even before
the mind came to participate in God. But the reason why
there is this image of the Trinity in the soul is not because it
remembers and knows and loves itself, but because in this it
manifests its capacity to remember, know, and love Him by
whom it has been made. Augustine then goes on to show how
the soul's capacity to remember, know, and love itself is its
capacity to cleave to God in remembering, knowing, and
loving Him: he speaks of

the force of the mind's love of itself, even when it is weak and erring through the mistaken love and pursuit of what is beneath it. Now it could not love itself, if it were altogether ignorant of itself, that is, if it had not memory of itself, and did not understand itself. Such potency it has by virtue of this image of God that is in it, that it can be strong to cleave to him whose image it is. It has been set in that place in the order of reality (which is no spatial order) where there is none above it but God. And when its cleaving to him has become absolute, it will be one spirit with him . . . The mind will be raised to the participation of his being, truth and bliss, though nothing thereby be added to the being, truth and bliss which is its own In that being, joined to it in perfect happiness, it will live a changeless life and enjoy the changeless vision of all that it will behold . . .

(XIX.xiv.20)

It is in this cleaving to God through its memory, understanding and will that the soul attains wisdom, and thus 'wisdom will be the mind's, not by its own illumination, but by partaking in that supreme Light, and only when it enters eternity will it reign in bliss' (XIV.xii.15).

So we come to the perfection of the image of God — the image of the Trinity — in the soul, when the soul attains wisdom, or rather receives wisdom, and remembers, understands, and loves God. Augustine is insistent that the soul can only be reformed in the image of God by God:

the beginning of the image's reforming must come from him who first formed it. The self which it was able to deform, it cannot of itself reform. (XIV.xvi.22)

It is not only reformation *by* God, but reformation *according to* God: reformation into the image of God. This renewal begins in a single moment, the moment of baptism, but the perfection of the image in man is the result of a long process:

The cure's beginning is to remove the cause of sickness: and that is done through the forgiveness of sins. Its furtherance is the healing of the sickness itself, which takes effect by gradual progress in the renewal of the image. (XIV.xvii.23)

The image that is being renewed in the spirit of the mind, in the knowledge of God, not outwardly but inwardly from day to day, will be made perfect by that vision, face to face, that shall be after the judgement — the vision which is now but a-growing, through a glass darkly. (XIV.xix.25)

And so the soul returns to God — not in a moment of ecstasy, but in a long process of renewal which will never end in this life, following a way that has been disclosed by the light of the doctrine of the Trinity and in which the Trinity is gradually disclosed in the heart of the Christian. Augustine's dogmatic theology passes over into spiritual theology and the end of both is contemplation, contemplation of the Trinity who is present in the soul through the Holy Spirit, who is that love that the soul has for God. 'God the Holy Spirit, who proceeds from God, when he is given to man, enkindles in him the love of God and his neighbour, and is that love' (XV.xvii.31). The soul's ecstasy — so important for Plotinus — is replaced, we might almost say (to use the language of Denys the Areopagite, which Augustine does not himself use), by God's ecstasy in the condescension of the Incarnation and the pouring forth of the Holy Spirit, as love, in the hearts of Christians. The way of the soul is the way of response to this love, a way of love and humility, by which we pass to the Trinity in whom, to quote Augustine, 'is the origin of all things, most perfect beauty and most happy delight.'

VIII.   DENYS THE AREOPAGITE

WITH Denys we come to the end of the development of
Patristic mystical theology. For with Denys are completed all
the main lines of the mystical theology of the Fathers: the
Origenist tradition has achieved its classical expression in the
realm of mystical theology in Evagrius, the Augustinian vision
has been articulated in the West, and in Denys the tradition of
apophatic theology, which has its roots in Philo and Gregory
of Nyssa, is summed up in the tiny, but immensely influential,
Mystical Theology.

> There is in God (some say)
> A deep, but dazzling darkness; As men here
> Say it is late and dusky, because they
> See not all clear
> O for that night! where I in him
> Might live invisible and dim.

So Henry Vaughan in his poem *The Night*. His 'some say'
refers to those who have been influenced — directly or
indirectly — by Denys (or Dionysius) the Areopagite. For
Denys is the most well-known exponent of the Negative or
Apophatic Way, where the soul flees from everything created
and is united with the Unknowable God in darkness. His
Mystical Theology is a brief and pregnant exposition of this
theme, and has been enormously influential. It was translated
into English in the fourteenth century by the author of the
Cloud of Unknowing — with the title *Hid Divinity* — and
fertilized that remarkable period of English mysticism. But he
is not just an exponent of the Negative Way. In the Middle
Ages he was equally well-known for his work on the nature
and ranks of the angels, the *Celestial Hierarchy*. Though its

influence was late and gradual (as late as St. Bernard we find
the angelology of St. Gregory the Great, rather than that of
Denys), by the period of High Scholasticism its ascendancy
was unquestioned. So Dante says, in his *Paradiso*:

> And Dionysius with so much desire
> Set about contemplating all these orders
> That he named them distinctly, as I have done.

> But Gregory departed a little from him;
> So that, as soon as his eyes were opened
> In this heaven, he smiled at himself.[1]

Denys' work, the *Divine Names*, on what we can say about
God, was much valued by Aquinas (if not completely understood). His *Ecclesiastical Hierarchy*, about the rites of the
Church and the ranks of the clergy and laity, was much less
influential in the West, presumably because it presupposed
the liturgical practices of the Byzantine East.

But it is for his mystical theology that Denys is best known,
and it is that which concerns us here. And yet we cannot
neglect his other writings. If in earlier chapters we have seen
that the mystical theology of a particular writer makes more
sense if we grasp its context — as we saw when we discussed
Evagrius' *praktike* or Augustine's use of the doctrine of the
Trinity to gain a greater understanding of the soul, to give two
very different examples — with Denys it is only as we begin to
understand the context of his mystical theology that we
perceive its real significance. For his mystical theology forms a
piece — the crowning piece — with the other ways of pursuing
theology that he discusses.[2]

During the Middle Ages, Denys was revered as the Athenian who had been converted by St. Paul's speech on the
Areopagus (Acts 17:34). In fact we first hear of him when in
533 some Severan Monophysites quoted (inaccurately) from
his third letter in order to claim virtual apostolic authority for
their position against the Orthodox. Not surprisingly the

---

[1] *Paradiso* XXVIII, 130–5. C. H. Sisson's translation of *The Divine Comedy*
(Carcanet New Press, 1980).
[2] This is something H. U. von Balthasar stresses in his important discussion of
Denys in *Herrlichkeit: eine theologische Ästhetik* (Einsiedeln, 1962), II/1, 147–214.

Orthodox rejected the authority of this new companion of the apostles. They pointed out that neither Athanasius, nor Cyril, nor any other of the Fathers seemed aware of this figure. None the less Denys' writings were rapidly adopted by Monophysite and Orthodox alike as genuine, and the doubts about their authenticity were short-lived. A collection of comments (*scholia*) was written on the Areopagitical corpus. This collection was begun by John of Scythopolis and later added to by Maximus the Confessor, and it is to the latter that the whole collection has been traditionally ascribed.[3] With his august approval — but also as modified by him — the Dionysian tradition entered and fertilized Byzantine theology.

If we want to try and fix a date for Denys, a *terminus ante quem* is clearly his citation by the Monophysites in 533. A *terminus post quem* can be derived from his account of the Christian liturgy in his *Ecclesiastical Hierarchy*, because it seems to include the singing of a creed. The singing of the creed (originally a baptismal creed) in the eucharistic liturgy is an innovation of the late fifth century, introduced among the Monophysites by Peter the Fuller in 476 or thereabouts. Denys, then, would seem to be late fifth century and appears to have come from a Syrian and Monophysite background — though his own writings are not unequivocally Monophysite in theology. None of that would be incongruous.

Before we go further it would be as well to say a little about Denys' philosophical background. We have seen that Augustine stands in the tradition of neo-Platonism which comes through Porphyry and Victorinus. Denys stands in the other tradition of neo-Platonism, that which passed through Iamblichus and at the end of the fourth century successfully took over the Academy at Athens. The most famous representative of this school is Proclus (410–85), who was *diadochus* — the successor of Plato — in the Academy from 437 or thereabouts. Denys has been called the Christian Proclus, and the general similarity between Proclus and Denys is very striking. There are even close verbal parallels — between *Divine Names* IV and Proclus' treatise *De Malorum Subsistentia*, for example.

[3] See von Balthasar, 'Das Scholienwerk des Johannes von Scythopolis', *Scholastik* 15 (1940), 16–38.

What is this Procline neo-Platonism?[4] In essence it is a systematization of Plotinus' teaching and, compared with Plotinus, much more sympathetic to the practices of pagan religion. Plotinus' three hypostases, that is, the One, Intelligence, and Soul, seen as a hierarchy, are drawn out: the hierarchy is developed and exaggerated. Proclus, one might say, produces a pattern out of the basic Plotinian vision: richer, in some ways, but less suggestive; at once dizzying and cramped. The themes of the pattern are various triads. There are three hypostases. There is a triad found in the process of emanation and return: a first term, rest — *mone* — is provided, and we have *mone*, *proodos*, *epistrophe* — rest, emanation, return. Another triad is found in his analysis of the modes of existence: Being, Life, Intelligence — *to on, zoe, nous*.

Much is made of the fact — which Plotinus had noted, and which Denys was to note also — that the hierarchy of existence is simple at both ends, top and bottom, and more complex in the middle. The One and Pure Matter — both simple — are respectively above and below Being, Life, and Intelligence. This observation provides the rational justification for theurgy — magic — which was important to Iamblichus and his successors (in marked contrast to Plotinus, who disapproved of magic). Since lower beings are simpler than intelligent beings, and therefore participate in higher hypostases, it might be argued that magical practices, using plants and potions, for example, are *more* likely to influence higher beings than the merely rational exercises of humans. So, whereas for Plotinus the only activity by which man draws nearer to the One is contemplation, *theoria*, for Iamblichus and Proclus theurgy, *theourgia*, magical operations with plants and animals (inspecting entrails and the use of magic potions, for example), is more likely to be effective. Proclus says of theurgical power that it is 'better than any human wisdom or knowledge'.[5] And Iamblichus' longest work, *De Mysteriis*, is about little else.

---

[4] Convenient accounts in English are by A. C. Lloyd, in A. H. Armstrong (ed.), *Cambridge History of later Greek and early Medieval Philosophy* (Cambridge, 1970), 302–25; and R. T. Wallis, *Neoplatonism* (London, 1972), 138–59. Fundamental is E. R. Dodds' edition of Proclus' *The Elements of Theology*, with important introduction and commentary (Oxford, 1933, 2nd ed., 1963).

[5] *Platonic Theology* I.25: in H. D. Saffrey and L. G. Westerink's edition (Paris, 1968), 113.

That gives some idea of the ingredients of Proclus' systematization of neo-Platonism; and the ingredients are easier to grasp than the resulting mixture, which is complicated to a degree. Proclus starts from Plotinus' three hypostases, the One, Intelligence, and Soul. From each of these issue replicas: from the One, *henads* or gods; from Intelligence, intelligences, or daemons, or angels; from Soul, souls — of humans, for example. Then by bringing into play the various triads a complicated set of interrelations is constructed and we have a sort of cosmic minuet, proceeding from rest, out through procession, and back again by reversion. The whole of reality is structured and everything has the right degree of being consistent with its own level of reality: 'all things are in all things, but in each according to its proper nature' (*El. Theol.* prop. 103).

If we turn to Denys we find many parallels with this. Proclus' three levels of reality — henads, intelligences, and souls — are paralleled in Denys' three hierarchies: the Thearchy, the celestial hierarchy, and the ecclesiastical hierarchy, that is, the Trinity, angels, and men. Denys makes use of Proclus' triads, and to them adds his own. All the hierarchies are triadic. The Thearchy is the Trinity. There are three ranks of the angelic beings and each rank contains three sorts. The ecclesiastical hierarchy is similarly divided into sets of three. There is, moreover, the triad — with antecedents, as we have seen, in the Christian tradition, and destined to have vast influence — of purification, illumination, and perfection or union (*katharsis, photismos, teleiosis* or *henosis*). Denys also makes use of the distinction between *theoria* (contemplation) and *theourgia* (theurgy). The ecclesiastical hierarchy fulfils its functions by 'intellectual contemplations and by diverse sensible symbols, and through these it is raised in a sacred manner to the divine' (*EH* V.i.2:501 C).[6] These sensible symbols — the sacraments (in a broad sense) — are sometimes referred to by the word *theourgia* and its derivatives. The oil of confirmation is called *theourgikotatos* — literally, 'most theurgical'. The use of the word is interesting, for it indicates that Denys thinks

---

[6] References to the divisions of the individual works as given in Migne (*PG* III), followed by column number. *DN* = *Divine Names, CH* = *Celestial Hierarchy, EH* = *Ecclesiastical Hierarchy, MT* = *Mystical Theology, Ep.* = *Letter.* The translations are my own.

of the sacraments as Christian theurgy — Christian magic, if you like — or, using less loaded words, a Christian use of material things to effect man's relationship with the divine. Here we see the 'Christian Proclus', using neo-Platonic language to express his understanding of the Christian sacraments. But, though he uses similar language, his meaning is basically different. For a neo-Platonist, theurgy — magic — worked because of some occult sympathy between the material elements used and the constitution of the divine. Theurgy, to a neo-Platonist, is natural — even if rather odd. The use of material elements in the sacraments, however, is a matter of institution, not of occult fitness: they are vehicles of grace not because of what they are materially, but because of their use in a certain symbolic context.

But what is this all about? In a word, it is about *theology*: *theologia,* in its proper sense, as the Fathers used it, not so much knowledge about God, but knowledge of God through communion with Him and contemplation of Him. Denys talks about various sorts of theology: symbolic, cataphatic, and apophatic — another triad. However we must beware of being mesmerized by these triads, and of playing games with them, like Proclus, in an attempt to relate them all one to another. This is not Denys' way. He makes use of his triads, but he is not trapped in fascination by them. Consequently it is difficult to reduce Denys' thought to anything systematic, and the temptation has to be resisted.

In Chapter III of the *Mystical Theology*, Denys discusses 'what are the cataphatic (affirmative) theologies and what the apophatic (negative)':

In the *Theological Outlines* we have celebrated that which is most proper to cataphatic theology, how the divine and good Nature is said to be single and how threefold; what is called in itself Fatherhood and what Sonship, and what the theology of the Spirit is intended to express; how from the heart of the immaterial and indivisible Good Itself there proceed the rays of that Goodness which are preserved inseparable by an eternally continuing regeneration, inseparable from Itself, in themselves and in one another; how Jesus, who is beyond being, becomes being in truly human form; and other such matters drawn from Scripture are celebrated in the *Theological Outlines*. In the book on the *Divine Names* we have celebrated how he is called Good, Being, Life, Wisdom and Power, and other such things relating to the spiritual naming of God. In the *Symbolic Theology* we have celebrated what conversions of names are necessary in changing their use from the realm of the senses to the service of the divine; what are the divine forms, the divine figures and parts and organs; what are the divine places and divine worlds, what the passions, what the griefs and wraths, what the inebriations and hangovers, what are the oaths and what are the curses, what the dreams and the awakenings and other likenesses belonging to the symbolic depiction of God that are sanctioned in the divine oracles. And I think you will see how much longer are the latter writings than the earlier. For it was necessary that the *Theological Outlines* and the *Divine Names* should be much briefer than the *Symbolic Theology*, seeing that the higher we ascend the more our words are straitened by the fact that what we understand is seen more and more altogether in a unifying and simplifying way; just as now on our entry into the darkness that is beyond understanding, we find not mere brevity of words, but complete wordlessness and failure of the understanding. And there as our reason descended from the most exalted to the lowest, the lower it descended, proportionately the more our understanding was broadened to encompass a multitude of notions, so now as our reason ascends from the lower to the transcendent, the more it ascends the more it is contracted, and when it has completely ascended it will become completely speechless, and be totally united with the Inexpressible.

(MT III: 1032 D–1033 C)

This passage introduces us to Denys' understanding of cataphatic theology and symbolic theology, and their relationship to apophatic theology. Cataphatic and symbolic theology are concerned with what we affirm about God: apophatic theology is concerned with our understanding of God, when, in the presence of God, speech and thought fail us and we are reduced to silence. Not all the works that Denys refers to in this passage have survived.[7] None the less we can develop what Denys suggests in this passage, since what the otherwise

---

[7] In this passage from the *Mystical Theology* and in several other places, Denys writes as if the writings we have of his (see n. 6) are only *part* of his complete works (supposedly written in the first century by St. Paul's Athenian convert). Whether the 'missing treatises' are really missing, or whether they are part of an attempt on Denys' part to create the impression that what we have is all that has survived from the first century, is a subject of dispute. Balthasar takes Denys' references to 'missing' treatises seriously (*Herrlichkeit* II/1, 157–67; cf. 151–4). For a contrary view, see R. Roques's article on Denys in *Dictionnaire de spiritualité* III, cols. 259–62.

unknown *Theological Outlines* is said to contain corresponds
pretty well with the first two chapters of the *Divine Names*, and
the subject of the otherwise unknown *Symbolic Theology* is
discussed in *Letter* IX, and also in the books on the hierarchies.

The first thing to notice about these various theologies is
that in them we learn how we can *celebrate* (*hymnein*). These
theologies are not about how we can predicate qualities of
God, but about how we can praise him. For Denys theology is
not concerned primarily with intellectual, academic matters
(though his *Divine Names* was used as a textbook on analogical
predication of God in the medieval West), rather it is concerned with the creature's response of praise and worship to
the Love of God.

The whole of creation has been brought into being by God
to manifest His glory, and each creature, as it fulfils the role
that God has assigned to it, manifests His glory and praises
Him. The *Divine Names* explores this theme by discussing the
manifestation of God in His creation. The first two chapters
(which correspond in content to the lost *Theological Outlines*)
discuss God's manifestation of Himself in the hidden life of the
Trinity. Denys distinguishes between 'unions' (*henoseis*) and
'distinctions' (*diakriseis*) in God. The 'unions' are ultimately
incomprehensible to us, for we can only know things by
making 'distinctions'. Nevertheless, behind the distinctions
lies the union or unity (*henosis*) which the distinctions unfold.
The primary significance of the 'distinctions' is the Persons of
the Trinity. These are distinctions in the ultimate and
unknowable unity, which yet remain in that unity and do not
serve to distinguish God from all else. If this is cataphatic
theology, in that it affirms something about God, it is clearly
no less apophatic, in that our affirmations are taking us
beyond what we can grasp: the doctrine of the Trinity reveals
God as unknowable, not so much beyond our powers of
comprehension as unknowable in Himself. As Vladimir
Lossky has said:

This is why the revelation of the Holy Trinity, which is the summit
of cataphatic theology, belongs also to apophatic theology, for 'if we
learn from the Scriptures that the Father is the source of divinity,
and Jesus and the Holy Spirit are the divine progeny, the divine

seeds, so to say, and flowers and lights that transcend being, we can neither say nor understand what that is.' (*DN* II. 7)[8]

But there is a further 'distinction', by which God is distinguished from all else, and this is the distinction in virtue of which God manifests Himself outside of Himself. This is the procession (*proodos*) of the divine union which is multiplied and diversified by the divine goodness. This going out of Himself in will and power is the creation of the world out of nothing, and its motive is the divine goodness: 'being Goodness Himself, He extends His goodness, simply by being good, to all that exists' (*DN* IV. 1: 693 B). Goodness, then, is the first of the affirmations about God discussed in the *Divine Names*. Various other attributes of God are discussed in the rest of the treatise: the order of the attributes (which may be imperfectly preserved) and the nature of the discussion owes a great deal to Denys' neo-Platonic background.[9] Indeed, discussions of the attributes of the divine are unknown in either Christian or pagan circles before Proclus, the first book of whose *Platonic Theology* is such a discussion, and whose example Denys seems to have followed.[10]

The *Divine Names* is, then, a treatise of cataphatic theology, a discussion of the affirmations with which we can praise God. But we are continually reminded that our affirmations fall short of God, that none of our concepts can reach Him who is unknowable. The affirmations we make in our praise can be made of God because God is genuinely manifested in the world. But He is not an object of knowledge, He cannot be known, and therefore at the same time as we make affirmations about God, we must deny what we are affirming — and this denial is more fundamental:

On no account therefore is it true to say that we know God, not indeed in His nature (for that is unknowable, and is beyond any reason and understanding), but by the order of all things that He has established, and which bears certain images and likenesses of His divine paradigms, we ascend step by step, so far as we can follow the

---

[8] In his article, 'La notion des "analogies" chez le Pseudo-Denys l'Aréopagite', *Archives d'histoire doctrinale et littéraire du Moyen Âge*, 5 (1930), 279–309, at p. 283.

[9] See E. von Ivánka, *Plato Christianus* (Einsiedeln, 1964), 228–42.

[10] See Saffrey and Westerink's introduction to their edition of the first book of the *Platonic Theology*, CXCI f.

way, to the Transcendent, by negating and transcending everything and by seeking the cause of all. Therefore God is known in all, and apart from all . . . For these things we rightly say of God, and He is praised in due proportion by everything among all those things of which He is the source. And this is, moreover, the most divine knowledge of God, that He is known through unknowing, according to the union which transcends the understanding, when the understanding withdraws from all, and abandons itself, and is united with the dazzling rays and in them and from them is enlightened by the unsearchable depths of wisdom.   (*DN* VII. 3: 869 C–872 B)

Here we have a clear assertion that God is really known, that He is really praised in our affirmations about Him. But it is none the less clear that the rejection of these affirmations is the path to a deeper knowledge of God.

Such is cataphatic theology. We find a not dissimilar pattern in symbolic theology. Here we are concerned with the 'conversion of what is taken from the realm of the senses to the service of the divine' (*MT* III: 1033 A). It is expounded in the books on the two hierarchies.[11]

These two hierarchies are the celestial and the ecclesiastical. The celestial hierarchy consists of three ranks, each consisting of three types of angelic being. The first rank consists of Seraphim, Cherubim, and Thrones; the second rank of Dominations, Powers, and Authorities; the third, of Principalities, Archangels, and Angels. The ecclesiastical hierarchy has what appears at first sight an odd characteristic, for, although it too consists of three ranks of three, the first rank consists not of beings but of rites — sacramental rites.[12] The first rank, then, consists of the mystery of *myron*, oil; of the Synaxis or the Eucharist; and of Baptism. The second rank is the rank of the sacred ministers: bishops, priests, and deacons or, to use Denys' own language, hierarchs, priests (*hiereis*), and ministers (*leitourgoi*). The third rank is the rank of the laity: monks, the baptized (the contemplative order, Denys calls them), and those who are excluded from the celebration of the mysteries — catechumens, penitents, and the possessed.

---

[11] On this, see R. Roques, *L'Univers dionysien: Structure hiérarchique du monde selon le Pseudo-Denys* (Paris, 1954).

[12] There are problems in any interpretation of the ecclesiastical hierarchy: see Roques, *L'Univers*, 196 ff.

We have seen that Denys regards symbolic theology as the 'conversion of what is taken from the realm of the senses to the service of the divine', and we can see already that in the ecclesiastical hierarchy this implies the taking up of the material order through the rites and sacraments of the Church into the praise of God. Bread, wine, water, oil, incense, painting, music — all is 'converted' from the realm of the senses to the service of God. As we have seen, Denys uses the neo-Platonic word *theourgia* to describe this. I think part of the reason for the use of what must have been rather a shocking term (it is as if we were to refer to the sacraments as magic) is an insistence — over against any merely spiritualizing interpretation — that we are using material things to accomplish something in the realm of the divine. It is perhaps not so clear, at first sight, how such a definition applies to the celestial hierarchy, which is, after all, immaterial. Here perhaps the meaning is that we understand the celestial hierarchy by means of analogies drawn from the realm of the senses: the most exalted of the celestial beings, the Seraphim, are apprehended by us through the analogy of fire, for example.

What is the point of all these hierarchies? Denys explains this himself in a long passage in the *Celestial Hierarchy*:

> Hierarchy is, as I understand it, a sacred order and knowledge and activity which is being assimilated as much as possible to likeness with God and, in response to the illuminations that are given it from God, raises itself to the imitation of Him in its own measure. The beauty which fitting to God, simple and good, the source of all perfection and unmingled with any unlikeness, lets each one participate, as far as it can, in its own light and perfects it by a most divine initiation, fashioning the initiate harmoniously to the unchanging likeness of its own form.

The end of hierarchy, then, is assimilation to God and union with Him as far as possible. It is God Himself who is our guide in all sacred knowledge and activity, and looking unwaveringly to his divine comeliness, the hierarchy receives his stamp as much as possible and makes its own members divine images, perfectly clear and spotless mirrors, receptive to the ray of the primordial and thearchic light, and divinely filled with the brilliance that has been given to it; and these in their turn, without envy, become sources of illumination for others, in accordance with the thearchic arrangements. For it is not permitted for any of those who have been

initiated into sacred matters or for those who are undergoing
initiation to do anything at all contrary to the sacred order of their
initiation, nor even to exist in any other mode, if they desire the
divine brilliance, and contemplate it with sacred propriety, and have
received its stamp according to the proportion proper to each of the
sacred spirits. Therefore he who speaks of hierarchies speaks in
general of a certain sacred arrangement, an image of the divine
splendour, which accomplishes in the orders and hierarchical
sciences the mysteries of its own illumination and is assimilated, as
far as it is permitted, to its own principle. For each being who is
assigned a role in a hierarchy, its perfection consists in its raising
itself to the imitation of God in its own measure. What could be
more divine than to become, in the words of the oracles, a 'fellow-
worker with God', and to shew forth the divine energy which is
manifested in oneself as much as one can. Thus since the order of
hierarchy will mean that some are being purified and others purify,
some are being enlightened while others enlighten, some are being
perfected while others complete the perfecting initiation for others,
each will imitate God in the way that is harmonious with its own
function. The Divine Blessedness, to speak in human terms, is free
from any unlikeness, full of eternal light, perfect and lacking no
perfection, itself purifying and enlightening and perfecting, or rather
purification itself, illumination itself and perfection itself, the primary source and principle by itself of all perfecting initiation, beyond
purification, beyond light, the source of all hierarchy, and yet
separated by its transcendence from anything that is sacred.

(CH III. 1 f.: 164 D–165 C)

The purpose of the hierarchies is assimilation to God and
union with him. This is accomplished by each being fulfilling
its proper role in the hierarchy. As each being accomplishes
this it becomes a fellow-worker with God — *theou synergos* —
and manifests the divine energy which is in it as much as
possible. The result of this assimilation to God — deification
— and union with Him is to make of the created order a
perfect theophany: each part in its own proportion manifest-
ing the glory of God. So symbolic theology and cataphatic
theology are not far apart: both are concerned with the
perfecting of our praise of God.

Now the system of the hierarchies both fulfils this function
— theophany — by being a glittering and ordered array of
symbols of God's majesty and glory, and also is the means for
bringing this about. As such, it embodies the threefold process

of purification, illumination, and perfection, and the system of triad upon triad fulfils this purpose. In every triad the highest is perfect or perfecting, the middle one is illuminated or illuminating, and the lowest is being purified or purifying. This may explain the odd feature of the ecclesiastical hierarchy, that its highest rank consists not of beings but of rites; for the rites, or mysteries, *perfect* us, the clergy *illuminate* us to receive the mysteries, and the laity are *being purified*. So the whole is a system of ordered activity and this activity Denys often calls *ascent*. But we must be careful: very rarely does ascent mean movement *up* the system of the hierarchies. Only the ascent from catechumen to contemplative, in Denys' language ('ordinary layman', as we would say), is normal; everything else is a matter of special divine ordination or vocation. The monks or servers[13] form a higher rank than the contemplative order, but the laity are not all expected to become monks. Nor are monks expected to join the ranks of the clergy, though that is a higher rank; indeed, in the Eastern Church, there is a tradition of resistance on the part of monks to being ordained. Nor are men expected to become angels in their ascent to union with God. What ascent means — at least in part — is a more perfect union with that divine energy (or will) which establishes one in the hierarchy. So one 'ascends' *into* the hierarchy rather than up it. One is reminded of Piccarda's reply to Dante's question as to whether she desires a higher place in Paradise, that she may 'see more and become more dear':

> Brother, the virtue of charity brings quiet
> To our will, so that we want only
> What we have, and thirst for nothing beyond that.
>
> If we desired to be higher up
> Our wishes would not be in accordance
> With the will of him who sets us here; . . .
>
> It is indeed the essence of this life
> That we keep ourselves within the divine will,
> So that our wills may be made one with his:

---

[13] *therapeutai* — so called 'from the pure service and worship they offer to God, and the single, undivided lives that they live as they strive for simplicity in a sacred folding together of all division into a God-like unity and the perfection of the love of God' (*EH* VI. i.3: 533A).

> So that, how we are at various thresholds
> Throughout this kingdom, pleases the whole kingdom
> As it does the king who rouses us to his will;
>
> And in his will we find our peace . . .
>   (*Paradiso* III. 70–5, 79–85, Sisson's translation)

We might say then that both cataphatic and symbolic theology are concerned with perfecting that theophany which is God's creation. They are concerned with bringing about as perfect an openness and transparency to the divine glory as possible. They are concerned with the manifestation of the effulgence of the divine energies in creation. They are not abstract and academic, but directly concerned with our vocation as Christians to live in accordance with the vocation God has allotted to us and there to manifest His glory.

We saw with cataphatic theology that the affirmation of God's manifestation leads to a more fundamental negation: there is an analogy to this in symbolic theology. Symbols may be either like that which they symbolize or unlike. When speaking of God Denys makes clear his preference for unlike symbols (*anomoia symbola*), for with them there is no danger of thinking that God is directly like that which the symbols call to mind. (If you say that God is fire, you don't mean that He is fire, and you *know* you don't mean He is fire. But if you say He is Perfect Beauty, you may think you mean just that.) 'Unlike' symbols, too, force the soul to rise above the symbols. 'If then negations concerning things divine are true, but the affirmations are inadequate to the hiddenness of the ineffable, revelation through representations unlike that which is revealed are more suitable to the invisible' (*CH* II. 3: 141 A).

Both cataphatic and symbolic theology, then, point beyond themselves to the way of negation — apophatic theology. The reason for this is fundamental and theological: God is unknowable in Himself, He is not an object of knowledge. With our understanding we can grasp God's manifestation of Himself in creation, but in the very act of understanding God's manifestation of Himself we realize that the One thus manifested transcends His manifestation. For the end of both cataphatic and symbolic theology is assimilation to God, union with God; and the more the soul knows and loves God in His manifestations, the more she longs for God in Himself. If she seeks to trace back God's manifestations to God Himself, she can only do this by negating these manifestations and moving — as we have seen in the passage quoted earlier from the *Mystical Theology* — through a state where less and less can be expressed until ultimately she 'becomes completely speechless and is entirely united to the Inexpressible.'

Like Gregory of Nyssa (and indeed the following passage has several close verbal parallels with Gregory's *Life of Moses*), Denys speaks of the ascent of the soul using the analogy of Moses' ascent of the holy mount:

This seems to me a marvellous thought, that the good cause of all is expressed in many words, and at the same time in few words or none at all, as there can neither be any account of Him nor any understanding of Him, since He transcends all in a manner beyond being, and manifests Himself without disguise and in truth only to those who have passed through ritual consecrations and purifications, and beyond all the ascents of all the holy summits, and have left behind all divine illuminations, and sounds and heavenly words, and have entered into the Darkness, where, as the Scriptures say, He who transcends all really is. For not simply is the divine Moses bidden first of all to purify himself and then to separate himself from those not thus purified; but after all purification, he hears the many-sounding trumpets and sees many lights which flash forth pure and widely diffused rays. Then he separates himself from the multitude and with the chosen priests he reaches the summit of the divine ascents. But not even here does he hold converse with God Himself, nor does he behold Him (for He is invisible), but only the place where He is. And this, I think, means that the most divine and exalted of the things that are seen with the eye or perceived by the mind are but suggestions that barely hint at the nature of that which transcends any conception whatever, a presence which sets but its feet upon the spiritual pinnacles of its most holy places. And then Moses is cut off from both things seen and those who see and enters into the darkness of unknowing, a truly hidden darkness, according to which he shuts his eyes to all apprehensions that convey knowledge, for he has passed into a realm quite beyond any feeling or seeing. Now, belonging wholly to that which is beyond all, and yet to nothing at all, and being neither himself, nor another, and united in his highest part in passivity (*anenergesia*) with Him who is completely unknowable, he knows by not knowing in a manner that transcends understanding. (*MT* I.3: 1000 B—1001 A)

Much of this is familiar. The apophatic way is only embarked on by a soul that has purified itself and has already ascended to the level of natural contemplation — contemplation of the world in God. The soul then ascends further by negating what it knows. Denys is still very Platonist here. This is clear from the passage quoted earlier from *MT* III, where the way of negation is represented as a stage beyond the level the soul reaches when it has rejected things of the senses and confined itself to purely intellectual understanding (the movement from many words to few words — and beyond that to the wordlessness of apophatic theology). But we must be careful not to misunderstand Denys here (or indeed Plato). Denys is not exalting some sort of 'pure thought' over involvement in the world of the senses as such. Rather it seems to me he is thinking of withdrawal from the inevitable fragmentariness of our involvement in the world of the senses to a more collected, unified state. This is what he has in mind in the passage from the *Mystical Theology* translated above as 'the higher we ascend the more our words are straitened by the fact that what we understand is seen more and more altogether in a unifying and simplifying way.'[14] The apophatic way is the next stage, when our words are completely straitened into speechlessness.

This 'negating' is, in part, something that we do. Denys — echoing Plotinus[15] — speaks of it thus:

For this is to see and to know truly, and to praise in a transcendent way Him who is beyond being through the negation of all things, just as those who make statues with their own hands cut away everything which obscures the clear beholding of the hidden form, and thus make it manifest its hidden beauty solely by the process of cutting away. (*MT* II: 1025 B)

But such negating as we do only takes us a certain way — to the place where He is, not to God Himself. Then the soul is caught up in the deep darkness where God is and in complete passivity (*anenergesia*) it is united with the unknowable God in an unknowable manner.

14 *MT* III: 1033 B; see 165 above.
15 See *Enn.* I.6.9; 6 ff. in Henry and Schwyzer's text, p. 63 in MacKenna's.

So Denys speaks of his teacher Hierotheus as one who 'did not so much learn about divine things, as suffer them and through his sympathy with them, if I may use such terms, was perfected to an untaught and hidden faith concerning them and union with them' (*DN* II.9, 648 B). In union with God the soul is passive, and suffers or finds a certain sympathy (literally, suffering with) the divine. It is not something it learns, and indeed it is unteachable (*adidaktos*), rather it is, as Roques says, 'contemplation due purely to grace, of a type at once unitive, ineffable and beyond the realm of the discursive understanding, something no longer distinct from ecstasy and pure love.'[16]

For Denys does speak of ecstasy in which the soul goes out of itself and is united with the divine. In this he seems to go beyond Gregory of Nyssa, to whom otherwise he is so close.[17] This ecstasy is a genuine 'going out of oneself' in which the soul is torn out of itself:

... by going out of yourself and everything, casting aside every restraint in pure and absolute ecstasy, you will raise yourself to the ray of Divine Darkness that is beyond being, leaving all behind and released from all.   (*MT* I.1: 997 B–1000 A)

But Denys does not stress the negative side of ecstasy, rather he sees ecstasy primarily as an ecstasy of love, as union and divinization (*henosis* and *theosis*).[18] Denys makes no distinction between *eros* and *agape* (though he says that *eros* is 'more divine' than *agape*) and he defines both as 'of a power that unites and binds together and effects an indissoluble fusion in the beautiful and the good' (*DN* IV.12: 709 C). This divine *eros* is ecstatic, meaning by that that 'those who are possessed by this love belong not to themselves, but to the objects of their longing' (ibid.: 712 A). Ecstasy draws the soul out of itself and centres it on the object of its love. Denys gives St. Paul as an example:

---

[16] In his article on 'Contemplation, extase et ténèbre chez le Pseudo-Denys' in *Dictionnaire de Spiritualité* II, col. 1895.

[17] W. Völker sees Denys as much closer to Gregory: see *Kontemplation und Ekstase bei Pseudo-Dionysius Areopagita* (Wiesbaden, 1958), 200 ff., disagreeing with Roques in the article cited, which we have followed here.

[18] See Roques, art. cit., col. 1897.

So also the great Paul, caught up in rapture by divine love and participating in its ecstatic power, said with inspired speech, 'I live and yet not I, but Christ lives in me'. As a true lover, caught up out of himself into God, he lives not his own life, but that life so much longed for, the life of his beloved.   (*DN* IV.13: 712 A)

Denys, however, speaks not only of the soul's ecstasy but (and here we have something inconceivable in Plotinus or in any neo-Platonist) of God's own ecstasy:

We must dare to add this as being no less true; that the Source of all things Himself, in His wonderful and good love for all things, through the excess of His loving goodness, is carried outside Himself, in His providential care for all that is, so enchanted is He in goodness and love and longing. Removed from His position above all and beyond all He descends to be in all according to an ecstatic and transcendent power which is yet inseparable from Himself.

(*DN* IV.13: 712 AB)

The soul in ecstasy meets God's ecstatic love for herself. Here is no union with Plotinus' One, immutable and unconscious either of Itself or of the soul.

How does the apophatic way relate to the other ways? And, in particular, how does this idea of union with God in ecstatic love relate to the idea of the hierarchies? The hierarchies seem to suggest intermediaries between the soul and God; ecstasy, on the other hand, speaks of a union between the soul and God, a state of immediacy of the soul to God. We have already seen that the hierarchies are not ladders up which we are expected to climb in our ascent to God. But we can say more: for all their similarity to, and even dependence on, the graded hierarchies of being that we find in the neo-Platonic systems, Denys is using them for another purpose. Denys does not believe in emanation. As a Christian, he believes in the doctrine of creation out of nothing by God. We do not receive our *being* from other creatures higher than us in the hierarchies, we are created immediately by God. Emanation, for Denys, seems to be ultimately a matter of light, illumination, and revelation, *not* of being. The hierarchical orders are only God's revealers and messengers. The theological principle behind Denys' apophatic theology is that each being is immediate to God in virtue of its creation by God. In union with God through ecstatic love, this immediate relationship is realized, or experienced.[19]

We might express this by saying that the hierarchies (and cataphatic theology) are concerned with God's manifestation of Himself in and through and to the cosmos. It is concerned with God's movement *outwards*. Apophatic theology is concerned with the secret, hidden relationship between the soul and God: it is concerned with the soul's movement *inwards* to God. Denys sometimes seems less clear than he might be on this because he uses one image only for the soul's movement Godwards, that of ascent. It is misleading because the most obvious ascent would be up the hierarchies, which is not at all what Denys is thinking of. An image that would have expressed his meaning better would have been that of movement *inwards* (an idea very common in Plotinus and Augustine). The soul is involved both in God's manifestation outwards through the soul and also in her own movement inwards into God; and the two are indissolubly linked. We have already seen that the soul's role within the hierarchy is to be as closely united as possible with that divine energy which establishes it in the hierarchy. The ultimate fulfilment of that role is by the way of apophatic, mystical union with God. Apophatic theology does not contradict cataphatic and symbolic theology. The movement inwards in no way detracts from God's movement outwards through the soul. The more deeply the soul is in God (ultimately in unknowable union) the more clearly and perfectly can it manifest the glory of God.

That is, then, in outline, Dionysian mysticism: a deeply significant mystical theology that puts the experience of mystical union with God in a context that preserves the fundamentally Christian insight that God is not the highest part of man, but beyond, transcendent — One who created all else out of nothing, essentially unknowable because of another order of reality altogether. But, alongside that, there is a deep awareness of the immanence of God in creation, for each created being depends immediately on God for its very being: 'Everything and any part of anything participates in the One, and on the existence of the One everything depends for its

---

[19] For all this, see von Ivánka's important article, 'Inwieweit ist Pseudo-Dionysius neuplatoniker?', reprinted in *Plato Christianus*, 262–89.

existence' (*DN* XIII.2: 977 C). This assertion of the immanence of God underlies the doctrine of the divine names.

Denys also gives us the idea of the cosmos as a glittering
sequence of hierarchies all serving to express and effect the
assimilation of all things in God. The lower part of this
hierarchy — the ecclesiastical — which takes up even the
material and sensible into assimilation to God, provides a
basis for the sacramental system. His *Ecclesiastical Hierarchy* is
the first example, so far as I know, of a genre very characteristic of Byzantine theology: a commentary on the liturgy, deeply
sensitive to the value of ritual and symbol, that represents the
interpenetration of the divine and human in the worship of
God. Later examples are the commentaries on the liturgy by
the fourteenth-century Nicholas Cabasilas and the
nineteenth-century Nicolai Gogol.

In conclusion, there is an essential connection between the
apophatic theology of the inexpressible and unutterable God
dwelling in the Divine Darkness, and the glittering array of
symbols, both spiritual and material, of the celestial and
ecclesiastical hierarchies. For, the assertion of the unknowability of God has radical significance for Denys. All symbols
and images are to be denied to God; none, not even lofty and
spiritual ones, are ultimately privileged. Indeed, *they* can be
especially misleading. Denys prefers *anomoia symbola* — unlike
symbols. That being so, *all* symbols and images may be
affirmed of him. 'God is known in all things, and apart from
all things . . .' (*DN* VII.3: 872 A). 'Therefore everything may
be ascribed to Him at one and the same time, and yet He is
none of these things' (*DN* V.8: 824 B).

Apophatic theology and symbolic theology — or iconic
theology, as we may call it — are two sides of the same coin.
Nowhere was that implication of the radical transcendence of
the God of the Christians, a God who creates out of nothing,
so clearly recognized as in Byzantium. And so, for all his deep
and diverse importance in the West, it is there that Denys
finds his true home.

IX. PATRISTIC MYSTICISM AND ST. JOHN OF THE CROSS

WE have traced the story of the origins of Christian mystical theology up to the figure of Denys the Areopagite. If we break off the story there it is not because the story in any way finishes with him but because by the time of Denys the various mystical traditions which the Patristic period bequeathed to later ages have all emerged.

We have seen, of these various mystical traditions, first in chapters four and five: Origen's mysticism of light, followed by Gregory of Nyssa's mysticism of divine darkness and, in between them, the anti-mysticism of Athansius' theology — of crucial importance in the conflict between Platonism and Christianity. Then, in chapter six, we have seen the traditions which prevailed in monastic circles, especially two sharply divergent ones, Evagrianism and Messalianism, Evagrius following the intellectualist tradition of the great Alexandrine theologians of the second and third century, Clement and Origen, while making of it another and intensely practical tradition, of precise help to the monk in the ordering of his life; and Messalianism, not at all intellectualist — even at times crudely materialistic — but nevertheless valued by the Eastern monks for its great stress on the primacy of prayer. And we have further seen how these two, apparently utterly diverse, traditions converge in the mystical theology of Diadochus of Photicē, and how the Patristic age thus bequeaths to later monasticism in the East the fruitful tensions arising from them.

In the same chapter, we noted that the Evagrian tradition was introduced to the West by John Cassian, but considerably modified in both its speculative and contemplative aspects so that it was Evagrius, the practical spiritual director, who was made known in the Latin world. And it is in this world that we find with Augustine the tradition of trinitarian mysticism — the ascent of the triune soul to the Triune God — which is to be the peculiar treasure of the Latin West and destined to influence profoundly the mystical theology of the Middle Ages. Finally, with Denys, we have seen a quite different tradition emerge, one which had its roots in Philo and reached Denys through Gregory of Nyssa: the ascent of the soul into the divine darkness.

Here we have, then, the 'basic patterns of thought which later theologians will take for granted'.[1] Beyond them all we have seen the fundamental co-inherence of mystical and dogmatic theology which, in the West, scarcely survived beyond St. Anselm in the eleventh century, for in the twelfth century, and notably in St. Bernard, we see a wedge being driven between heart and head.[2]

All that is another story, but there is one point we might well raise here. This book has been concerned with the origins of the Christian mystical tradition, and there is no doubt that the developments in the Patristic period influenced later Christian mystical theology. But what sort of an influence is it? Is it a purely literary influence — the influence of ideas and images — or is there a genuine continuity between the mysticism of the Fathers and the great flowering of mysticism in the later Middle Ages and beyond? For, when we think of Christian mysticism, it is usually of this period that we think — at least in the West — and in particular of the teaching of the great Carmelite mystics of the sixteenth century, St. Teresa of Ávila and St. John of the Cross. We are indeed encouraged in this by the fact that they have both been declared doctors of the Church, John of the Cross himself being designated *doctor mysticus*, the mystical doctor. If this is Christian mysticism, does the mystical theology we have discussed in this book, the mysticism of the Fathers, belong to it?

---

[1] xi, above.
[2] See my article, 'Bernard and Affective Mysticism', in *The Influence of St. Bernard*, ed. Sr Benedicta Ward (Fairacres Publications 60, 1976), 1–10.

Divine Darkness and the Dark Night

This is a question which cannot be treated exhaustively here, but there is one issue we can make the centre of our discussion. We have seen in some of the Fathers the doctrine that as the soul approaches God it is plunged into the Divine Darkness where God dwells. This appears to bear some similarity to the doctrine of the Dark Night of the soul that is central to the mystical theology of St. John of the Cross. How closely related are these two doctrines: the Patristic doctrine of the Divine Darkness and the sanjuanist doctrine of the Dark Night of the Soul? Opinions differ and differ very widely. It is, however, an indisputable *fact* that the medieval tradition which culminates in the Dark Night of St. John of the Cross was fertilized by the writings of Denys the Areopagite and especially his *Mystical Theology*. St. John himself often quotes him in support of his discussion. Can we simply say, then, that the Divine Darkness tradition which we find running through Philo, Gregory of Nyssa, and culminating in Denys is absolutely *identical* with St. John's Dark Night?

As we shall see, there are problems with this view. None the less, Daniélou, in his work on Gregory of Nyssa's mystical theology, *Platonisme et théologie mystique*, relates Gregory to St. John of the Cross without hesitation. He speaks of a night of the senses and a night of the spirit,[3] and finds a very sanjuanist mysticism in Gregory — though he says that Gregory has more of Bernard's *suavitas* than St. John.[4] But others are more cautious. H.-C. Puech, in an important article,[5] 'La ténèbre mystique chez le pseudo-Denys', concludes his discussion of the theme of divine darkness in Patristic and especially Dionysian theology by making four points. First, the 'Night' spoken of in the Bible (in the Moses account and so forth) does spark off the mystical 'dark night'. However, in the Fathers it appears only as an allegorical theme illustrating a dogmatic point. It remains abstract and theoretical. The Cloud, the Darkness, the Night do not appear to correspond to the immanent symbols of mystical experience; they are, rather, external and occasional motifs, used by

[3] See, e.g., 134
[4] 224.
[5] *Études carmélitaines*, 23, II (1938), 33–53.

doctrinal speculation anxious to mark the limits, or to fix certain necessary modalities, of the mystical vision of God.

Secondly, Puech says, the language of Divine Darkness does have a peculiar place within Judaeo-Christian monotheistic mysticism. In pagan thought, on the other hand, darkness in one's approach to God is transient and has a pejorative significance. It is due only to matter, the body, the senses, with which the soul is entangled. But, according to Philo and Christian mystics, the Divine Darkness bears witness to the radical disproportion between the created subject and the transcendent object of its vision.

Thirdly, Denys' *Mystical Theology* belongs to this Patristic tradition. And in it, words for darkness like *gnophos* and *skotos* are theoretical in import and do not bear witness to any experience. The dramatic and affective character of the Night of the later mystics is missing, nor does purificatory love seem to characterize its fundamental nature.

Fourthly, if one wants to find something closer to the concrete content of St. John's Dark Night, one must look rather to Origen's experience of the alternation of exaltation and dryness in the 'spiritual marriage', or to Gregory of Nyssa, who, says Puech, depicts the loving and desperate pursuit for the Infinite God with an accent and an emotion which can only arise out of genuine experience.

Broadly speaking, then, Puech's point is that language about the Divine Darkness in the Fathers, and especially in Denys, is not really the same as language about the Dark Night in later mystics such as St. John of the Cross; and so St. John's Dark Night does not derive directly from Denys. His main argument in favour of this conclusion is the contrast between the theoretical character of Patristic language about the Divine Darkness and the dramatic, affective character of the language of St. John of the Cross. On that point, however, we must enter a query and a qualification. For this contrast is not simply between the language of the Fathers and St. John of the Cross on the Dark Night; it is a contrast between the whole style of Patristic writing and that of late medieval and Renaissance literature. We have already noted, when contrasting the Eastern Fathers and Augustine, the objective, theoretical character of Eastern mystical theology. Personal language is rare.[6] But this does not mean — obviously it does not mean — that they *had* no experiences, only that it was not their way to talk about them. As we have seen above, truth, for the Fathers generally, was to be found in Scripture and therefore their theology took the form of exposition of Scripture. An appeal to experience, convincing for us and for most Westerners, did not have the same importance for them. The difference that leads Puech to postulate a difference between Patristic thought on Divine Darkness and St. John on the Dark Night is, in fact, a difference of genre more general than he suggests. If we are to judge on that criterion alone we must pronounce *non liquet*.

The problem of the origins of the theme of the Dark Night in St. John's sense is indeed very difficult. Whatever its roots in Patristic mysticism, what we find in St. John of the Cross has been influenced by a medieval development which provided a different context for Denys' apophaticism. For Denys, as we have seen, in ecstasy the soul transcends the intellect, and in that way negates it: but the intellect is only rejected because it is *no longer* useful, not because it is of no use at all. On the contrary, the stage of intellectual purification can only be accomplished by means of the intellect. During the Middle Ages there develops the idea that the mystical organ in the soul is not intellectual at all but *affective*: it is in virtue of the *principalis affectio*, which is the *apex mentis*, the summit of the mind, that the soul has contact with the divine. In the context of such a tradition, the teaching of Denys's *Mystical Theology* takes on a different light: the insistence that the intellect must be transcended is interpreted as a rejection of the intellect in favour of the will or feeling. So we find in the *Cloud of Unknowing*, which is a good example of the influence of Denys on medieval mysticism, the dictum: 'by love he can be gotten and holden, but by thought never.'[7] St. John is in contact with this tradition[8] and it must have influenced his understanding of the Dark Night of the Soul. Part of this

---

[6] Cf. I. Hausherr, 'Les Orientaux connaissent-ils les "nuits" de S. Jean de la Croix', *Hesychasme et prière*, 95: 'Ce qui rend la réponse plus difficile, c'est que la spiritualité orientale répugne profondément aux autobiographies.'

[7] See E. von Ivánka, *Plato Christianus*, 309–85.

[8] See *Medieval Mystical Tradition and St. John of the Cross*, by a Benedictine of Stanbrook Abbey (London, 1954).

influence can be seen in the way such a development of affective mysticism serves to emphasize the contrast between the theoretical character of Patristic mysticism and the dramatic and affective character of later Western mysticism which we have already noticed. But the question is really, what is the significance of this difference? Is it simply a matter of style, or does it go deeper? It is worth mentioning in this context that, in contrast with much medieval mysticism, St. John does not work with a contrast between the knowledge of God (which cannot lead to union with Him) and the love of God (which can effect such union): the Dark Night is the dark night of *faith* when images and concepts are stripped from the intellect as part of its preparation for union.[9]

One way of posing the question is to take the central point being made by the Patristic theology of the Divine Darkness, namely, that this is a symbol of the radical distance between the created soul and the Uncreated God, and ask how far this is central to the theology of the Dark Night of St. John of the Cross. If we try and transpose this into the language of Western mysticism, it might be taken to mean that the Dark Night is the soul's experience of the absolute transcendence of God. In other words, that in the Dark Night the soul is learning to know the infinite God, and the pain and distress of this learning is because the soul, naturally finite, is being prepared for an experience that is beyond its natural powers.

Is this what the Dark Night of the Soul means for St. John of the Cross? In the *Dark Night* (Book II, chapter v) St. John explains that 'this dark night is an inflow of God into the soul, which purges it of its habitual ignorances and imperfections, natural and spiritual, and which contemplatives call infused contemplation or mystical theology' (II.v.1).[10] It is an inflow of divine light into the soul which purifies it and prepares it for union with God. But, St. John of the Cross goes on to ask, why is it called a dark *night*, if it is in fact the illuminating and purifying presence of divine *light*? He replies thus:

[9] A point made by J. P. H. Clark, 'The "Cloud of Unknowing", Walter Hilton and St. John of the Cross: A Comparison', *Downside Review* (Oct. 1978), 285.

[10] All quotations from St. John of the Cross are taken from *The Collected Works of St. John of the Cross*, translated by K. Kavanaugh and O. Rodriguez (Nelson, 1966).

In answer to this, there are two reasons why this divine wisdom is not only night and darkness for the soul, but also affliction and torment. First, because of the height of the divine wisdom which exceeds the capacity of the soul. Second, because of the soul's baseness and impurity; and on this account it is painful, afflictive, and also dark for the soul. (II.v.2)

The first reason does correspond to the basic motif behind the Patristic theme of the Divine Darkness, but not the second. Not that the Fathers lack any sense of the seriousness of sin, but it is not involved in their understanding of the Divine Darkness in which the soul finds itself close to God. For Gregory of Nyssa, for example, the soul begins in a kind of darkness, the darkness of ignorance and sin, but as it responds to God it experiences illumination. The entry into the Divine Darkness is a further stage, beyond that of purification from sin.

There is clearly a contrast here between St. John of the Cross and the Fathers, but this contrast is misunderstood if we simply say that for the Fathers the Divine Darkness is due to human finitude, whereas for St. John the Dark Night is due not just to human finitude, but also to sin. For the doctrine of St. John of the Cross is more radical than such a summary suggests: it is not that sin causes the Dark Night, but rather that the Dark Night discloses the soul's sinfulness. In reality we do not begin the search for God with a genuine sense of sin; often enough what we take for a sense of sin is only a sense of failure, or wounded pride. Rather it is as we draw close to God that we begin to realize the depths of our sinfulness. And for St. John of the Cross we draw close to God in being called upon to relinquish ways of prayer and devotion that give satisfaction in themselves and, out of love for God in Himself, to enter on the night of contemplation. So John says:

The first and chief benefit of this dry and dark night of contemplation is the knowledge of self and of one's own misery. Besides the fact that all the favours God imparts to the soul are ordinarily enwrapped in this knowledge, the aridities and voids of the faculties in relation to the abundance previously experienced, and the difficulty encountered in the practice of virtue, make the soul recognize its own lowliness and misery, which was not apparent in the time of its prosperity. (*Dark Night* I.xii.2)

Nor is it adequate to say of the Father's understanding of
the Divine Darkness that it is simply the finite soul's experience of the infinite transcendence of God. For with all the
Fathers we have been that the mystic ascent is a result of the
soul's longing for God as He is in Himself. The love that the
soul has for God cannot be satisfied with anything less than
God and the soul passes into the Divine Darkness as it
relinquishes the comfort of anything less than God, and seeks
God alone. For the Fathers such a pure love is only possible
when the soul has relinquished sin and freed itself from the
attraction of sin to devote itself to God alone. It is a *purified*
love that enters into the Divine Darkness, whereas for St. John
of the Cross it is in the Dark Night that the soul experiences
purifying love: is this then the contrast between St. John of the
Cross and the Fathers?

Perhaps it is, but if so, what we have here is, it seems to me,
a difference of perspective rather than anything more fundamental. It is the contrast we have noted already between St.
John's more introspective, experiential approach and the
objective, theoretical character of Patristic theology. St. John
of the Cross is discussing the soul's experience as it seeks God
in love; St. Gregory of Nyssa, for example, is discussing what
is involved, at an 'objective', theological level, in the soul's
loving pursuit of God. It is only a purified love that can attain
God — so Gregory; it is only in being purified that the loving
soul is prepared for union with God — so St. John of the
Cross. It is a difference of perspective, and once this difference
is granted it is not difficult to find the characteristic emphases
of each in the other. Thus, Gregory knows that the closer the
soul comes to God, the more it is aware of sinfulness and the
necessity for purification (though he does not dwell on it):

Even after that complete stripping of herself she still finds something
further to remove. So it is with our ascent towards God: each stage
that we reach always reveals something heavy weighing on the soul.
Thus in comparison with her new-found purity, that very stripping
of her tunic now becomes a kind of garment which those who find
her must once again remove.   (*Comm. on the Song* XII: 1029)

And he goes on to explain this in terms of the 'beating and
wounding' of the bride spoken of in the Song of Songs. For St.

John the greatest suffering the soul experiences in the Night is just before it is united to God, and in his explanation of this he seems to dwell on the soul's experience of an intolerable emptiness — an emptiness experienced because it has now been totally purified and is ready to experience the infinite unfathomableness of God. St. John speaks of the 'deep caverns of feeling' within the soul, and says:

> It is an amazing thing that the least of these goods is enough so to encumber these faculties, capable of infinite goods, that they cannot receive these infinite goods until they are completely empty, as we shall see. Yet when these caverns are empty and pure [namely, when the soul is in complete detachment] the thirst, hunger, and yearning of the spiritual feeling is intolerable. Since they have deep cavities they suffer profoundly, for the food they lack, which as I say is God, is also profound.   (*Living Flame of Love*, Stanza III.18)

This is the experience of darkness and emptiness of *purified* love. In the Dark Night the soul is purified and prepared for union with God, and the fundamental nature of this Night is perhaps most clearly revealed when its purpose is on the verge of being achieved — the subject of the *Living Flame*

It is, however, the case that many Eastern Orthodox writers find in St. John of the Cross something quite foreign to their own tradition — which for them is a tradition stretching back to that of the Fathers. It may be, then, that we are touching here on an area where there is a fundamental contrast between the ways of East and West. So Vladimir Lossky writes that 'both the heroic attitude of the great saints of Western Christendom, a prey to the sorrow of a tragic separation from God, and the dark night of the soul considered as a way, as a spiritual necessity, are unknown in the spirituality of the Eastern Church.'[11] In a series of articles, now published as a book, [12] Mme Myrrha Lot-Borodine finds very much the same contrast between Eastern and Western spirituality that Lossky indicates. It is a contrast between a passionate, tortured devotion to the sufferings of our Lord's sacred humanity in the West and a more austere, serene

---

[11] *The Mystical Theology of the Eastern Church* (London, 1957), 226; though cf. his modifying remarks, 227 n.
[12] *La Déification de l'homme* (Paris, 1970).

devotion to the royal Victor in the Byzantine East[13] – the contrast between the crucified Christ in Matthias Grünewald's *Isenheim Altarpiece* and the figures in an icon by Andrei Rublyov. The Byzantine (and Russian) East continues the tradition of the Fathers; but in the West the Church began to depart from this tradition with Augustine, and with him Mme Lot-Borodine finds the beginnings of a new tradition guided by poignant personal experience.[14]

The Western Christian's reaction to this is probably to find such language rather startling and not altogether convincing. In the *Ascent of Mount Carmel* St. John does devote a chapter (II.7) to the way of the Cross, but it is difficult to find here the tortured devotion of which Mme Lot-Borodine speaks. None the less there is some sort of a contrast here, even if it is not fully present in any particular individual: the contrast between Grünewald and Rublyov does seem typical, indicating a contrast between (to use her own words) 'tout l'inépuisable trésor de la sensibilité pathétique' of the West and a Byzantine 'frisson sacré'.

For Mme Lot-Borodine the fundamental theological point at issue between these two traditions is the question of synergism. The idea that at every point the soul works together with God is for her basic to the mystical theology of the Eastern Church[15] and stands in marked contrast to the Western, Augustinian doctrine of grace, according to which the soul does not work *with* God so much as simply responds to his prevenient action. Such synergism is optimistic in that there is no doubt that God will support the efforts of the soul and thus it is to be contrasted both with the 'sterile fatalism' of gnosticism and also with the 'anguished distress of Saint Augustine which has left an indelible mark on the whole of Christian Europe.'[16] It is this contrast between synergism and an Augustinian doctrine of grace which Mme Lot-Borodine discerns behind the East's rejection of the peculiarly Western doctrine of the Immaculate Conception of our Lady,[17] rather than the way in which this doctrine seems to presuppose an

---

[13] Ibid. 61–6.   [14] 29, 49 f.
[15] 86 ff.; cf. Lossky, op. cit., 197 ff.   [16] *La Déification*, 87.
[17] See Daniélou's introduction to Lot-Borodine's book, 15.

Augustinian notion of inherited, original sin. For her the Immaculate Conception expresses the idea that Mary's response to God was purely due to her preparation in grace; it is an outright rejection of the possibility of synergism and thus incompatible with Eastern Orthodox theology.

A contrast between synergism and a radical doctrine of grace: it is this that Mme Lot-Borodine sees at the heart of the contrast between Eastern and Western theology. And, in general terms, such a contrast may be allowed; in Western and especially Protestant theology 'synergism' often carries overtones of 'Pelagianism' or, at least, 'semi-Pelagianism'. But has this anything to do with the contrast between the mysticism of the Dark Night of St. John of the Cross and Eastern mystical theology, as Lossky suggests when he singles out the idea of the Dark Night as symbolic of the radical difference between East and West? Perhaps it has, for central to St. John's understanding of the Dark Night is the idea that here the soul is being purified so as to be capable of a pure response to God. St. John of the Cross lays great stress on the soul's learning to be passive, at any rate as the Dark Night deepens, a passivity, to be sure, that is the fruit of great effort, but still a passivity that gives the impression that the soul is not so much working with God (syn-ergism) as becoming purely transparent to Him.[18] In one passage St. John expounds this notion of the soul's passivity by means of the analogy of an artist painting a portrait, an analogy we have already found used several times in the Patristic tradition:

If a person should desire to do something himself with his interior faculties, he would hinder and lose the goods which God engraves upon his soul through that peace and idleness. If a model for a painting or retouching of a portrait should move because of a desire to do something, the artist would be unable to finish, and his work would be disturbed. Similarly any operation, affection or advertency a soul might desire when it wants to abide in interior peace and idleness, would cause distraction and disquietude, and make it feel sensory dryness and emptiness.   (*Dark Night* I.x.5)

[18] Lossky sees in the idea of the *passive* parts of the Dark Night something quite foreign to Denys and the rest of the Patristic tradition (*In the Image and Likeness of God* (1974), 38), but this seems to me to be an over-simplification, see above 174 f.

For Macarius[19] the point of the analogy of the portrait painter is that the soul be *attentive*; for St. John it is that the soul be *still*. So perhaps to see the contrast between Eastern synergism and a Western doctrine of pure response to grace being worked out in St. John's doctrine of the Dark Night is justified.

All the same, it would seem to me to be a difference of emphasis. For there is no fundamental contrast between the idea of our responding to God and the idea of our working with God. There would indeed be such a contrast if God were external to me, if God were not the One who has created me and holds me in being, if God were not *interior intimo meo*. But, in responding to God, 'in whose service is perfect freedom', I find true freedom and so become a fellow-worker (*synergos*) with God. It is a paradox that St. Paul lays hold of when he says, 'Work out your own salvation with fear and trembling. For it is God which worketh in you both to will and to do of his good pleasure': here the ideas of our own effort, God's grace, and the fact that the fruits of our efforts in obedience are the work of God, both at the level of deed and at the deeper level of the inspiring will, are united. Here is true synergism that cannot be opposed to the idea of response.

There may, however, be a difference of *style* according to whether one is influenced by teaching on synergism or response as keys to interpret mystical experience, and these different styles draw out different areas of mystical experience. If East and West display different styles in the way they explain the same experience of the soul's engagement with God, this is but evidence of a tension within a deeper unity, and suggests that East and West have much to learn from one another here.

---

[19] See above, 121, and cf. Diadochus' use of the same analogy, 130 above.

X.   THE MYSTICAL LIFE AND THE MYSTICAL BODY

In almost any discussion of Christian mysticism there arises the question as to its uniqueness: what is the relationship between Christian mysticism and other forms of mysticism? Evelyn Underhill spoke of the mystics' 'impassioned love of the Absolute . . . which transcends the dogmatic language in which it is clothed and becomes applicable to mystics of every race and creed':[1] at its core all mysticism is one. Such an opinion is very widespread, so much so, that R. Zaehner remarked that it had become a platitude to say that all mysticism is 'essentially one and the same',[2] a platitude he went on to question. In the context of a discussion of Patristic mystical theology the problem is effectively narrowed down to that of the influence on Patristic mysticism of the Platonic tradition, which is fundamentally mystical, especially in the form the Fathers encountered it. This is a matter we raised in our introduction.

Platonism and Mysticism

The issue is not so much whether the mystical theology of the Fathers has been influenced by Platonism, for clearly it has. 'When the Fathers "think" their mysticism, they platonize',[3] Père Festugière rightly says. The issue comes to the surface in his next sentence: 'There is nothing original in the edifice.' For him the mysticism of the Fathers is pure Platonism.

---

[1] *Mysticism* (London, 1940), 86.
[2] *Mysticism — Sacred and Profane* (Oxford, 1957), x.
[3] *Contemplation*, 5.

The charge that the mystical strain in Christianity is alien to Christianity is a charge frequently made. Perhaps the most elaborate, and certainly the most influential, presentation of this case is that of Anders Nygren in his book, *Agape and Eros*.[4] For Nygren mysticism is an incursion of the *eros* motif into Christianity, where it is quite alien because Christianity is grounded purely in the *agape* motif:

> The thought of the mystical vision of God, for instance, which is one of the more prominent features of Eros religion, has always been able to attach itself to the text, 'Blessed are the pure in heart, for they shall see God', without any notice being taken of the deep cleavage between the mystical and the eschatological vision of God, of which alone the text speaks and which is only another way of speaking about perfected fellowship with God.[5]

Nygren's own theory is too highly wrought and too detailed to be discussed here.[6] It will be more profitable to discuss Festugière's very similar case, which is more specifically related to the mysticism of the Fathers. This can be found in three short articles published together in the volume, *L'Enfant d'Agrigente*.[7]

In the first two of these articles, Père Festugière records his impression of the utter contrast between the religious ideals of Hellenistic religions and of Christianity;[8] and as one of the greatest living authorities on Hellenistic religion such an opinion is not lightly to be set aside. The Hellenistic religions are concerned with seeing God and understanding mysteries; Christianity is simply concerned with following Jesus, and the only mystery is love, *agape*. In the third article, 'Ascèse et Contemplation', Festugière applies this to the mysticism of the Fathers. In contrast to the truly Christian spirituality of the evangelists and the apostles, Ignatius, Irenaeus, the martyrs, all the great monastic founders, the heroes of the *Apophthegmata*, Basil, John Chrysostom, Jerome, Cassian, and

---

[4] Translated by P. S. Watson (London, 1957).
[5] 228 f.
[6] There are discussions of Nygren's thesis in M. C. D'Arcy, *The Mind and Heart of Love* (London, 1945) *passim*, and John Burnaby, *Amor Dei* (London, 1938), ch. 1, 'The Embarrassment of the Anti-Mystic', 3–21.
[7] Paris, 1950. Briefly discussed by V. Lossky in *The Vision of God* (London, 1963), 39.   [8] 110–26, and 127–33.

Benedict, he finds another tradition of what he calls 'philosophical spirituality'. 'The origin of this movement is quite clear: it is the Alexandrine school, Clement and Origen. And the links in the chain can be easily discerned: in the East they are all the teachers of contemplation, Evagrius, Gregory of Nyssa, Diadochus of Photicē, Pseudo-Denys; and in the West, Augustine and (to the extent that he follows Augustine) Gregory the Great.'[9] This tradition of 'philosophical spirituality' is not necessarily anti-Christian, but it is essentially independent of Christianity. It betrays its independence in that it is a form of mysticism: 'to be perfect is to contemplate and that is to see God in an immediate vision';[10] it is intellectualist or super-intellectualist: in other words, in contemplation (*theoria*) the mind (*nous*) is united with God, or goes out of itself in ecstasy to find union with God; and finally it presents as an ideal a form of life that is exclusively contemplative and has no place for action, even if that action is inspired by love. What this amounts to is the assertion that the philosophical spirituality of these Fathers is simply a variant of Platonist mysticism — 'there is nothing original in the edifice' — and, further, that the fundamental fault of such mystical spirituality is that the purely contemplative nature of this mysticism excludes Christian love or *agape*. Is this in fact the case?

First of all let us remind ourselves what Platonic mysticism looks like. Man, it says, lives in a transient world of sensible phenomena and of conjecture, or opinion, based on it. But his soul belongs to a higher, truer world which is eternal and immutable. To regain its kinship with that world the soul must purify itself from this world; it must seek to die to this world, to live now the life it hopes it may lead after death. This purification has two sides: moral and intellectual. Moral purification will restore to the soul transcendence over the body; the body will cease to disturb its endeavours after contemplation. Intellectual purification, or dialectic, trains the soul in abstract thought; it weans the soul from dependence on the world of sense and accustoms it to the more austere, but also more real because eternal, world of the

[9] 141.   [10] 142.

Forms or Ideas. When the soul has sufficiently purified itself it may — suddenly and without warning — attain contemplation, *theoria*, of the highest of the Forms, the Beautiful or the Good, for which it has longed. In this gratuitous act of *theoria* the whole world of ultimate reality is seen as a single whole, and the meaning even of sensible reality becomes clear. This sudden ultimate act of *theoria* is experienced as ecstasy: the soul seems to transcend itself, to be rapt out of itself. At the same time, this ecstasy is a sort of *home-coming*. The soul becomes what it truly is in its deepest self; its kinship with ultimate reality becomes something experienced. In Plotinus we find all this with two refinements: the ascent of the soul is seen more as withdrawal into itself than as ascent; and secondly, the nature of ultimate reality — the One — is beyond the Forms instead of only equivocally so as in Plato's Idea of the Good, and is more clearly defined. This final ecstasy for Plotinus really transcends *theoria*: it is contact or presence or ecstasy, inexpressible and ineffable.

Now quite clearly what we have found in Patristic mysticism is very similar to this. Even intellectual dialectic finds a place:

We shall understand the method of purification by confession, and the visionary method by analysis, attaining to the primary intelligence by analysis, beginning at its basic principles. We take away from the body its natural qualities, removing the dimension of height, and then that of breadth and then that of length. The point that remains is a unit, as it were, having position; if we take away everything concerned with bodies and the things called incorporeal, and cast ourselves into the greatness of Christ, and so advance into the immeasurable by holiness, we might perhaps attain to the conception of the Almighty, knowing not what He is but what He is not.   (Clement of Alexandria, *Stromateis* V.11.71)

And there are other examples.

But though we can see Patristic mysticism taking its cue from Platonist mysticism when it tries to achieve intellectual expression — and such is hardly surprising — it seems to me that at several points this intellectual background is modified. Let us consider three points: first, the concept of God; second, the idea of the soul's relationship to God; and third, the understanding of the moral virtues.

First, the concept of God. In Plato himself there is no clear and unequivocal concept of God at all. The summit of the soul's quest, the Idea of the Good and the Beautiful, is certainly the highest and most ultimate being and gives form and meaning to everything else. But whether one can call this God is uncertain. For, to call it God is to suggest that it is some sort of personal, even if supra-personal, being; and it is not clear that Plato's Good is this. With Plotinus we can more obviously regard the One as God — though he does not characteristically use *theos* of the One. Even so, we have to recognize that for Plotinus the One transcends any personal categories; it is unconscious even of itself, let alone of anything outside of itself. It is the object of the soul's quest; but it is not actively involved in that quest.

Now it is true that God's impassibility is an important premiss in the theology of the Fathers. But, even so, in their mystical theology we find that, though God's impassibility is not explicitly denied, the Fathers feel compelled to use personal language of God that consorts ill with it. For the Platonists God is an impersonal (or supra-personal) ultimate principle; for the Fathers God is a Person. It is not an experience of ultimacy they are concerned with, but an experience of God. God is not unconscious of the soul's quest for Him, but actively engaged on the soul's behalf in her quest. The concept of grace, present though it is in a sense in Platonist and neo-Platonist mysticism, is much more vivid in Patristic mysticism. In Platonist mysticism it is no more than the firmly held belief that mystical experience is not something the soul can achieve, but something that comes upon it.[11]. In Christian mysticism grace is God's gift to the soul of communion with Himself, without which not even the soul's search for God would be possible.

The extent to which the concept of God is immeasurably enlarged and a thoroughly Christian understanding of grace introduced can be seen — paradoxically enough — in the two Fathers we have discussed who are most indebted to neo-Platonism: Augustine and Denys. Augustine's account of his

---

[11] Festugière points out the inadequacy of the notion of grace in Platonist mysticism (op. cit. 131 f.), but he does not inquire how far this understanding of grace is held by the Fathers.

discovery of God in Book X of the *Confessions* begins in a very Platonist vein. God is supreme, eternal Beauty:

Late have I loved Thee, O Beauty so ancient and so new; late have I loved Thee! For behold Thou wert within me, and I outside; and I sought Thee outside and in my loveliness fell upon those lovely things that Thou hast made. Thou wert with me, and I was not with Thee. I was kept from Thee by those things, yet had they not been in Thee, they would not have been at all . . .

All this could be paralleled in Plotinus, but not the continuation:

Thou didst call and cry to me and break open my deafness: and Thou didst send forth Thy beams and shine upon me and chase away my blindness: Thou didst breathe fragrance upon me, and I drew in my breath and do now pant for Thee: I tasted Thee, and now hunger and thirst for Thee: Thou didst touch me, and I have burned for Thy peace.

This is not Plotinus' One, unconscious of itself and of the soul's quest for itself. When Augustine finds God, he finds One who is most urgently searching for him and it is only because of God's initiative that he has been able to find Him at all. Similarly, in Denys the Areopagite we have the idea of *God's* ecstasy:

We must dare to add this as being no less true that the Source of all things Himself, in His wonderful and good love for all things, through the excess of His loving goodness, is carried outside Himself, in His providential care for all that is, so enchanted is He in goodness and love and longing. Removed from His position above all and beyond all He descends to be in all according to an ecstatic and transcendent power which is yet inseparable from Himself.

(*Divine Names* IV.13: 712AB)

Clearly Denys wants to preserve the idea of God's serenity and impassibility, and so the idea of God's ecstasy is paradoxical; yet still he must affirm it. The soul's ecstatic love for God is her response to God's love for herself. It is the desire to affirm a genuinely personal grace in God that leads the Fathers to qualify the Platonist concept of the divine.

This can, and indeed must, be put more strongly. The Fathers' emphasis on grace in their mysticism is derived from their experience of the love of the *Incarnate* Christ. For the Platonist mysticism is about the soul's withdrawal and ascent; for the Christian it is about the soul's response to God's descent and condescension in the Incarnation. Grace is not just the soul's awareness that it is experiencing something beyond its own powers, it is God's love for man which underlies the very possibility of man's response in love.

We find similarly that the understanding of the soul's relationship to God is modified and rethought. For Plato the soul was divine, it was akin to the divine realm of the Forms, it belonged there. The soul's ascent was a process of becoming what it most truly was, of realizing its innate divinity. So it was thought of as divinization, assimilation to God. Such language we find in the Fathers, and it is very important to them. In Origen we have seen that there is a real kinship between the *Logos* and the soul, and both are eternal. But it is precisely this aspect of Origenism that is so unacceptable to most of his successors (Evagrius being a notable exception). From Athanasius onwards there is the necessity of working out the consequences of the peculiarly Christian notion of *creatio ex nihilo*. With Athanasius this leads to an anti-mystical tendency. But then, in different ways, there follow attempts to think through a mysticism which does not infringe this fundamentally Christian insight into the relationship between the Creator God and his creatures. With Gregory of Nyssa and Denys they lead to the theme of the Divine Darkness — a theme without parallel in Platonism. So, far from the Fathers swallowing uncritically the Platonist premiss of the soul's kinship with the divine, they have, on the contrary, a clear perception of its fundamental foreignness to the Christian understanding of the creature's relationship to God. And this leads them to real originality in a mysticism which remains faithful both to experience and to the radical doctrine of *creatio ex nihilo*. Platonists spoke of 'becoming like God as much as is possible', but for them the qualification 'as much as is possible' referred to the limitation imposed by the soul's inhabiting a body. With Christians it is a radical qualification indicating the fundamentally creaturely mode of divinization proper to humanity.

Thirdly, there is the understanding of the moral virtues. For the Platonists the moral virtues are the ways in which the soul controls the body so as to be as free from it as possible. They are essentially purificatory. And this idea is strengthened and emphasized in Plotinus who draws a distinction between civic and purificatory virtues — only the latter being of significance for the soul's mystic quest. But within Christian theology the moral virtues are the fruits of the Spirit, the evidences of the indwelling of Christ in the soul of the Christian. To the Platonist, virtues seen as purificatory have a purely negative significance: they effect in a moral way the separation of soul and body which will be finally brought about by death. But for the Christian, seen as fruits of the Spirit, evidence of the indwelling Christ, virtues are positive: they are that in virtue of which the soul is becoming divinized. They still have purificatory significance for the Fathers — for, to cultivate the virtues is to extirpate the corresponding vices — but they are more. So Gregory of Nyssa puts it like this:

It is impossible for the living Word to be present in us — I mean that pure, invisible Spouse who unites the soul to Himself by sanctity and incorruptibility — unless by the mortification of our bodies on earth we tear away the veil of the flesh, and in this way open the door to the Word that He may come and dwell in the soul.
(*Comm. on the Song* XII:1016 C)

The Fathers still readily use Platonist language but it is transfigured by the context in which they use it. So, in these three ways at least, Patristic mysticism transforms Platonist mysticism while finding its language and forms convenient to use.

Festugière's other — and more fundamental — point against the philosophical spirituality he detects in some of the Fathers is that it leads to a purely contemplative form of the Christian life that has no place for action even if inspired by love. He insists again and again that there is something fundamentally un-Christian about an understanding of *agape* that sees it as simply a means to an end. There he is right, but this criticism does not hold when the moral virtues are no longer seen simply as means to purify the soul so that it can contemplate, but as the fruits of the indwelling Christ; for fruits are not means but ends. The problem is that Festugière oversimplfies the Christian religion in seeing it as no more than moral imitation of Christ, thus canonizing a kind of Christianity which has little support in the New Testament. It is participation, not moral imitation, which stands at the centre in the New Testament. And behind Festugière's oversimplification there is, one suspects, an assumption that too easily opposes the contemplative and the active, and sees Christian *agape* as essentially active.

Just as theology and spirituality ought not to be separated, and are not in the Fathers, nor should contemplation and action be separated. Gregory of Nyssa's treatise on the Lord's Prayer provides a good example of the way in which the contemplative and the active are united in the Fathers; it is *because* prayer is contemplative that it flows out in acts of love. For Gregory prayer 'is intimacy with God and contemplation of the invisible. It satisfies our yearnings and makes us equal to the angels.'[12] Such prayer, however, implies not simply the individual's acts of love, but an awareness of the relationship of prayer to the social dimensions of Christian *agape*:

You are the master of your prayer if abundance does not come from another's property, and is not the result of another's tears; if no one is hungry or distressed because you are fully satisfied. For the bread of God is above all the fruit of justice, the ear of the corn of peace, pure and without any admixture of the seed of tares.[13]

Realization of the social dimension of Christian love springs, for Gregory, from the experience of the society of angels, but also — as for all Christians — from something more.

The Communion of Saints

It is precisely here, as we perceive that contemplation and action are held together in Christian love, that we begin to discern what is truly distinctive in Christian mysticism, what it is that distinguishes it from Platonic mysticism and, indeed, from any non-Christian mysticism. For Christian love is the love of Christ which unites us to him and through him to one

[12] *The Lord's Prayer*, Sermon I: 1124 B (Graef translation, 24).
[13] Ibid., Sermon IV:1173 BC (Graef translation, 67), commenting on the petition, 'Give us this day our daily bread.'

another. And so Christian theology, and in particular Christian mystical theology, is ecclesial, it is the fruit of participation in the mystery of Christ, which is inseparable from the mystery of the Church.

Within the Platonic tradition the mystic is an individual, or at best the member of an intellectual élite; the whole business of moral, and especially intellectual, purification is something to be pursued by a small, cultured group with sufficient means to provide the leisure to devote to it. When Augustine retired to Cassiciacum this was the sort of enterprise he was engaged on; but it is noteworthy that it was a stage he passed through rapidly. For the Christian the mystical life is the flowering of the baptismal life, and baptism is incorporation into the Body of Christ, his Church. The contrast, then, is between the final vision of the *Enneads*, which beholds, as it were, the 'flight of the alone to the Alone', and the final vision of the Bible: 'After this I beheld, and lo, a great multitude, which no man could number . . .' (Rev. 7:9). The Christian mystic's search for God takes place within the Church and has no significance apart from the Church. Thus the author of the Epistle to the Hebrews, after extolling those who have embarked on the search for God, concludes: 'And all these, having obtained a good report through faith, received not the promise; God having provided some better thing for us, that they without us should not be made perfect' (Heb. 11:39 f.).

When we discussed Origen's interpretation of the Song of Songs as the relationship of the soul with God we thought of this as being the more mystical interpretation compared with the ecclesiological one found in Hippolytus. But there is, clearly, a mystical interpretation in the ecclesiological, and neither can be separated from the other, for the relationship of the bride to the Bridegroom is both singular and corporate, inasmuch as each individual soul baptized into Christ's Body *is* the whole Church while remaining uniquely personal. In recent theology no one, perhaps, has seen this more clearly than Hans Urs von Balthasar. The symbol of the bride and Bridegroom — love calling forth love — lies at the heart of this theology; but it is a symbol both of the soul accepting God's love and of the Church — in indissoluble unity. 'It is therefore clear', he says, that the one who receives the Word can never be the reader, the researcher, or the one who prays, in isolation. The 'key of know-ledge' (Lk. 11:52) is delivered by the bearer of the keys (Rev. 1:18) and the opener of the seals (Rev. 5:5) to him who symbolizes the Church (Mt. 16:19). And it is in his incorporation into the Church in the Spirit that the individual finds his meaning as individual, for we saw that the Church in her hidden core is an individual — 'anima *mea*', 'spiritus *meus*', 'beatam *me* dicant omnes' (Lk. 1:47 f.) — and therefore is the universal justification for the individual (but never the isolated one) in his decision of faith and love.[14]

The mutual co-inherence of the mystical and the ecclesiological is, indeed, a striking feature of the mystical theology of many of the Fathers, though it is a pervasive colouring rather than a specific theme. We noted this with Origen, for whom the Song of Songs is the song of the soul united with God, but also the song of the Church. For the Song of Songs is seen as the seventh and the highest of the songs of the Old Testament, the first of them being the Song of Moses, sung after the crossing of the Red Sea, which sym-bolizes baptism, incorporation into the Church, the Body of Christ. We have seen this co-inherence in Denys the Areopa-gite in our attempt to correlate his mystical theology and his doctrine of the hierarchies. It is, however, perhaps most developed in Gregory of Nyssa. In his two principal treatises on the mystical life we have what seems at first sight to be a single figure ascending to God — Moses, in *The Life of Moses*, and the bride, in the *Commentary on the Song of Songs*. But, if we look more carefully, we see that Moses is not solitary, he is ascending the mount on behalf of the people of God, and indeed in Gregory's *Life* is always surrounded by his people. Nor is the bride alone in her search for the Beloved, but accompanied by a band of maidens. Daniélou comments:

Thus the soul's ascent is never presented as a solitary ascent. The soul ascends surrounded by a retinue of other souls who are attached to her. The graces of sanctification which she receives she receives not for herself but that she may sanctify the others. The mystical graces have an apostolic purpose. They are all in a sense charismatic graces. To this apostolic aspect of the mystical life there corresponds inversely the mystical aspect of the apostolic life. By that I mean

[14] *Herrlichkeit: eine theologische Ästhetik*, III 2 (Einsiedeln, 1969), 93.

that it is above all in attaining personal sanctity that the soul becomes a source of grace for others. Thus sanctification, far from separating her from the others, is on the contrary that which enables her to serve them. The image which Gregory gives us is that of a soul wholly turned towards God, who only draws others to herself for the sake of him.[15]

It is a constant theme with the mystics of the Church. We might point to St. John of the Cross who says of the grace of contemplative union with God that 'a little of this pure love is more precious to God and the soul and more beneficial to the Church, even though it seems one is doing nothing, than all those other works put together' (*Spiritual Canticle*, Stanza 29, para. 2); or to St. Thérèse of Lisieux with her conviction that the contemplative vocation is the most fruitful of all *apostolates*. But we might also, and more fundamentally, point to the apostle Paul in whom we find a fully ecclesial mysticism, and an asceticism which is intrinsic to the mystical life and wholly for the sake of the Body: 'Now I rejoice in my sufferings for your sake, and in my flesh I complete what is lacking in Christ's afflictions for the sake of his Body, that is, the Church' (Col. 1:24).

St. Paul was one who had been caught up to the third heaven and heard unspeakable words (II Cor. 12:1–10); he was one who could say, 'I live, and yet not I, but Christ liveth in me' (Gal. 2:20). He was, as St. Denys has it, a 'true lover, caught up out of himself into God, living not his own life, but that life so much longed for, the life of the beloved' (*DN* IV.13:712 A). But this union with Christ is with the One whose Body is the Church. His sufferings unite him to Christ — 'always bearing about in the body the dying of the Lord Jesus, that the life also of Jesus might be made manifest in our body' (II Cor. 4:10) — but all this is 'for the sake of his Body, that is, the Church.' 'So then death worketh in us, but life in you' (II Cor. 4:12). Thus it is that when Augustine wants an example of the love of the apostle Paul, something that 'kindles the fire in our hearts', it is II Corinthians 6 that he quotes — a passage describing Paul's apostolic sufferings:

---

[15] *Platonisme et théologie mystique*, 310; and see the whole section, 309–14.

In all things approving ourselves as the ministers of God, in much patience, in afflictions, in necessities, in distresses, in stripes, in imprisonments, in tumults, in labours, in watchings, in fastings; by pureness, by knowledge, by long-suffering, by kindness, by the Holy Ghost, by love unfeigned, by the word of truth, by the power of God, by the armour of righteousness on the right hand and on the left, by honour and dishonour, by evil report and good report; as deceivers, and yet true; as unknown, and yet well known; as dying, and, behold, we live; as chastened, and not killed; as sorrowful, yet always rejoicing; as poor, yet making many rich; as having nothing, and yet possessing all things.

It is an account of Paul's sufferings for the sake of the Church that 'stirs in us . . . a more burning love. So that the stronger burns our love for God, the more sure and unclouded is our vision of him', as Augustine puts it (*De Trin.* VIII.ix.13).

Greek philosophy has bequeathed to the Church the idea that there are two lives, the active and the contemplative, and that the contemplative life is superior.[15] In Plato these two lives were held together within the notion of the city state, and only for some, an intellectual élite, and for them successively so that the life of contemplation, once achieved, was broken by spells of activity for the sake of the city state. In Aristotle these two lives are distinct, and the contemplative life presented as the ideal. This theme is important in the Fathers and often symbolized by the contrast between Mary and Martha — a contrast first drawn out, it would seem, by Origen, and repeated ever since. There is a tension between Mary, the contemplative, who seeks God for Himself, and Martha, the active one who is 'cumbered about much serving' in attending to the needs of those around her. But perhaps this equation of Martha's bustle with the active life has been misleading — if helpful in persuading to prayer. For the true active life is as much a call from God to the highest of which a man is capable as is the contemplative life. And so Augustine, who understood both lives and, indeed, lived both to the full in his own person, could write sublimely in the last of his homilies on St. John's Gospel of these twin pillars at the heart of the Church:

[15] See the discussion of this topic in C. Butler, *Western Mysticism*, (London, 1922), 195–293.

Two lives, therefore, preached and commended to her by God, the Church knows: of which, one is in faith, the other in vision; one in time of sojourning, the other in eternity of abiding; one in labour, the other in rest; one on the way, the other in its home; one in the work of action, the other in the reward of contemplation; one declines from evil and does good, the other has no evil to decline from and has great good to enjoy; one fights with the enemy, the other reigns without an enemy; one is courageous in things adverse, the other has no sense of anything adverse; one curbs carnal lusts, the other is wholly given up to spiritual delights; one is anxious with care of getting the victory, the other in the peace of victory is without care; one in temptations is helped, the other without any temptations rejoices in the Helper himself; one succours the needy, the other is there where it finds none needy; one forgives others' sins that its own may be forgiven, the other neither has anything done to it that it need forgive, nor does anything that it need ask to be forgiven; one is scourged by evils that it be not lifted up in its good things, the other with such fulness of grace is free from all evil that without any temptation to pride it cleaves to the Supreme Good; one discerns between good and evil, the other beholds the things that alone are good: therefore the one is good but as yet wretched, the other better and blessed. The former is signified by the apostle Peter, the latter by John. The former is wholly carried out here until the end of this world, and there finds an end; the last is deferred, to be completed after the end of this world, but in the world to come has no end . . . Let perfected action *follow me*, informed by the example of my Passion: but let contemplation that has been begun, *tarry till I come*, to be perfected when I come.

(CXXIV.5)

Bibliography

This is not in any way intended as an exhaustive bibliography; attention is drawn in what follows to those books which themselves have good bibliographies. It is intended as an indication of the literary sources of my own thought, and a guide to further reading.

General. The general literature on mysticism and mystical theology is vast, and much of it only tangentially relevant to this work. The older books by F. Heiler, R. Otto, Baron F. von Hügel, and Evelyn Underhill still retain their importance. Of these the following have been most useful:

F. Heiler, *Prayer* (E. T. London, 1932).

R. Otto, *The Idea of the Holy* (E.T. London, 1923).

F. von Hügel, *The Mystical Element of Religion*, 2 vols. (2nd edn. London, 1923).

E. Underhill, *Mysticism* (London, 1911); *Worship* (London, 1936).

One of the most important books of recent years on mysticism has been: R. C. Zaehner, *Mysticism — Sacred and Profane* (Oxford, 1957). For a good bibliography of more recent literature see P. G. Moore's article, 'Recent Studies of Mysticism: a critical survey' in *Religion*, III/2 (Autumn 1973), 146–56.

General studies of Patristic mystical theology. While there is nothing precisely on the subject, relevant material is found in three types of work: (a) general studies of the history of Christian mysticism or spirituality, (b) studies of the influence of philosophy (especially Platonism) on the Christian tradition, and (c) studies of Orthodox, or Byzantine, theology and spirituality. Particularly important in these categories are:

(a) Hilda C. Graef, *The Light and the Rainbow* (London, 1959).
Rowan Williams, *The Wound of Knowledge* (London, 1979).

(b) A. H. Armstrong (ed.), *Cambridge History of Later Greek and Early Medieval Philosophy* (Cambridge, 1970), which has a good bibliography.
Endre von Ivánka, *Plato Christianus* (Einsiedeln, 1964).

(c)   Vladimir Lossky, *The Mystical Theology of the Eastern Church* (E.
T. London, 1957).
The Vision of God (E.T. London, 1963).
M. Lot-Borodine, *La Déification de l'homme* (Paris, 1970).
Paul Evdokimov, *La Connaissance de Dieu* (Lyons, 1967).
Also important for Patristic mystical theology in general:
    G. B. Ladner, *The Idea of Reform: its Impact on Christian Thought
    and Action in the Age of the Fathers* (Cambridge, Mass., 1959).

Chapter I   Plato. There are many translations of Plato. I have
used the following:
    F. M. Cornford, *The Republic of Plato* (Oxford, 1941).
    R. Hackforth, *Plato's Phaedrus* (Cambridge, 1952).
    Timaeus, translated by H. D. P. Lee (Harmondsworth, 1965).
For the *Phaedo* I have used H. N. Fowler's translation in the *Loeb
Classical Library* (1914), and for the *Symposium* (or the *Banquet*) that
by the poet, Shelley. The following books I have found particularly
useful:
W. Jaeger, *Paideia: the Ideals of Greek Culture*, vol. II (*In Search of the
    Divine Centre*) and parts of vol. III (Oxford, 1944).
A.-J. Festugière, *Contemplation et vie contemplative selon Platon* (Paris,
    1967).

Chapter II   Philo. Philo's works are available in the *Loeb Classical
Library*, edited and translated by F. H. Colson and G. H. Whitaker,
with indices by J. W. Earp (10 vols., London, 1929–71). There are
two supplementary volumes with a translation (only, from the
Armenian, by Ralph Marcus) of the *Questions and Answers on Genesis
and Exodus* (London, 1961). The best thing on Philo's mysticism is
Marguerite Harl's introduction to her edition of *Quis rerum divinarum
heres sit* (Paris, 1966). See also:
    E. Bréhier, *Les Idées philosophiques et religieuses de Philon d'Alexandrie*
    (Paris, 1925).
J. Daniélou, *Philon d'Alexandrie* (Paris, 1958).
And more generally on Hellenistic philosophy and religion:
    A.-J. Festugière, *La Révélation d'Hermès Trismégiste* (4 vols., Paris,
    1944–54).

Chapter III Plotinus. The standard edition of the text of Plotinus is
    P. Henry and H.-R. Schwyzer, *Plotini Opera*, 3 vols. (Paris and
    Brussels, 1951–73).
Translations:
    Plotinus: The Enneads, tr. by Stephen MacKenna, rev. by B. S.
    Page (London, 1969).

A. H. Armstrong's translation in the *Loeb Classical Library* is as yet incomplete.
See also:
R. Arnou, *Le Désir de Dieu dans la philosophie de Plotin* (2nd edn. Rome, 1967).
E. R. Dodds, 'Tradition and Personal Achievement in the Philosophy of Plotinus', in *The Ancient Concept of Progress* (Oxford, 1973), 126–39.
P. Hadot, *Plotin, ou la simplicité du regard* (Paris, 1963).
J. M. Rist, *Plotinus: the Road to Reality* (Cambridge, 1967).
J. Trouillard, *La Purification plotinienne* (Paris, 1955).

Chapter IV Origen. Most of Origen's works are edited in *Die Griechischen Christlichen Schriftsteller*, various editors, Leipzig and (later) Berlin, 1899 ff. The following translations have been used:
R. P. Lawson, *Origen: The Song of Songs — Commentary and Homilies* (London, 1957).
G. W. Butterworth, *Origen: On First Principles* (London, 1936).
See also:
H. U. von Balthasar, *Parole et mystère chez Origène* (Paris, 1957).
H. Crouzel, *Origène et la «connaissance mystique»* (Paris, 1961), with an almost exhaustive bibliography of works on Origen.
J. Daniélou, *Origène* (Paris, 1948; E.T. London, 1955).
M. Harl, *Origène et la fonction révélatrice du Verbe incarné* (Paris, 1958).
Hal Koch, *Pronoia und Paideusis: Studien über Origenes und sein Verhältnis zum Platonismus* (Leipzig, 1932).
H. de Lubac, *Histoire et esprit* (Paris, 1950).
C. Macleod, 'Allegory and Mysticism in Origen and Gregory of Nyssa', *Journal of Theological Studies* XXII (1971), 362–79.

Chapter V Nicene Orthodoxy. There is little on Athanasius. The edition used for the text of *Contra Gentes* and *De Incarnatione* is that by R. W. Thomson in the series, *Oxford Early Christian Texts* (Oxford, 1971).

There is a new edition of the Greek Text of Gregory of Nyssa, edited under the supervision of W. Jaeger: *Gregorii Nysseni Opera* (Leiden, 1960 ff.). In addition an edition of the *Life of Moses* with translation and introduction by Jean Daniélou (in *Sources Chrétiennes* (=*SC*), no. 1, 3rd edn., Paris, 1968). Translations used:
J. Daniélou, *From Glory to Glory*, tr. by H. Musurillo with Introduction by Daniélou (London, 1962) — translation of extracts mainly from the *Life of Moses* and the *Commentary on the Song of Songs*.

Hilda C. Graef, *St Gregory of Nyssa: The Lord's Prayer, the Beatitudes* (London, 1954).
Now available in the series, *Classics of Western Spirituality*, but too late for my use:
  The Life of Moses, tr. by E. Ferguson and A. J. Malherbe (London, 1979).
See also:
  H. U. von Balthasar, *Présence et penséee: Essai sur la philosophie de Grégoire de Nysse* (Paris, 1942).
  J. Daniélou, *Platonisme et théologie mystique* (2nd edn., Paris, 1953).
  J. Gaïth, *La Conception de la liberté chez Grégoire de Nysse* (Paris, 1953).
  R. Leys, *L'Image de Dieu chez Saint Grégoire de Nysse* (Paris, 1951).
  W. Völker, *Gregor von Nyssa als Mystiker* (Wiesbaden, 1955).

Chapter VI   The Monastic Contribution:
  Évagre le Pontique, *Traité Pratique ou Le Moine* (*SC* 170 f., Paris, 1971): Text and translation of the *Praktikos*, with an important introduction, by A. and C. Guillaumont.
  Text of *On Prayer* in *Philocalia* (Venice, 1782), 155–65 (ascribed to Nilus). (=PG 79, 1165–1200, though there the enumeration is somewhat different.)
  Text of *Kephalaia Gnostica* in *Patrologia Orientalis* XXVIII, 1 (Paris, 1958) ed. with translation by A. Guillaumont.
  H. Dörries, E. Klostermann and M. Kroeger, *Die 50 Geistlichen Homilien des Makarios* (Berlin, 1964). A critical edition of the text produced in Migne of which there is a translation:
  Macarius, *Fifty Spiritual Homilies*, tr. by A. J. Mason (London, 1921).
  Makarios/Symeon, *Reden und Briefe: Die Sammlung I des Vaticanus Graecus 694 (B)*, by Heinz Berthold (2 vols., Berlin, 1973).
  Diadoque de Photicé, *Œuvres Spirituelles*, edited by E. des Places (*SC* 5, 3rd edn., Paris, 1966).
There are translations of *On Prayer* and of Diadochus's *Gnostic Chapters* (the first into English from the Greek of the latter) in
  G. E. H. Palmer, Philip Sherrard, and Kallistos Ware, *The Philokalia: the Complete Text*, vol. I (London, 1979), which has good introductions and notes.
  J. E. Bamberger, *Evagrios: The Praktikos and 153 Chapters on Prayer* (Spencer, Mass., 1970) is another translation of the important works by Evagrius preserved in Greek.
See also:
  A. Guillaumont, *Les 'Kephalaia Gnostica' d'Évagre le Pontique et l'histoire de l'origénisme chez les Grecs et chez les Syriens* (Paris, 1962).
  I. Hausherr, *Hesychasme et prière* (Rome, 1966).

Introduction to his edition of the *Liber Graduum* in *Patrologia Syriaca*
III (Paris, 1926) by M. Kmosko.
W. Jaeger, *Two Rediscovered Works of Ancient Christian Literature:
Gregory of Nyssa and Macarius* (Leiden, 1954).
R. Staats, *Gregor von Nyssa und die Messalianer* (Berlin, 1968).
E. A. David, *Das Bild vom neuen Menschen* (Salzburg and Munich,
1968).
H. Chadwick, 'Messalianerne — en evangelisk bevegelse i det 4.
århundre', *Tidsskrift for Teologi og Kirke* 3/1979, 161–72.
H. Dörries, *Symeon von Mesopotamien* (Leipzig, 1941).
Die Theologie des Makarios/Symeon (Göttingen, 1978).
I. Hausherr, 'L'erreur fondamentale et la logique de la Mes-
salianisme', *Orientalis Christiana Periodica* I (1935), 328–60.
F. Dörr, *Diadochus von Photkie und die Messalianer* (Freiburg im
Breisgau, 1937).

Chapter VII Augustine:
Confessiones, ed. by M. Skutella, rev. by H. Juergens and W.
Schaub (Stuttgart, 1969).
La Trinité, vol. 1: intr. by E. Hendrikx, tr. and notes by M. Mellet
and Th. Camelot; vol. 2: tr. by P. Agaësse, and notes with J.
Moingt (Paris, 1955).
Confessions, tr. by F. J. Sheed (London, 1944).
Books VIII-X, XIV and XV of *De Trinitate* translated in
Augustine: Later Writings, tr. with intro. and notes by John Burnaby
(London, 1955).
See also:
P. Brown, *Augustine of Hippo* (London, 1967).
J. Burnaby, *Amor Dei* (London, 1938).
C. Butler, *Western Mysticism* (London, 1922).
F. Cayré, *La Contemplation augustinienne* (Paris, 1954).
P. Henry, *La Vision d'Ostie* (Paris, 1938).
R. Holte, *Béatitude et sagesse* (Paris, 1962).

Chapter VIII Denys the Areopagite. The Greek text in Migne
PG 3 is all there is, apart from
La Hiérarchie céleste, intr. by R. Roques, text by G. Heil, tr. and
notes by M. de Gandillac (*SC* 58, 2nd edn., Paris, 1970).
The only complete translation into English (which I have not used)
is
The Works of Dionysius the Areopagite, by J. Parker (London and
Oxford, 1897, 1899).
Divine Names and Mystical Theology, by C. E. Rolt (London, 1920
and often reprinted) is unreliable.

There is a useful French translation:
Œuvres complètes du pseudo-Denys l'Aréopagite, by M. de Gandillac (Paris, 1943).
See also:
H. U. von Balthasar, *Herrlichkeit: eine theologische Ästhetik*, chapter on Dionysius, vol. II/1, 147–214 (Einsiedeln, 1962).
V. Lossky, 'La notion des "analogies" chez le ps. Denys l'Aréopagite', *Archives d'histoire doctrinale et littéraire du Moyen Âge*, 5 (1930), 279–309.
'La théologie négative dans la doctrine de Denys l'Aréopagite', *Revue des sciences philosophiques et théologiques*, 28 (1939), 204–21.
R. Roques, *L'Univers dionysien* (Paris, 1954), and his articles on 'contemplation' and 'Denys' in *Dictionnaire de Spiritualité*, vol. 2, col. 1777–87, 1885–1911; vol. 3, col. 244–86.
W. Völker, *Kontemplation und Ekstase bei ps.-Dionysius Areopagita* (Wiesbaden, 1958).

Chapter IX   Patristic Mysticism and St. John of the Cross:
H.-C. Puech, 'La ténèbre mystique chez le pseudo-Denys', in *Études Carmélitaines*, 23, II (1938), 33–53.
Collected Works of St. John of the Cross, tr. by Kieran Kavanaugh and Otilio Rodriguez (London, 1966).
A Benedictine of Stanbrook, *Medieval Mystical Tradition and St. John of the Cross* (London, 1954).
E. W. Trueman Dicken, *The Crucible of Love* (London, 1963).
Ruth Burrows, *Guidelines for Mystical Prayer* (London, 1976).

Chapter X   The Mystical Life and the Mystical Body:
A.-J. Festugière, *L'Enfant d'Agrigente* (Paris, 1950).
Anders Nygren, *Agape and Eros*, tr. by P. S. Watson (London, 1957).
M. C. D'Arcy, *The Mind and Heart of Love* (London, 1945).
H. U. von Balthasar, *Herrlichkeit* III/2, part 2 (Einsiedeln, 1969).

INDEX